A TREASURY OF PLAYS
FOR WOMEN

EDITED BY

FRANK SHAY

BOSTON
LITTLE, BROWN, AND COMPANY
1922

TO MY MOTHER
J. M. S

FOREWORD

When the Editor conceived the idea of bringing together in one volume a selection of the best plays requiring only women to cast, it was with the sublime faith that is born of ignorance. Anthology making is not an art: there are no chairs dedicated to it in our universities: it is merely the application of common sense to a selective problem. The editor can only select from the available material those plays he considers worthy and then write the various authors for permission to reprint.

It was not until the Editor began to assemble the plays that came within the present classification that he realized how meagre the field is. Drama, he argued, was a conflict between two or more persons usually of opposite sexes. This is not quite a truism. The mind of the average dramatist deals only with conflicts that have both men and women as principals. He does not always see the problems that persons of the same sex have to meet and deal with. These problems, however, do exist and are, at times, quite potent. Witness Miss Alice Brown's "Joint Owners in Spain", and Gustave Wied's "Autum Fires."

Plays requiring only women to cast were more or less plentiful in the beginning. It early became apparent that most of them had been written for girls' schools, Sunday Schools and institutions of like nature. They were neither dramatic nor interesting.

Of all these plays the Editor found but twenty worthy of inclusion. Of these Miss Brown's delightful little play was not available owing to copyrights, and Miss Alice Gerstenberg's "Overtones" has had such wide circulation it was decided it would be better to have other plays by the same author. As the volume stands before the reader, it is the Editor's firm belief that it contains the best plays the field affords.

Certain plays in this collection have male characters. Miss Millay's beautiful play has several. It is included because it was written for an all-girl cast and was produced at Vassar College in the Summer of 1921 with just such a cast. Miss Dransfield's play is a favorite with women's clubs and has been produced more often with a woman cast than otherwise. Miss McCauley's "Conflict"; Alfred Kreymborg's "Manikin and Minikin", Maeterlinck's "The Death of Tintagiles", require boys, a character that even in legitimate theatres is usually given to a woman.

At the end of the volume the reader will find lists of published plays requiring only women to cast, and titles of books which will be of help in production.

It is a pleasure to acknowledge the gracious help in compiling this volume to Mrs. Jane Dransfield Stone, Miss Evelyn Emig, Miss Alice Gerstenberg, Miss Florence Clay Knox, Miss Clarice Vallette McCauley, Miss Edna St. Vincent Millay, Messrs. Colin Clements, Alfred Kreymborg, Christopher Morley, Eugene G. O'Neill, Eugene Pillot, and Howard Forman Smith, for permission to include examples of their work. To Mr. Norman Lee Swartout and Mr. Holland Hudson thanks are also due for many helpful suggestions.

F. S.

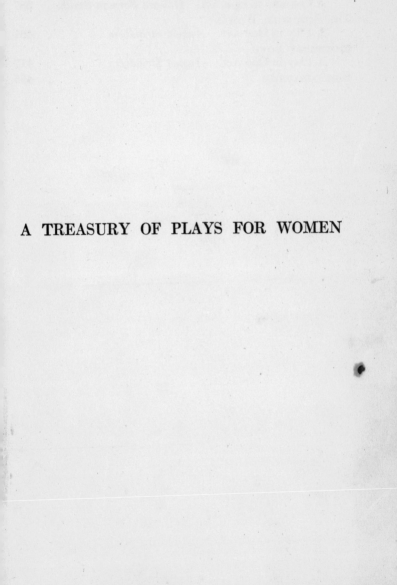

A TREASURY OF PLAYS FOR WOMEN

THE SIEGE

COLUMBINE

COLIN CAMPBELL CLEMENTS

COLIN CAMPBELL CLEMENTS was, until recently, connected with the American Relief Committee in the Near East. It was there that he got the material for "The Siege." He has written several plays, and has contributed to the magazines. He makes his home at Lawrenceville, N. J.

THE SIEGE

A PLAY IN ONE ACT

By COLIN CAMPBELL CLEMENTS

Characters

ZANAB
BISHARA, her old nurse
GAZNIA, a servant

THE SIEGE

A room in an Oriental house. At the right is an arched door, leading to another part of the house. A door at the left, partly hidden by a large Oriental screen of carved wood and inlaid pearl, opens into a bedroom. At the back, up one step, is a balcony with latticed windows overlooking the city. A low round table with a copper water jar stands near the screen. The only other piece of furniture is a low couch, over which a rug is thrown, near the center of the room.

When the curtains part, the room, gray and somber, is empty. The old servant enters from the right. She arranges the pillows on the couch and sees that the water jar is full. As she moves quietly about the room she glances now and then at the closed windows, — each time with a little exclamation of fear. Once she starts as if to open the shutters, moves as far as the step, stops for a moment and then with a little sob hurries from the room. There is quietness. The wail of a street dog is heard, then quietness again. Zanab enters from the bedroom. She stands, slowly turning from left to right. Bishara enters.

ZANAB. I thought — I thought I heard you here.

BISHARA. No — I have not been here. Perhaps it was Old Gaznia filling the water jar you heard.

ZANAB. Yes — perhaps it was Old Gaznia. But she has not opened the shutters.

BISHARA. I shall open them.

ZANAB. Yes — yes.

[Bishara goes to the windows.

Zanab turns quickly.

No — no, no.

BISHARA (*she comes to Zanab*). Why are you up with the away?

ZANAB. You, also, are here.

BISHARA. I came because I heard you.

ZANAB. I was very quiet.

BISHARA. You did not sleep, Pretty One?

ZANAB. Sleep! All night I listened — for sixty days an[d] sixty long nights I have been listening. No — no, I hav[e] not slept!

BISHARA. But the prisoners have gone now. Last night a[t] midnight they went away.

ZANAB. Last night at midnight — so quietly, so quietly I stood at my window. There was only a flash and then I heard the carts as they moved away in the darkness. [I] heard the rumble of wooden wheels over the stones in the darkness. They moved away to the little white road that wanders through the mountains. Once a dog barked, then all was quiet again. (*She sighs*) They are gone. Those people who came to bring peace to us who have never known peace, who came to bring civilization to us who have never known civilization — they have gone away. They have been driven away. Oh, Bishara, must we always, always, always be caged things? I am afraid! (*She puts out her hand to meet Bishara's*) I — am — afraid.

BISHARA. It is over now, the siege has been lifted and the prisoners have been allowed to go away in safety.

ZANAB. The siege! For sixty days without food — without water, and still they fought! They were surrounded — they were like rats in a trap. And still they fought! Always I prayed Allah to send them help. Always I sat at that window —

BISHARA. I know — I know.

ZANAB. Waiting — waiting for help. (*She turns her head away*) Waiting for help that never came. Bishara, I am afraid for them.

BISHARA. Saeed promised them safety to the border of [the] land — he will keep his word.

ZANAB. Can he keep his word? (*Bishara moves*) Saeed is a coward. *Can* he keep his word? Ca[n a] coward keep his word?

BISHARA. Saeed is your betrothed.

ZANAB (*her arms fall to her side*). I am his prisoner. (*A low chant is heard from the city. Zanab starts*) What — what is that?

BISHARA. It is — it is the muezzin calling the morning prayer.

ZANAB. But the sun cannot be up yet. It is not time for the morning prayer. Open the windows! (*Bishara starts toward the balcony*) No, no — let them be shut. I am afraid. Bishara, I am afraid — for him! No, do not open the windows.

BISHARA. But it is daylight.

ZANAB. They went through the mountains — the mountains are treacherous.

BISHARA. Ah, they have surely reached the plains beyond the mountains. It is daylight.

[*The chant is heard again.*

ZANAB. Hear — what is that?

BISHARA (*as she listens*). Yes, it is daylight. The muezzin is calling the morning prayer — calling his people to prayer.

ZANAB. His call is dismal.

BISHARA. Calling his people to prayer.

ZANAB. To prayer! To pray one must first love. What do the muezzin's people know of love? (*She turns*) Oh, they could have learned but they have driven love away. They could have learned. They could have learned! (*She covers her face*) My love! My love! My love! They have driven love away — André — André — André. (*She runs to the window and with her head against the closed shutters, sobs*) André — they have driven you away. The little white road has carried you away through the mountains and beyond — beyond. I heard the wooden carts as they moved away in the darkness, André. You went with them! But I shall be here waiting for you always — always. André, your Zanab — your little Zanab will wait for you — always. She will watch the little white road

for your return. You promised you would come bac
André — André.

BISHARA. Sh-h-h! He'll kill us. Saeed will hear you. I
has spies everywhere. He will kill us.

ZANAB. Kill — kill us? Who is afraid of death, here?

BISHARA (*she takes Zanab by the arm and leads her to the couch*
No — no. Oh, they have reached the plains beyond th
mountains and André with his brave men are on the wic
road now, the wide road that leads to their own countr

ZANAB. On the wide road — yes. André must be on th
wide road that leads to his own country! I shall not l
afraid any more. His own country. Do you remembe
Bishara, do you remember how he used to tell us about h
country? (*Bishara slips to the floor beside the couch an
listens*) You remember he told us about those great gree
trees — those great green poplar trees that reach to th
stars? To the stars, he said — and underneath were wic
green places full of flowers and butterflies and laughte
He smiled so when he told us about it. I shan't forge
how he smiled. And do you remember the day he told u
about the boats — little boats with blue and yellow sails —
and he made a paper boat for us. Do you remember
And Gaznia put it sailing in a silver bowl? I should lik
to have ridden in a boat, over the water — so — and so —
and so — And he told us of the fisher folk who go dow
to the sea, the fisher folk who always sing. (*She sings*
snatch of a French song) And, Bishara, do you remembe
when he told us the story of — Ah, yes, yes, I know yo
do remember, for there is laughter in your eyes. An
the young girls, the pretty young girls who wear whit
headdresses. Oh, they must be lovely, those pretty
young girls! He said — he said I could have a headdres
too and —

BISHARA (*she comes to Zanab and takes her hand*). Littl
Sweet —

ZANAB. Lovely girls — and they never lived, like us, beh
barred windows or went about with their faces alwa

covered — and they danced hand-in-hand through the
gold of sunset, like white butterflies. Do you remember
when André told us —

BISHARA. Sh-h-h.

ZANAB. But —

BISHARA. Saeed will kill us!

ZANAB. Perhaps — perhaps, but I shall tell him —

BISHARA (*she draws away*). No, no — no! Promise me you
will not do that — promise me, promise me you won't do
that! (*Weeping, she sinks to her knees at Zanab's feet*)
Promise me you will not tell Saeed!

ZANAB. I — shall — not - - tell — him.

BISHARA. Oh!

ZANAB. You and I shall have that secret always — forever
You and I. Just us. Alone, we shall talk of the popla
trees that reach to the stars and the little boats with bl
and —

BISHARA. You must forget. It is best to forget.

ZANAB (*she rises*). Forget — forget? It is impossibl to
forget one's — heart. No, I can never forget. — I hall
always remember.

BISHARA. He has gone back to his own country.

ZANAB (*she talks very slowly*). To his own country — Ah.
To his own country. Yes, he was different from this —
all this. So happy, so gay — so kind. Yes, he was quite
different. Bishara, do you remember you used o go out
and bring him to me? (*She laughs softly*) D you remember? He was so funny in that long black coat — so
funny!

BISHARA (*she covers her mouth with her hand*). Sh-h-h. You
must forget. André was of another life; he was of another
chapter and the leaf has been turned over. We go on to
new stories. You must forget even as he has forgotten.

ZANAB. Forgotten? Do you believe he will forget? Do
you believe he has already forgotten me? Yes — yes,
perhaps a man always forgets — because he is a man. Oh,
but a woman, a woman never forgets, eh, Bishara? A

woma never forgets.   Surely he can't forget everything
Do y remember the night during Ramadan when you
bro it him through — that door?   And he threw o
his oak like this — and stood before me like some strange
go from the skies — like some strange god from an old
st y book?   Bishara, his hair was like spun gold!   He
   s like —

B ARA.   Sh-h-h!   Some one may hear you!   Allah!

Z AB.   And Gaznia brought us sweetmeats from the
bazaars and played for us on the pipes — and I danced
Oh — the jasmine was in bloom, then.   I think it will neve
never be so sweet again as it was that night — never s
sweet again.   And the stars were very bright; they hun
from the skies like silver lamps.   I think the stars wi
never come so close to earth again.   (*Softly*)   Bishara —
life was sweet then.

BISHARA.   Little Bird — Little Bird, he has gone awa
You must forget.   He has gone away.   He will forge
It is best to forget.   Life is like that — it is best t
forget.

ZANAB.   But I shall never forget.   Why do you talk to m
so?   I can never forget — all through the nights I shal
dream of him, as I saw him last, here before me — al
through the nights I shall dream of him and all throug
the days I shall think of him — André.   What is, *is* —
we cannot change it, Bishara.   (*She throws out her arms*
In my dreams I shall be with him there in his own countr
— even as I was with him here, with him, under the tree
and the stars, with him in the little blue boats upon th
water, with him —

[*The door at the back opens.   Gaznia enters.   She is carry*
ing a large silver tray.

BISHARA.   Sh-h-h!   Sh-h-h!

[*Zanab sits down again.   Gaznia places the tray upon a sma*
table near the couch and brings the water jar and a silver bow
from the screen.   She pours fresh water over Zanab's hand

ZANAB.   You look very tired, Gaznia.

GAZNIA. Little sister of the moon. — I — I am very tired.

ZANAB. You have not slept well?

GAZNIA (*she glances around the room with frightened eyes*).
I — I did not sleep.

ZANAB (*she laughs*). You are in love?

BISHARA. Sh-h-h!

ZANAB. You are in love, Gaznia?

GAZNIA (*softly*). I was in love with love.

BISHARA (*she turns and whispers*). We shall all be killed!

ZANAB. In love with love? In — love — with — love.
Gaznia, let in the sunlight. Open the windows wide. We
shall need the sunshine to-day.

[*Gaznia moves toward the windows. Zanab begins to drink
the coffee which has been placed before her. She is about to
put down the cup when Bishara moves toward her.*

BISHARA. Little one —

ZANAB. The coffee is so black.

BISHARA. My Lovely One, let me put the water of roses in
your cup.

[*She pours from a small silver pitcher. Zanab tastes the
coffee.*

ZANAB. It is so sweet — too sweet.

[*Gaznia reaches out her hand to swing open the windows but,
in fear, draws back her hand.*

GAZNIA. Oh-h-h.

ZANAB (*she has not seen Gaznia's fear of opening the window.*)
Let in the sunlight — swing open the windows, Gaznia.
(*She gives Bishara the cup*) Put it down, I cannot drink
this morning, I cannot drink. No, I shall watch the sun
make patterns through the lattice. I shall watch the sun
chase the little frightened shadows across the marble
floor. Open the windows, Gaznia.

[*Gaznia swings open the windows. Terrified, she stands
looking down into the streets, then begins to weep.*

BISHARA (*she runs to the window*). What is it, Gaznia? (*She
looks out*) What is it? There is — there is — there is no
one in the streets!

ZANAB. There is no one in the streets? What does it mean? What does it mean?

GAZNIA. Hear me — the muezzin this morning, the muezzin, even before dawn, called out for all good Mohammedans to go out — to go out upon the white road — out into the mountains and overtake the freed prisoners. There is no one in the streets. (*She covers her face with her hands*) There is no one in the streets! They have all gone! They have all gone out into the mountains.

[*She flees from the room.*

ZANAB. The muezzin — this morning — before dawn — called — You told me it was the call to prayer! You lied!

BISHARA (*who has sunk to the floor*). I did not know! I did not know!

ZANAB. They have gone out to overtake the soldiers — to kill them! They have gone out to kill the Christians! They have gone to the mountains! The muezzin has called them. Saeed has broken his word — he has lied! Saeed always lies! He is a coward — a coward — he lied! Bishara, do you hear, the muezzin has called them — they have gone — the streets are empty! Saeed has broken his word. Every man has gone out to — gone out into the mountains to — kill. Bishara, do you hear — to kill!

BISHARA. The prisoners were given permission to go in honor — they have their guns and their ammunition with them. They will again fight.

ZANAB. The muezzin has called — perhaps — perhaps, Saeed had men hidden in the mountains waiting — waiting, like thieves, like murderers, like — They will cut off the camels and the little wooden carts and then —

BISHARA. Ah — but surely they have reached the plains beyond the mountains. They surely have reached the plains — the plains —

ZANAB. A camel train moves slowly and the wooden carts —

BISHARA (*bravely*). But surely — yes, yes, they have reached the plains beyond the mountains. They are safe.

[*Shouts and firing from afar are heard.*

COLUMBINE

A FANTASY IN ONE ACT

By COLIN CAMPBELL CLEMENTS

Characters

MINNIE
SALLY
ONE UNSEEN

kind. But they never invite us into *their* homes, do they?
(*She lights a cigarette*) Sal, you ought to go out more.

SALLY. I've been waiting.

MINNIE. Waiting! Oh — o. Say, you don't expect anybody to just come and find you waiting, do you? You sit
here alone night after night, just sit. And when you go
down to work, what have you got to think about during
the whole day? What have you got to laugh about?
What have you got to tell the other girls? Then, like
everybody else, you keep getting older and older. What
are you going to do then?

SALLY. I suppose everybody must come to the end — sometime.

MINNIE (*walking to the center of the room, she turns*). I don't
want to think about that! I don't want to think about
the — end! I'm young! I want to laugh! I want to feel!
I want to live! I want to hear the music — and see the
lights — and be part of the big crowd, just as long as I
can. It's all there is to do — for me. (*She stands for a
moment and then with an hysterical little laugh turns toward
Sally*) My Gaud — who's been hanging flowers on you!
(*Sally's hand goes quickly over the white rose at her belt*)
Sal, who's been pinning white roses on you?

SALLY. It's from a boy who —

MINNIE. A boy! (*She comes closer*) Sally — don't tell me
you 're in love with a man.

SALLY. I think — yes, I *am* in love.

MINNIE. You! You in love! (*She sinks into a chair*) Gaud,
this is the last straw! Now I'll have to stay home nights
and chaperon you.

SALLY. I've hoped and waited and waited and now —

MINNIE. And missed a lot of fun just waiting for — nothing.

SALLY. And at last he has come — love has come.

MINNIE. Poor little mouse. Love! Oh, if you only knew
what I know. Love isn't made for our kind.

SALLY. Why, love is for everybody. Every girl dreams of
having a home all of her own sometime.

MINNIE. Do you know what that means? It means frying greasy potatoes and washing clothes — and getting old and hard and ugly. It's all there is for us, just that. I'm going to get away from it all, I'm going to be free until — until the end.

SALLY. But if a man loves a woman —

MINNIE. He doesn't marry her. Men don't marry women they *really* love.

SALLY. Oh!

MINNIE. The only reason men ever get married is so they won't have to wash their own socks!

SALLY. No — no — no.

MINNIE. It takes more than love to get over the hard places — it takes more than love to keep live. Romance has to be fed with three square meals a day, take it from me, or it don't last long. Oh, it's all right in books but it don't work out in real life. I've seen it tried again and again and again. It's filthy.

SALLY. No! Real love is clean — clean as is white rose.

MINNIE (*taking the rose*). As this white rose. Who knows — even it may have a worm eating at its heart. White rose, grown in a greenhouse, sheltered from the dirt of the city — that's what it is. But you don't find 'em growing down on these dirty streets and black holes where we live, Sally, you don't. Maybe if you and me had always been taken care of and lived in a clean place where there was sun and flowers, instead of a place like this — where it's always dark and smelly and noisy — well, perhaps we would be different too. (*She sighs*) But we weren't and it's too late to change now. There's nothing to do but just go on as we are until — just keep on as we are. Love! It ain't real, Sally. (*She pauses*) I wish — I wish to Gaud I could believe it was! (*She rises and with a little shudder, throws the flower on the table. She walks slowly toward the door. Turning*) Who's the fellow?

SALLY. A boy — Harlequin.

MINNIE. Harlequin what?

SALLY. Just Harlequin, that's all.

MINNIE. Just Harlequin — sounds suspicious.

SALLY. He's wonderful.

MINNIE. Of course you'd think so, until to-morrow — or the day after.

SALLY. I shall think so always. (*Very low*) And to-night — to-night he's coming with the new moon to take me away from all this — to a place where there is always sun and flowers and birds. The sort of a place you said —

MINNIE. But is he —

SALLY. And we're going to live in a little house with holly-hocks against the red brick wall and little green boxes of red geraniums at all the windows and dotted swiss curtains inside and —

MINNIE. Hm-m. Sounds like stories they tell about heaven. Say, where, where did you meet this guy — Harlequin?

SALLY. In the park first — almost a week ago.

MINNIE. Oh, that's what's been the matter with you lately. Why didn't you tell me about it?

SALLY. You wouldn't have believed me.

MINNIE. I don't — not all that stuff about hollyhocks against red brick walls and the rest of it. (*She laughs*) What's he do?

SALLY. He is a painter — and he sings songs and he made some sketches of me in the park one day and sang me a little song and —

MINNIE. You mean he's an artist?

SALLY. Yes.

MINNIE. That finishes it, worst kind — them artists. Regular bums, no money, no nothing but a lot of foolish ideas and a lot of green paint. Oh, I know that sort. I fell for one once myself. Gee, he was swell to look at — long curly hair and one of them soft bow ties and every-thing, you know. Gaud, but he was hansome and he made cartoons for a Sunday paper. But come to find out he already had a wife and three kids besides. (*She laughs*) "And dotted swiss curtains inside!"

SALLY. But he isn't a bum! He works — he works in a florist's shop during the mornings and in the afternoons he paints —

MINNIE. Oh, in a flores' shop. Thus the flowers, eh! Stingy — with only giving you one rose. Say, if I'd a fellow what worked in a greenhouse I'd go to bed every night with roses at my head and lilies at my feet.

SALLY. He paints pictures.

MINNIE. That struggling sort — bah!

SALLY. He's sold some of them too — and saved the money. That's how we're going to build the little place in the country and live together, and work together — until the end. One can't be afraid that way, Minnie.

MINNIE. I used to get like that too — pipe dreams.

SALLY. Only you think so. You know my mother used to be a dancer. I always wanted to be one too but my father thought millinery was better — that's how we happened to come to New York. But we all loved the country — specially my mother — she liked the birds so. My father used to call her his little dream girl and then after she — died, I became his little dream girl — that's the reason I believe in dreams — and dreams do come true.

MINNIE. You mean —

SALLY. Dreams *do* come true. And so to-night — to-night with the new moon, Harlequin is coming to take away his Columbine.

MINNIE. Who's that?

SALLY. Why — why, that's what he calls me!

MINNIE (*throwing the hat, which she has been bending into shape, down on the bed*). He's coming here? To-night? Then I'm staying home to-night!

SALLY. You — staying — home?

MINNIE. Straight, Sally. I don't like fellows who go around drawing pictures of girls in the park, specially you.

SALLY. But he doesn't draw every girl's picture. He was eating his lunch — and so was I. That's how it all began.

MINNIE. Oh! and then —

SALLY. He sang a little song for me. A little song I've known ever since I was a child and when he sang, it seemed as if I had known him forever and ever.

MINNIE. Yes, I know. You fell for him — fell for him hard. And now he wants to come and — carry you off, in the night!

SALLY. But I want to go! He was perfectly willing to come in broad daylight. But night — night seemed more sort of romantic. It was me who suggested his coming at night.

MINNIE. You, Sally, you?

SALLY (*coming forward*). Yes, me — and I'm not ashamed of it! Every girl wants a romance. Every girl wants the man she loves — and I've found my man. I'm going to help him — work for him, live for him, love him — always. I suppose every man plays around with girls; they are all alike to him until he comes to the right one — the one that is meant to be his mate and then — then she's got to let him know it. Men! Why, they're all alike — just big stupid boys. Every man needs a woman to take care of him. And I've found my man!

MINNIE (*she takes Sally's hand*). I'm not really such a bad sort, Sally. I've seen a lot more than you have, that's all. Why, you're only a kid. I'm not going to let you go through what I have. After all, it ain't worth the candle. Perhaps there is something in dreams. — I wish I could believe so.

SALLY. I know there is!

MINNIE. That's the reason I'm going to stay home with you to-night. I want you to go on believing in dreams. (*With a sigh of resignation she sits down. After a long pause*) They was going to have a real jazz band. (*Another long pause*) I wonder if the drummer from St. Louis is still waiting for me!

SALLY (*she walks over and puts her hand on Minnie's shoulder*). I don't want you to stay here with me to-night. I want to be alone — all alone when he comes for me. He's not

at all what you think he is. Oh, I've had men try to flirt
with me and try to talk to me and all that. I know that
kind. But a woman can always tell a good man from a
bad one.

MINNIE. I wonder? I think only a very bad woman can
tell a good man from a bad one. (*Pause*) Sally, don't
you know what a woman is what goes away and lives with
a man — without being married to him?

SALLY (*backing away*). Oh! You didn't think that of me!
You couldn't think that!

MINNIE. What else could I think?

SALLY. But we are going to be married, like anybody else.

MINNIE. Who suggested that?

SALLY. Why, Harlequin, of course. We're to be just Harlequin and Columbine forever — so please go away and let
me be alone when he comes. You *shan't* spoil it! Nobody
shall.

MINNIE (*with a shrug of her shoulders*). Of course — (*She
rises*) Oh, well, if you want to be alone. But he won't
come for you — hell, he won't come. (*She puts on her
hat*) You'll just sit here waiting and waiting, until you're
all tired out, and then you'll go to bed and cry till your
poor little heart is broke. I waited for a fellow once!
You see I'm still waiting!

SALLY. You mean you —

MINNIE. Yes. We were going to live in a flat and have a
baby grand piano, and a imitation palm with red tissue
paper around the pot and all that. I never saw him again.
[*She laughs as she walks toward the door.*

SALLY. But Harlequin *will* come.

MINNIE. Maybe. But not to take you to a little red house
with hollyhocks! He'll want to postpone that until next
week. Wait and see.
[*She starts to go.*

SALLY (*running to her*). Good-by, Minnie.

MINNIE. Naw, not good-by — just so long. So long, Sally,
poor little kid. (*She turns at the door*) Say, if you don't

mind, stay on your own side and weep.   I hate sleeping on
a damp pillow!

[*Sally closes the door softly after her and walks toward the
table.   The moon begins to peep in at the back window.   The
room grows brighter.   Sally picks up the rose from the table
and kisses it; she moves toward the window where she stands
waiting as the moon slowly rises.   After a long pause Sally,
with a little catch in her throat, walks toward the center of the
room.   Slowly she pulls the petals from the rose and lets them
fall through her fingers one by one.   The lamp suddenly
flickers and goes out.   A voice, distant at first but coming
nearer and nearer, is heard:*

> I will give you the keys of my heart,
> We shall be married until death do us **part,**
> Lady, will you walk,
> Lady, will you talk,
> Lady, will you walk and talk with me?

[*Some one is running up the stairs outside.   Sally turns
toward the door which flies open as the curtain falls.*

THE LOST PLEIAD

JANE DRANSFIELD

JANE DRANSFIELD was born in Rochester, New York, and was educated in the city schools. She later attended Vassar College for two and one half years. Miss Dransfield is a contributor to many magazines and lectures on dramatic criticism at Columbia University.

Her plays are "The Romance of Melrose Hall" (Ms.), "The Lost Pleiad", and the following one-act plays: "The White Window", "Joe, a Hudson Valley Play", "The Baroness", "Two Women".

THE LOST PLEIAD

A FANTASY IN TWO ACTS

By JANE DRANSFIELD

FOREWORD

THE suggestion for this fantasy lay in the Greek myth of the Pleiad, who came to earth to marry a mortal. The Pleiades were the seven beautiful daughters of Atlas and the ocean nymph Pleione. By command of Zeus they became a constellation, shining by night as stars; but by day, in the form of doves, they winged their way to the far Hesperides to fetch ambrosia for the Olympian King. All were content with their fate except Merope, the youngest, who, having fallen in love with Sisyphus, founder and first King of Corinth, slipped down to earth to become the bride of the mortal of her choice. For this act she was forbidden to resume her heavenly station. Compensation was hers however, since it was her grandson, Bellerophon, who, beside the magic spring Peirene, captured Pegasus, the winged horse of the Muses, thereby securing forever for mortals the service of poetry.

This classical story has been used in the present play neither with desire, nor attempt, to produce, either in form, or in feeling, a Greek drama. Pleasure, outbreaking the beautiful spirit of the myth, has been the only aim.

JANE DRANSFIELD.

The first performance of "The Lost Pleiad" was given in the Academy of Music, Brooklyn, New York, December 28, 1910.

Characters

SISYPHUS, *King of Corinth*
TOLMID, *who plots to be king*
LEONTES, *friend to* SISYPHUS
MERCURY, *messenger of heaven*
ISIDORE, *a toy vender*
AN OLD FISHERMAN
BION, *the fisherman's son*
MASTER WORKMAN
FIRST WORKMAN
SECOND WORKMAN
MEROPE, *the Pleiad*
DIAN, *the huntress*
PLEIONE, *mother of the Pleiades*
IRIS, *messenger of dreams*
HERSE, *sister to* BION

PROTO,
THETIS, } *Nereids*
GALENE,

Tree-nymphs, Fauns, Nereids, the Pleiades, Sun Maidens
SCENE: *A wooded seashore near Corinth. A spring night.*

THE LOST PLEIAD

PROLOGUE

(Spoken before the Curtain)

All gentle hearers, humbly we entreat
Your courtesy for this, our Fancy's play;
That it is writ in rhythmic lines, forgive,
If rhyming be not to your taste, since what
Is born poetic must its essence show,
No other form could clothe so airy frame.
And if, perchance, you quarrel with the theme,
That it harks back to ancient things forgot,
Old myths outgrown, remember, then, that art,
Presenting truth, no present knows, nor past.

Remember, too, if still inclined to chide,
That poets haply wait on circumstance;
Their themes chose them, not they their themes, ofttimes;
For with their minds at leisure, roaming free,
Browsing the hills of romance, vales of song,
Or wandering through the woods of legendry,
Sudden a figure starts from those dim realms,
And, why he knows not, bids the poet "Write!"
For poets are but instruments through which
Strange voices from far worlds articulate.

Within the slow procession of the stars,
Which nightly moves in majesty through heaven,
In Taurus shine the wistful Pleiades, —
That group whose rising here marks winter's reign,
But which in Argolis bespeak the spring,
Bidding the farmer hopeful sow his grain,
The mariner put forth his boats to sea;

Six sisters, you may count them with the eye,
But there's a story they were seven once,
Ere that the youngest member of the group,
The gentle Merope, slipped down to earth,
Obedient to the dictum of her heart,
As often maids, against all elder rule,
And for forbidden love, high heaven lost.
Yet so without regret, since this is truth, —
That earth from heaven is no different,
If one doth harbor heaven in the thought.
This, then, is simple matter of our tale; —
How Merope, the Pleiad, Dian's maid,
Forsook her sisters on a summer night,
And swiftly down the azure hill of heaven,
Sped unto earth to marry Sisyphus,
First king of Corinth, in fair Argolis;
How Sisyphus had vision of her grace
In god-sent dream, which he in steadfast faith
Believed, and let the vision rule his deed;
How Dian, in whose train ran Merope,
With hair unbound, all ardent to the chase,
Besought her, though in vain, to heaven return;
And how her sisters, lonesome as the heart
Which finds not in a throng the one face loved.
Found heaven a solitude, once she had fled.

So on your kindness let our play begin,
And if thereby you shall be entertained,
Finding some pleasant things, or wise, herein,
We who have striven, have our end attained.

ACT ONE

The scene represents a wooded seashore. Massive rocks to the sides, with an open grassy glade to the front, and a pool at the base of a rock. There are entrances to left, and right. In the far distance Mt. Helicon is visible. It is sunset. Enter Iris.

IRIS.   There went a voice through heaven, plaintive, low,
  Yet heard to farthest limits, "She is lost!
  Our little sister Merope is lost."
  It swept along like south wind through the trees
  All wet with tears, or note of instrument
  Responding to a heart's complaining tone.
  Acteon heard, and let the wild stag go
  To listen.   Ceres stopped her golden scythe;
  Apollo's lute sighed soft in unison,
  While Daphne caught the quiver in her leaves.
  By every god and goddess, then, it passed,
  Till Echo took the sound in her thin hands,
  And carried it aloft to where Zeus sat,
  On magisterial throne, studded with stars.
  There standing near, I, Iris, heard the news,
  And swift sped down to summon Sisyphus
  To meet his bride, new disappeared from heaven.
  Here on this spot where first he dreamed of her,
  Swift destiny shall lead them soon to meet.
  Who comes?
  [*Enter Hermes, cloaked.*

HERMES (*uncloaks*).   I come.

IRIS.   'Tis Hermes, Maia's son.

HERMES.   But one brief moment since, and I, aloft,
  Stood near the circle of the Pleiades.
  With trembling lips, and tender, they told me
  Of Merope, their sister, whom they love,
  How she had fled from them, they deem to earth.
  They bid me come ere that the mischief's done,
  And married to a mortal, she lose heaven.

IRIS.   Why came not they themselves?

HERMES.   The Pleiades
  In Taurus must remain until the dawn;
  Then, in the form of milk-white doves released,
  They fly to far Hesperides to fetch
  Ambrosia to the Olympian king.   The dawn
  They fear will be too late.

IRIS.   'Tis now too late.

HERMES.   As earth checks time, scarce 'tis an hour ago
That Merope left heaven.

IRIS.   Yet 'tis too late.
Time with the bond of love has naught to do.

HERMES.   Love, fickle, may be changed before 'tis law.

IRIS.   Love's law itself, if it be truly love.

HERMES.   I know you, Iris, and the spell you cast
On men by reason of the dreams you send.
Yet even you act not without command.
Who sent you to arrange, or to suggest
Such undesired marriage?

IRIS.   Pleione.

HERMES.   Now will the sisters doubly mourn that she,
Their mother, has played false.

IRIS.   Not false! Most true!
For Merope, wed on the earth shall win
A greater fame than had she stayed in heaven.
Farewell! sweet Hermes.   You and I, though fleet,
Have much to do, ere we again shall meet.
[*Exit Iris.*

HERMES.   The Pleiades shall learn this latest move.
Against Pleione shall they pit Dian.
Persuasion often wins, where fails command.
Yet ere I go, I would learn certain news
Of Merope, that she is here, or no,
And so speed Dian without loss of time.
Some one about, for gods need men, as men
Need gods, perchance can give me news of her.
(*Looks out on the right.*)
Ah! to my wish, a peasant comes.   'Tis good!
I'll question him, pretending I'm from court.
(*Enter the old fisherman.   Hermes draws his cloak about him
closely, and retires rear.   The fisherman seats himself upon
the rocks, and throws in his line.   Hermes approaches him,
imperiously*)
Stranger, be off!   Go! get you home at once.

FISHERMAN (*unabashed*). I would like nothing better, sir.
  What news?

HERMES. This place is spot predestined, where to-night
  The king of Corinth comes to meet his bride,
  The youngest of the seven Pleiades.

FISHERMAN. I know not any neighbor Pleiades.

HERMES. The Pleiades, my friend, are stars in heaven.

FISHERMAN. A woman, or a star, 'tis all the same.
  To wed is to be caught within a net.
  And so our young king is to marry?

HERMES. Yes.

FISHERMAN. Not even kings escape love's malady.
  Well, I can't go, till I have caught a fish.

HERMES. You should not labor when the sun is set.
  That is but great ambition's need.

FISHERMAN. 'Tis plain
  You, sir, are young.

HERMES. Not old!

FISHERMAN. Unmarried, too.

HERMES. How can that matter, even grant it true?

FISHERMAN. No matter, save it mars your judgment,
    friend.
  If you were married, and not quite so young,
  You'd know ambition's not the only spur
  To set a man to work. His wife, —

HERMES (*impatient*). My friend, —

FISHERMAN. An hour ago there knocked upon our door
  A pretty maid —

HERMES (*interested*). Indeed!

FISHERMAN. Sir, you mistake.
  I am beyond the age of escapades.

HERMES. You interrupt yourself. "A pretty maid" —
  I am impatient for your story, friend.

FISHERMAN. Well, being young, and it near night, and she
  Alone, my wife and children bid her in;
  One way or other, she impressed them so,
  My wife was shamed to offer her our food,

So bid me out to fetch a fish for supper,
As if she needed better food than we.
I'm like to sit here, sir, from now till dawn.
That's all the women know of fishing art.

HERMES (*with greater interest*). Whence came the stranger?

FISHERMAN. That I know not, sir.
She gave us no account. She said her name
Was Merope. That's all I know, my friend.

HERMES (*turns*). She's close about, somewhere. (*Returns to the fisherman*) Have patience, sir,
And keep on fishing.

FISHERMAN. That I'm like to do.

HERMES (*shows the wings on his cap*).
Look, there! Be careful, now. You have a bite.

FISHERMAN (*astonished*). Why, so I have.

HERMES (*shows his winged heels*). Another, now!

FISHERMAN (*excited*). Hark ye!
Loud talking's bad, though fishes have no ears.

HERMES (*strikes the fisherman's pole with his caduceus*).
There! Look, you now, a fish!

FISHERMAN (*draws in a large fish*). I've landed him.

HERMES (*as a god*).
Hermes rewards you, friend, for service given.

FISHERMAN (*recognizes the god*).
Thou art a god! (*Kneels*)
I bend my aged knees.
Do me no harm. I swear that I fear thee.

HERMES (*raises the fisherman to his feet*).
If men but knew how close divinity
Doth walk to them in forms unrecognized,
They would have less of fear, and more of power.
You have no cause to fear. Arise, my friend!
'Tis meant for man to walk erect on earth.

FISHERMAN (*rises*).
Oh, take from me my bitter sting of years.

HERMES. Years have no sting unless ill spent. Go, now!
By reason of this fish, persuade your wife

You're still the family's head.   Tell Merope
That Hermes sends Diana here.   Farewell!
[*Exit Hermes.*

FISHERMAN (*stands a moment in astonishment too great for
words, recovers, examines himself curiously*).
Well, well! Still I'm myself for all of this;
Sound head, sound legs, the selfsame hands, and feet,
As though I'd not been talking to a god.
What's more, I've landed now a three-pound fish,
And I'll be off with it, before night comes.
(*Looks out left, hastily takes up the fish*)
There's two men coming down the woodsy path, —
Two well appearing men, — that is, they look
Like men, but may be Zeus and Hercules,
For all I know. I'll not be sure of men,
Or gods, hereafter.   Let me go before
My wits forget that I be I.   One god
May give a fish, another take it back.
[*Conceals the fish under his jacket, exists hastily.   Enter,
left, Sisyphus and Leontes, cloaked.*

SISYPHUS. No more, Leontes.   No more warnings, now,
Nor fears, nor doubts, nor any tiresome things.
No, I'll not listen.   Come! you are my friend,
And friends should catch the mood of those they love.

LEONTES.   I am your friend, and subject, so obey.
I'll say no more, my king, at least, not now.

SISYPHUS. This is the place of dreams; the slumbering sea,
The woods to left and right, and these dark rocks
Which over Corinth stand like Titan guard,
Shooting by day the sun's bright arrows back,
But feeding night with silence.   Yea, the place
Of dreams!   Here, by this unstirred magic pool,
Whose source unseen was struck at my command
By Aesopus from barren rock, I lay
And dreamed of Merope.

LEONTES.   The Pleiad!   Well,
Some dreams come true, they say.

SISYPHUS (*lays his hand on Leontes' shoulder*). Incredulous,
　　still.
　　Yet such distrust is kinder than some faith,
　　Winning more confidence. Upon this spot
　　Came first light touch of Merope's fleet feet.
LEONTES (*affects belief*). You saw her fall to earth, my lord?
SISYPHUS. Not fall; —
　　No lawless passenger through frightened space,
　　No outcast hurled from high Olympian throne,
　　As Ate was, dark daughter of discord:
　　But through the clouds descending on safe way,
　　Swift as a meteor whose silent trail
　　Makes night mysterious. Here, then, she came,
　　Slender and fair as some young poplar tree,
　　Whose new leaves shimmer to an April moon.
　　But, ah! the star upon her forehead went.
LEONTES. If such sweet visions fed my dreaming eyes,
　　I'd ever choose to sleep.
SISYPHUS. I say I dreamed.
　　It was, however, no fancy of the night,
　　No bright impossible figment of the mind,
　　No common sleep; — but as through open door,
　　I seemed to look into another world,
　　And what I saw I knew I must believe. (*With a change*)
　　But I for other purpose brought you here
　　Than to describe what soon will be a deed.
　　This is the spot where you, my friend, must lead
　　A merry festival to-morrow. Here
　　Let young and old join me in happiness.
LEONTES. You have more faith than I thought possible,
　　So to believe and act upon a dream.
　　I could not so, though I might willing be,
　　By dreams to be so sweetly entertained;
　　In dreams upon my spirit to take flight
　　From this dull world, and soaring, wing light way,
　　More swift than is the slender swallow's flight,
　　Above strange seas, through groves of spice and balm,

By rivers clear, and lake's pellucid stream;
In dreams to shake the cares that cloak the day,
And find for fretted mind divertisement
Mid scenes of childhood, all too near forgot,
Or early friendships pleasantly renew;
To see in dreams not only things we know,
But Lethe dipped to things that are, to go
Like bold discoverer into new realms,
Our souls like Ariel speeding through the night,
Whilst our dull bodies lie at home in bed.
I would I knew this entertaining art.

SISYPHUS. Your raillery, Leontes, has no sting;
Beneath it lies a true and loyal heart.
If we would prove, we must believe our visions;
Believing them, we then must act them out.
You see the place. Make pleasure business,
In honor of my bride.

LEONTES. My lord, I will.
The peasantry shall long recall the day.

SISYPHUS (*leads Leontes left*). Now all the earth to drowsy
    quietude sinks;
Soft silence reigns. Let us return, dear friend.
There's naught to do here, yet. My dream did read
That not till dawn would I meet Merope.
At dawn I will return alone.

LEONTES. Alone?
Now let me speak as friend, as subject, too.
This dream, and your attendant actions strange,
Afford, my lord, an opportunity
Long sought by Tolmid. Here you say you come
Alone at dawn. You must have known, ere this,
How jealous Tolmid's of you, how he seeks
To be acclaimed as king next in your stead.

SISYPHUS (*stops, astonished*). No, I've not heard this news.
What, is it true?
'Tis unbelievable. Tolmid and I
Were boys together.

LEONTES.   There's the rankling cause.
  You were not born a king, he says, no more
  Than he.   Fortune has favored you.
SISYPHUS.   I grant
  I was not born a king, who now am king,
  Yet from a boy I knew my destiny.
  Deep in my heart burned consciousness of power,
  Resistless flame that feeds, and yet consumes —
  A cruel goad, and yet, a solacer.
  To be a king it is to act a king,
  To prove in thought and deed true majesty.
  Yet so 'tis ever said.   Whoso succeeds
  It is called luck.   There's no such thing as luck.
  Our fates upon our own decisions wait,
  And our decisions on a consciousness
  Which we can not explain, yet must obey.
  I have no fear of Tolmid.
LEONTES.   Yet to-night
  He seeks your life.   And his excuse is this, —
  You are no longer fit to rule as king,
  Since swayed by fantasies.   Therefore, I beg,
  If come you must, come not alone at dawn.
  Bring trusty friends with you.
SISYPHUS.   One friend, — no more.
  To ease you, I consent to company.
  Will you return with me?
LEONTES.   Gladly, my lord.

[*Exeunt Sisyphus and Leontes, left.   It grows darker.   Enter
Bion and Herse, right.   Herse carries a small basket.*

HERSE.   Do you think we shall ever find her, Bion?   Mother
  said I must give her back these yellow stones she left on the
  table.
BION (*searches about*).   Of course we'll find her.   It isn't an
  hour since she knocked on our door, and mother sent father
  out to catch a fish.   She can't have gone very far.   She
  may be asleep hereabouts.

HERSE (*glances about apprehensively*). The woods are so still. I feel afraid.

BION. That's just like a girl. You want to come along, but you don't want to stick it out. Well, go home, then, fraidy. You may see strange sights, after sunset. (*Mysteriously*) They tell me, though with what truth I know not, that at this time of day, and it's the same before dawn, when nature stops to take breath, and it's neither night, nor day, neither light, nor dark, that then the woods do not belong to mortals, not to boys and girls, like us, but to creatures we cannot see, —

HERSE (*frightened*). Oh, —

BION. Fauns, tree nymphs, and nereids!

HERSE (*more frightened*). Oh, dear, —

BION (*reassuringly*). Never mind! I'll take care of you.

HERSE. Bion, do you suppose Merope was one of those creatures? She didn't look like us.

BION. Well, what if she was?

HERSE. Then she'd never marry you.

BION. Who said I wanted her to marry me?

HERSE. Why, when she came, you put on your best suit.

BION (*shyly*). The other seemed so coarse.

VOICE OF A CHILD (*sings*).

Little creatures of the wood,
Fauns and nymphs, O,
Spring from out your leafy bowers,
Cease your slumbers midst the flowers;
Now 'tis neither night, nor day,
Fauns and nymphs, O,
Time it is for us to play,
Nymphs and fauns, O.

HERSE (*clings to Bion*). What is that?

BION. Be still. Don't move.

(*Bion and Herse cling together, at one side, in the shade of a rock. Enter a troop of little tree nymphs and fauns. They dance, music playing softly outside. Then a toy whistle is heard, which imitates a bird. The nymphs and fauns stop;*

the whistle is repeated, they run off, frightened. Bion drops Herse, and steps forward. Herse follows)

There, didn't I tell you? When 'tis neither night, nor day.

HERSE. I'm not afraid now. They are no bigger than I.

BION. Herse, perhaps they'd help us find Merope. Come!
[*Starts to pull Herse out. The whistle is heard again. Herse stops.*

HERSE. What kind of a bird is that?

BION. Hurry!
[*Drags Herse to the exit at the left. They run into Isidore, who is entering, blowing on a toy whistle. He carries a lighted lantern, and over his shoulder is suspended a basket containing terra-cotta statuettes and colored balls. The scene grows lighter, as it would from the light of a lantern.*

ISIDORE. Stop, now! Not so fast! What, would you knock Isidore down?

HERSE. Please excuse me.

ISIDORE (*adjusts his wares*). No harm done. The populace assembles already for the king's festival. I'm none too early with my wares. The first at the jug skims the cream.
[*Offers his wares.*

HERSE. Oh, what pretty balls!

BION (*tries to draw Herse away*). We're wasting time.

HERSE. I would like a ball, Bion, or a doll.

ISIDORE. Buy something, young sir? It's a gentleman's privilege to satisfy his lady's desires.

BION. I've no money.

ISIDORE. What? No money to spend at the king's wedding?

BION (*tries to draw Herse away*). We are from the country, sir, and know nothing of the king's wedding.

ISIDORE. Your indifference is explained. 'Tis the wine of enthusiasm which opens the purse strings. Curb your haste, and by the aid of my dolls, which the little lady admires, I will tell you the whole pretty story. Timeliness is the spirit of trade.

HERSE (*resisting Bion*). Please, Bion.
[*Examines the wares.*

ISIDORE. Now, here is Atlas, the bride's father, a care-worn man, since he carries the weight of the world. Here you see Pleione, her mother, and all the ladies of the family. We must not be ignorant of our best people. Here's Maia, the eldest daughter, goddess of spring, and mother of Hermes. Here's Electra, Taygete, Sterope, Alcyone, Celaeno, and last and best, Merope, the bride herself.

BION. Merope!

HERSE. Merope!

ISIDORE (*offers the statuette to Bion*). The king's bride! A bargain.

BION (*awed*). The king's bride! Herse, we'd better go home.
[*Bion tries again to draw Herse away from the dolls, fails, runs out alone.*

ISIDORE (*aside*). I scent news. I'll draw it forth.
(*Tosses a ball into the air, then a second, and a third; keeps the three balls going*)
Little lady, watch the balls! Now this one, now that, now this. Quite a trick, eh? Ah! One falls, another, and the third. 'Tis the darkness.
[*Herse searches for the balls. Finds one.*

HERSE. Here's one.

ISIDORE. Never mind. Come to-morrow, and find them. Little lady, I have told you about my Merope. Tell me about yours.

HERSE. Why, Merope came to our house about an hour ago, while we were just sitting down to supper. Then, while we were waiting for my father to bring back the fish, suddenly she saw some one she knew, though we saw no one at all, and crying out "Iris", or something like that, she went away. We've been looking for her. She left these yellow stones on the table.
[*Holds out her basket.*

ISIDORE (*examines the stones. Conceals his delight*). Worthless stones! However, I will make a bargain with you. You give me the pebbles. I'll give you the doll Merope.

[*Holds out the statuette to Herse, who takes it with pleasure.*

HERSE. Oh, thank you. Only it doesn't look like Merope.

ISIDORE. An ideal likeness, my dear, a figment of the artist's imagination. Most ladies prefer such. Good night.

HERSE. Good night, and thank you again.

[*Exit Herse.*

ISIDORE (*counts the nuggets*). So the king's dream is like to come true. Upon this mundane sphere Merope has set foot. An item of information worth its weight in gold. I can serve thereby the love-sick king, or the jealous Tolmid. Like an editor, I can argue with equal skill on either side. He that is shrewdest closes the best bargain. (*Slips the nuggets into a pocket beneath his cloak*) And to all appearances I was wasting breath. One can never tell when good luck's about to fall. Impatience is the sting of little minds. Therefore I won the nuggets. Now, for a wink of cat's sleep, one eye open. (*Lies down*) Isidore, thou dealer in gods and goddesses, wilt thou say prayers? Nay, except as wares, I have no use for gods. They sit and laugh in heaven, while we, poor devils, toil and die. Why worship them, and beg with servile spirit the good that should be ours unasked? The gods never gave me a night's lodging. The sky's my roof, the wind's my broom, the rain's my pail, nature's my housekeeper. (*Yawns*) Come, sleep! thou silent well of uncreated thought. In thee I sink myself, unfathomed friend. But first, let me put out my light. I am economical.

[*Isidore puts out his lantern. The scene is darkened. He settles himself for sleep. The moon rises. Upon the rocks in the rear appear the Nereids, disporting themselves joyously.*

PROTO. Like foam upon the water swift we glide;
Upon the tide
We drift to shore,
Then out again to moor beneath the moon.

THETIS. There sporting round a rock we dive for pearls,
While swiftly whirls
The water round our ears,

Ere there appears
The mermaid's room,
The chambers where they comb their long wet hair;
And where they wear
Green gowns, whose sheen
Is dimly seen,
As soft they play
Sad tunes upon an instrument of bone.

GALENE. No bound we own,
But free as wind,
New paths we find,
By night, or day,
Across the seas, to south, to east, to west;
In gay unrest,
Like morning light,
That glances bright
Upon the waves,
Or thoughts of poets as they idly muse.

PROTO. Or if we choose,
We sink below
The undertow,
To the still caves,
Grotesquely carved from rocks on ocean's floor;
There to explore
The rooms and aisles,
Or swift, meanwhiles,
A banquet call
On coral table set with cups of shell.

ALL. Then in cool dell,
Softly we slumber,
Fifty in number,
Nereids all.

[*The Nereids come over the rocks upon the glade. Thetis discovers Isidore, who pretends sleep.*

THETIS. Oh! Proto, look!

PROTO. A man!

[*They examine Isidore curiously.*

GALENE. It may be Phoebus playing he's a man,
Wearing disguise for love of idle tricks.
Those hyacinthine curls, those limbs divine,
Where tireless strength is married to fair form,
Often assume less god-like shape than this.

PROTO. No, no! The sleep that sits upon these lids
Is not the sleep of gods.

THETIS (*discovers the basket of toys*). Why, what are these?
Some balls! Catch, Nereids, catch!
[*The Nereids play ball.*

GALENE (*empties the basket of balls, and then of the statuettes*).
Such tiny men.

PROTO. They have form, but not breath.

GALENE. A lucky find.
[*Throws the empty basket down. It hits Isidore, who waits
until the Nereids are at play again, then pushes the basket
aside, and watches the Nereids with a wry face.*

ISIDORE (*aside*). Lucky for them, but as for Isidore, —
[*The Nereids exclaim with delight over the toys.*

A NEREID. Mine's best.

ANOTHER. No, — mine.

ANOTHER. No, — mine.

ISIDORE. Enchanting thieves!
[*A voice sings outside. It is Merope, approaching.*

MEROPE'S SONG
Where lilies blow, and roses grow,
And fragrant zephyrs die,
Midst daffodils and hyacinths,
In dalliance dwell I
The wanton wind I often bind,
And drive it as my steed;
With clouds for reins, and stars for spurs,
Across the skies I speed.
[*The Nereids stop play, and frightened, retreat rear to the
rocks. Enter Merope, singing the last of the song. She bears
wood flowers in her hands, with garlands about her neck.*

PROTO. A mortal comes! Away!

GALENE. Away!

[*In confusion the Nereids disappear over the rocks. Merope pursues them.*

MEROPE. Proto! Galene!

(*One or two Nereids turn, look at Merope, do not recognize her, all disappear. Merope comes forward, puzzled, and disappointed*)

Are they afraid of me? Am I then changed?
Nay! Rather are the Nereids at fault.
Their eyes see naught but surface form of things.
I am no different than when I kept
My place among the Pleiades in heaven.

(*Looks up into heaven*)

Ah! heaven doth seem doubly fair from earth.

(*Caresses the flowers*)

Yet sweet is earth. The woods, bright with spring flowers,
Frail bluets, hairbells, hypaticas, and cress,
Bid me dear welcome. I shall not regret,
But will be happy in this new sought sphere.

(*Sees the reflection of the stars in the pool*)

The stars! Caught here as fallen from heaven.
Sweet prisoners, companion me on earth.
The nymphs shall tangle you within their hair,
Drawing you down to sport beneath the waves,
With pearls and coral red enticing you.

(*Isidore watches Merope closely, from beneath the basket, which lies over his head. He pushes it aside, about to rise, when the sound of a hunting horn is heard. He hides again beneath the basket. Merope springs up*)

I know the sound. 'Tis Dian's silver horn.
She seeks me, having missed me from her maids.
I dread her loving eloquence, yet stand
Firm on my own decision.

[*Enter Dian with hounds in leash.*

DIAN. Merope!
My little maid. (*Embraces Merope. The dogs run off*)
What idle trick is this?

This dress, this spot, what does it mean?   Play you
A tree nymph, new released from aged elm,
Or naiad from the brook?   Tease me no more
By absence, but return with me to-night.

MEROPE.   I cannot, Dian, even though I would.

DIAN.   To-night the Pleiades in heaven less bright
Than wonted shine.

MEROPE.   One more, one less, naught should
Be difference.

DIAN.   Can you forget your birth, —
Your heritage?   Your golden goblet waits.
Pour out the wine of memory and quaff
It deep.   Without you heaven is forlorn.
Your sisters mourn.   Remember now their love;
Let pure affection in your heart have sway.

MEROPE.   Unchanged my love for them, Dian, and thee.
How heard you I was here in Argolis?

DIAN.   As sped I through heaven's winding avenues,
The devious pathways wide between the stars,
Came Hermes to me, telling you were here.
My little one!   Dian doth plead with you.
To women I belong, their cause I serve;
Not in their several states as sweethearts, wives,
Or mothers, but as women.   Ah! I would
That they had conscious pride that they were women,
And loved attainment as they now love men.

MEROPE.   Dian, I'm sorry to have caused you grief.

DIAN.   Beneath a clear cold moon sat Pleione,
And spun for you this web of human fate.
It cannot be of your own will you left
The star-sown fields.   Your mother loves the earth.
The name she gave you — Merope — proves that.

MEROPE.   My mother told me of the earth, 'tis true.
My childish ears she charmed with wondrous tales
Of crisp curled waters breaking on white shores;
Of moss-grown grottos, lulled by purling streams,
In whose cool depths the clear-eyed fishes sport;

Of sounds of soft winds stirring new-leaved trees,
At whose slim base the pale blue violets grow;
She told me, too, of men. I grant this true,
Yet came I down of my own will, that will
Determined by necessity. I had
To come, and I am happiest so, Dian.

DIAN. Where lay necessity?

MEROPE. Within my heart.

DIAN. O Echo! carry not these words afar,
But bury them in some dim cavern deep!
Can it be, then, that you who followed me,
Are caught within that net of earthly weave
Which men call love? For shame, my little maid;
Be not so weak! Take pattern by Dian.

MEROPE. Your heart is stern. You never have known
love.

DIAN. Is there no love but that 'twixt man and maid?
What, then, is deep desire for mankind's good?
Oh! I could weep when I look down on men.
They sell their souls for evanescent things;
They build false worlds, in which they suffer pain;
They call swift passion love, and foolish, take
Deceptive seeming for the truth that saves,
And then expect to reap reward. No, child!
Become not one of them. They are not wise.

MEROPE. In heaven you never spoke to me like this.

DIAN. I had no cause. Now, there is need to warn.
Earth's mystery has subtle, siren power;
Love, as men wish it, is but passion wild,
And woman is the plaything of the race;
Yet doth she know she has a soul, and craves
Some recognition of herself beyond
The lure of sex. Diana's state is best.

MEROPE. There must be some mistake. This can't be true.

DIAN. Experience alone to many minds
Conviction brings. Whom is it that you love?

MEROPE. His name is Sisyphus.

DIAN.   Corinth's great king!
  How came you to this choice?
MEROPE.   One night I looked
  From heaven to earth, and there did lie asleep
  Here by this pool, like some young god, the king·
  And he did dream of me.
DIAN.   This is the work
  Of Iris, wrought by dreams.   'Tis ever thus
  Her rainbow fingers slip to deep recess
  Within the mind, attuning some fine sense
  To expectation of a bliss divine.
  Yet even so, Dian will not despair.
  I surely have some power, and dare to say,
  Between us you must choose.
MEROPE.   My choice is made.
DIAN.   You wish me gone?
MEROPE.   Confuse not my desire.
  [*Isidore, from under his basket, chances to sneeze.*
DIAN (*alarmed*).   Hush!   What was that?
MEROPE (*puzzled*).   I do not know.   'Twas strange.
DIAN.   Some mortal's near.   Come, ere too late, away!
  Return, sweet bird, to that ethereal tree
  Where hangs your nest.   Let earth go as it will;
  For if men darken their own lives through pain,
  Because they will not act the good they know.
  Even pity has no power to succor them.
  Choose freedom!   Come!
MEROPE.   My freedom is to stay.
DIAN (*turns from Merope*).   More words were vain.   Yet
  with regret I go.
  (*Blows her horn.   The dogs return*)
  Ho! dogs, the gift of Pan;
  Scent up the prey.
  Ho! hounds, and fare ye forth,
  Ere burns the day.
  Ye six of spotted coat,
  Hunt lion's lair;

Ye Spartan seven swift,
Stir fauns and hare.
Now through the grey greenwood,
Crash through the brush;
After we have passed there falls,
In wake of us, a hush.
[*Exit Dian with the hounds.*

MEROPE (*starts after Dian*). Dian! Desert not now your little
    maid.
    The woods will empty be, when you are fled. (*Stops*)
    No, Merope! Let Dian go her way.
    The heart's good choice the will must consummate.
ISIDORE (*pushes off the basket; whispers*). Now is my chance.
    (*Starts to rise; Merope sees some one approaching on the
    left, comes forward. Isidore conceals himself again*)
    Not yet.
MEROPE (*looks left*). On evil errand bound this stranger is.
    No light surrounds his spirit as he walks,
    But like the night, his soul is robed in black.
    I would not meet with him; he wills naught good.
    [*Searches for a hiding place, discovers a cave formed by the
    rocks in the rear which she enters. Isidore rises, and lies
    down across the entrance to the cave.*

ISIDORE. The bird is safe. This cave's the cage, this rock
    The door, and I, the lock upon the door,
    That's fitted only with a golden key.
    Whoever entrance gains must first pay me.
    Knowledge is golden; therefore I'll be wise.
    [*Feigns sleep. Enter Tolmid left.*

TOLMID. Why should I, Tolmid, bow to Sisyphus?
    Injustice fans my hate, for why should he
    Be ever fortunate, and always gain
    What he desires, while ever I remain
    In name, place, state, to him inferior.
    (*Comes upon Isidore*)
    What fellow's this, asleep upon wet grass?
    [*Kicks Isidore, who starts up, feigning anger.*

ISIDORE. Who kicked me?

TOLMID. The pleasure was mine.

ISIDORE. Apologize.

TOLMID (*laughs cynically*). The fellow's drunk.

ISIDORE. I deny it.

TOLMID. Why do you sleep here?

ISIDORE (*aside, recognizing Tolmid*). 'Tis Tolmid. Lucky Isidore! (*Turns to Tolmid*) My head being top-heavy with the weight of some newly acquired information, I laid down, master. I had not meant to sleep. I am waiting for Tolmid.

TOLMID. Tolmid?

ISIDORE. Aye, the great Tolmid, — he who stands second to the king.

TOLMID. Second?

ISIDORE. Yes, master. But in my opinion, and there be many who agree with me, a man more fit to be king than the present royal dreamer.

TOLMID. My friend, you speak boldly.

ISIDORE. He who thinks boldly must speak so.

TOLMID. Since you wait for Tolmid, what can he do for you?

ISIDORE. The question is, rather, what can Isidore do for Tolmid? Much, master, much.

TOLMID. I am friend to Tolmid. I promise you his good will.

ISIDORE. Assist me to rise. (*Holds out his hand to Tolmid, who hesitates to take it*) Well, I need more sleep.

[*Lies down again.*

TOLMID (*offers his hand to Isidore*). Pardon, friend.

ISIDORE (*rises, with Tolmid's aid*). 'Tis wise to be democratic these days. Thanks, master. Allow me to light my lantern. Moonlight may suit lovers, but for affairs of business, give me real light. (*Lights his lantern. The scene grows brighter*) So! Master, have I your word that this is a little matter of business? Were I dealing directly with Tolmid, —

TOLMID. Let this speak for Tolmid.

[*Gives Isidore money.*

ISIDORE (*counts the money*). Thank you. All trade is built on trust. (*Slips the coins into his pocket*) This, I take it, is but an appetiser. The feast's to follow. For this sum, master, you might obtain a peasant maid, but I can offer you, of course, on sufficient inducement, —

TOLMID (*impatient*). To your point.

ISIDORE. Master, do you believe in dreams?

TOLMID. I play no fool to fantasies.

ISIDORE. Nor I. My reason guides my will. Still, one must believe one's eyes, and with these eyes that look on you, I've seen to-night, here on this spot, this very spot, —

TOLMID (*more impatient*). Well, talker, whom have you seen?

ISIDORE. The thieving nereids. They robbed me of my wares. Proof, — my empty basket.

TOLMID (*starts left*). I've no time for nereids.

ISIDORE. Wait! Also, I have seen Diana, goddess of chastity.

TOLMID. The lady does not interest me.

ISIDORE. Listen! Also, I have seen Merope, the king's bride.

[*Watches Tolmid, for the effect of his speech.*

TOLMID (*alert*). The king's bride, —

ISIDORE. The Pleiad, come to earth, a miracle. Just as the king dreamed.

TOLMID (*affects indifference*). What matters that to Tolmid?

ISIDORE. My lord, either you are exceedingly sly, or exceedingly slow. I incline to the former opinion, but will reply as if my wits were dull.

TOLMID (*turns from Isidore*). Talk, talk, talk! (*Turns back to Isidore*) Well, I'll hear you out.

ISIDORE. 'Twill pay you, master, to listen to Isidore. The Pleiad's here. If Tolmid should send her back to heaven whence she came, the king could not marry her. His dream would not come true, all Corinth would say he was crazy, and laugh him out. Once make a man ridiculous, and he's lost.

TOLMID. If the Pleiad loves the king, she'll not return to heaven.

ISIDORE. She'll have to, if you send her there. (*Makes the motion of killing some one with the sword*). Since she's on earth, she's mortal, just like any of us.

TOLMID (*aside*). My daytime sense yields to this night's spell. (*Gives Isidore more money*) There's for reason gone. Where is the Pleiad?

ISIDORE (*counts the money*). Sufficient crumbs may in time make a loaf. Double this, master.

TOLMID. No more. Furthermore, if you are lying to me, and there's no Pleiad here, I shall run you through, and send your own soul back to heaven. (*Half draws his sword*) I'll recover my money.

ISIDORE (*frightened*). I assure you, that will be unnecessary. My soul is not prepared for heaven. This way, master. (*Leads Tolmid to the cave; whispers*) The Pleiad's here.

TOLMID. If this is a trick, remember, —

[*Enters the cave.*

ISIDORE. If I'm caught lying, I'm run through with the sword, and lose my money. Merope may have escaped. I'm off! Good luck to you, Tolmid. I'll conceal my going with noise. (*Picks up his empty basket, and his lantern. Goes off singing. The scene is lighted again by moonlight*)

For he's a fool who does but act
Upon a person's word;
Yet he's a fool who does not act
Upon what he has heard.

[*The song concluded, Tolmid reenters from the cave, leading Merope, who resists him, frightened.*]

TOLMID. The churl spoke truth for once. At least, I've found a maid, — a pretty one.

MEROPE. Pray, let me go!

TOLMID. But whether you're the Pleiad, ——

(*Draws her into the bright moonlight*)

Here's more light.

Come! Let me look at you. A pretty face,

A slender form, a hand that's fine, with eyes
That would do Venus honor. Well, and good!
Yet many a mortal maid is just as fair.
Give me some sign that you have come from heaven.

MEROPE. No sign have I but truth within my heart.
I wore a star in heaven, but it was quenched
When I touched earth. I beg you, let me go.

TOLMID. I half believe I have the Pleiad here.
Each gentle word makes your release less sure.
Know you who I am?

MEROPE. Tolmid! — he who plots
Against the king.

TOLMID. Nay! He who shall be king.

MEROPE. Brazen assertion is but barren proof.

TOLMID. You love the king?

MEROPE. At dawn I'll be his bride.

TOLMID (*grasps her roughly*). I dream no dreams, but you are
in my power.
You think to marry Sisyphus, and so
Confirm his confidence that he shall mount
To higher place in public honor.   No!
I'll take no risks that you are not from heaven.
No Pleaid bride shall aid the man I hate.
(*Forces Merope to her knees, and draws his sword. Clouds
obscure the moon. The scene grows dark*)
Now fate is kind to me at last.

MEROPE (*in terror*). Good sir,
What ill have I done you, that you harm me?

TOLMID. Your beauty pleads for you, but all in vain.
Though you were thrice as fair, my will I'd work.
A weak will at the end thwarts ablest plan.

MEROPE (*stays Tolmid's hand, which holds the sword*). The ill
you seek to do me, will rebound
Upon yourself. I pray you, harm me not.
Such deeds, Pandora like, bear cask of woe.

TOLMID. Let come a woe more deep than Tartarus,
More black than Stygian waters, and more fell

Than Hydra's hiss, yet welcome would it be,
So it came after I'd obtained my will.
You shall not be the bride of Sisyphus.

[*Frees his hand, raises his sword. The scene grows so dark the figures of Merope and Tolmid are scarcely visible. It thunders.*

MEROPE. Grant me one prayer, before you strike me down.

TOLMID. Prayers do no harm. But come, be quick! I wait.

MEROPE (*in supplication*). Oh, mother, dear Pleione, lend thy aid.

Fate tangles destiny for one thou lovest.

You bade me come to earth. Oh, save me now!

TOLMID (*about to kill Merope*). Now goes your soul to heaven whence it came.

[*A white light appears upon the scene. Tolmid drops as if struck by lightning. Pleione is revealed. She goes quickly to Merope, raising her.*

PLEIONE. My child?

MEROPE. My mother, — you have come!

PLEIONE. I heard

Your cry, and came, swift through the trembling night.

For when a soul doth utter such a prayer,

The ether trembles to the outmost zone,

And he who has the power to answer, heeds.

MEROPE (*points to Tolmid*). He wills to kill me.

PLEIONE. Child, he has no power,

Save what you give him by this mortal fear.

MEROPE. I knew not earth was thus; it looked so fair.

Oh, take me back with you to heaven kind.

PLEIONE. Speak you such timid words? Recall them, swift!

Have you lost faith in your high destiny?

Then learn this truth, and having learned it, live

On earth immortal as you were in heaven,

Until your work is done. Take courage, child.

Let not the earth thought weight your spirit down.

Death has no power save fear in minds of men.

Repeat my words.

MEROPE (*humbly*). Death has no power but fear

In minds of men. Forgive me, Pleione.

I shall remain on earth. I am rebuked.

PLEIONE. Now speak you like my child, my Merope.

Yet Hermes comes with firm command of Zeus

That you return. Already is he near.

MEROPE. I shall not change.

PLEIONE. Kiss me farewell!

MEROPE. Farewell!

(*Kisses Pleione, who immediately goes away. The white light remains about Merope, although somewhat dimmer. Merope stands an instant in thought; Tolmid stirs, turns. Merope goes to him*)

This man hates Sisyphus.

(*Takes up Tolmid's sword, raises it as if to kill him, suddenly throws it down in horror*)

Did I this deed,

I'd rank the same as Tolmid.

[*The falling sword rouses Tolmid. He sits up, dazed. Merope retreats. He does not see her at first.*

TOLMID (*notices the light*). What! 'Tis day?

I must have lain for hours. (*Reaches for his sword*)

My trusty sword!

The lightning struck me, paralyzed my hand.

(*Rises, sees Merope, stops, astonished. Merope faces him fearlessly*)

Still here? The Pleiad? Good! You said at dawn

You should be bride. My sword will wed with you.

[*Approaches Merope with menace.*

MEROPE (*with dauntless conviction*). Against the Pleiad has the sword no power.

[*Tolmid's hand drops.*

TOLMID. The second time I fail. Well, be it so!

(*Laughs harshly*)

"Against the Pleiad has the sword no power!"
(*Raises his sword*)
But — Sisyphus! My sword has power there.
[*Laughs again. Goes out with uplifted sword.*

MEROPE. I sense his dreadful meaning! Sisyphus!
My king! my lover! This must never be.
The sword of Tolmid must be rendered dull.
[*Merope turns to follow Tolmid. Enter Hermes.*

HERMES. Daughter of Pleione, —

MEROPE. Nay, stop me not!

HERMES. From Zeus I come to summon you to heaven.

MEROPE. To heaven! When my love is in danger? No!
Command of Zeus is less than mother's wish,
And mother's wish less than decree of fate,
But fate itself less than demand of love.
I go to Sisyphus, ere 'tis too late.

HERMES. You will, then, to remain on earth?

MEROPE. I must.

HERMES. Farewell! I bear, though loath, the news aloft.
High heaven's lost to you forevermore.
[*Exit Hermes. As he goes, the white light fades from about
Merope. The scene is lighted again only by moonlight.
Merope stands with upraised hands.*

MEROPE. One heaven lost! Another to be gained.

CURTAIN

ACT TWO

*The scene is the same as Act One. Dim light, which slowly
changes to colors of the dawn. Six Pleiades are disclosed, dancing in stately measure. They wear garments of filmy texture, and
on the forehead of each shines a star. They sing. Soft music.*

CHORUS OF THE PLEIADES.
Nightly we shone,
Sisters seven,
Brightly we graced
Earth and heaven;

But of the fair, fairest of all,
She whom we sing, she whom we call,
Merope! Merope!
Sister ours!
Weary the waiting, weary the hours;
Why didst thou leave us?
Why thus so grieve us?

Lovely as Hebe
Walked she heaven,
Followed by leash hound,
By Dian given.
Golden her hair that gold fillet bound,
Golden her girdle that cinctured her round.
Merope! Merope!
Sister ours!
Vacant thy place is, withered the flowers,
Gathered at morning
For thy adorning.

Daughters of Atlas,
Born of Pleione,
Ocean sprung, mountain sprung,
Mountain Cyllene;
Maia, Electra, Taygete named,
Sterope, Celaeno, Alcyone famed,
Abiding in heaven,
Must we deny thee?
Merope! Merope!
Where dost thou hide thee?

Sister-love sending,
Swiftly we fly,
Searching all places we can descry;
Warm is the warmth of love, in love abiding;
Strong is the strength of love, in love confiding.
Merope! Merope!
Little one dear!

Could we but see thee, could we but hear,
Thy laughter ringing,
Thy tender singing!
[*The song concluded, the Pleiades pass quickly out to the left.
Enter Merope, from the right, dejected.*

MEROPE. It was decreed we could not meet till dawn.
All night I've searched for him in vain. I pray
He come now, as he dreamed, unharmed.
(*Six white doves fly in from the left. They flutter above
Merope*)
The doves!
My sisters! gentle Pleiades! You fly
To far Hesperides to fetch for Zeus
Ambrosia.   Not seven, now, you go,
But shorn of your dear sister, sadly six.
(*Caresses the doves*)
Such sadness, though, is kind of happiness,
Like tender music played in minor key.
I'll not return to you, yet I am glad,
Like scent to flower, clings sister-love to me.
(*Lets the doves go*)
Each night I'll look to heaven, and send you prayers.
[*The doves fly out to sea. Merope kisses her hands to them.
Enter Iris. The dawn grows brighter. Merope stands in
the rear, unseen by Iris.*

IRIS.   Now dim-eyed night with cloud-encircled form,
Doth creep to Tartarus, as forth steps day,
Robed in a garment woven of frail light,
And gazing with blue eyes upon the world;
Now tune the birds their matin orchestra,
When robin's lusty note outshouts the rest;
Now is the time consummate.   At the dawn
Shall Merope meet Sisyphus. I call
The willing actors to their several parts.
Ho! Sisyphus — ho! Sisyphus — the king.
Ho! Merope — ho! Merope — the queen.
[*Merope runs forward.*

MEROPE. O Iris, is he safe? Where is the king?
 Has harm befallen him? Oh, I must hear.
IRIS. Now comes he with Leontes through the wood,
 To meet you here.
MEROPE. Oh, happy, happy dawn!
IRIS. Lo! see the east —
 The dawn has changed to rose. I must away!
 I shall be visible to you no more;
 But when in after dawnings you awake,
 As from strange, joyous dream unmemorized,
 Know you have been with Iris in far fields.
 Men call it rest in sleep; 'tis heaven, instead,
 Which touches them, though they be unaware.
MEROPE. Then heaven's not lost to me?
IRIS. If kept within
 The heart, heaven is never lost. Farewell!
 [*Exit Iris.*
MEROPE. He comes! He comes! Then Tolmid wrought no ill.
 Oh, I am glad! I'll hide within the wood;
 'Twould not be maidenly to seem in haste.
 I'd rather he should search for me awhile.
 (*Goes right, stops*)
 What if he know me not, but ask some proof
 That I am Merope, as Tolmid did?
 Nay! that's impossible. It could not be.
 I've but to show him love within my eyes.
 [*Merope runs out, right. Enter Tolmid, left, cloaked.*
TOLMID. I would that it keep dark. The night were best,
 For then is most effective that fell brood
 Which night ununioned bore: — fate, death, and sleep,
 Oblivion, wanton love, oaths, fraud, and pain;
 Contentions, doubts, disputes, and homicides —
 The pitiless instruments that men must use
 To gain their will. I thought that Sisyphus
 Would come, ere now. (*Looks out left*)
 Ah! who is this, with lights,
 As if it still were night? I'll not be seen.

[*Tolmid retreats rear. Enter from the left three workmen, carrying lighted lanterns, which they blow out, as they set them down.*

MASTER WORKMAN (*to First Workman*). Have you the written measurements?

FIRST WORKMAN (*fumbles in his blouse*). I think so, master. (*Takes out a paper*) Yes, here they are.

MASTER WORKMAN (*takes the paper, reads*). A platform to be erected, forty paces long, and thirty paces wide. For the dance, I suppose.
(*Folds the paper, puts it in his belt*)
Get to work, men.

SECOND WORKMAN. We ought to have started this work before.

MASTER WORKMAN. My lord Leontes only gave me the order at midnight. He sent to my door, and roused me from as sound a sleep as I've had in moons.

FIRST WORKMAN. Of what is the platform to be made?

MASTER WORKMAN. Of board planks. Did you think it was to be the platform of a political party, to exist only on paper?
[*Laughs at his joke.*

SECOND WORKMAN. Where are the boards?

FIRST WORKMAN. Not arrived.

SECOND WORKMAN. Shall we hew down trees, and make our own planks?

FIRST WORKMAN (*sits down*). We must wait for the material.

MASTER WORKMAN (*rouses up First Workman. Bustles about*). Wait! Not on your life. Get to work, there. Measure off the space.

FIRST WORKMAN. I left my measure in the shop. I'll go back for it, master.

MASTER WORKMAN. Not this evening. This job is not a time job. We're on contract. Every man to finish as quick as he can. Get to work everybody. Pace the space. Quick!

SECOND WORKMAN. How long shall I pace, master?

MASTER WORKMAN. To the full of your stretch.

FIRST WORKMAN (*aside to Second Workman*). The master sells lumber. He, he! To the full of your stretch.

[*Second Workman overpaces, and falls.*

MASTER WORKMAN (*angry at Second Workman*). What are you wasting your time for?

SECOND WORKMAN. I overstretched, master, pacing for lumber.

MASTER WORKMAN (*to First Workman*). Where are your tools?

[*Second Workman rises.*

FIRST WORKMAN. I will go for the tools, master.

MASTER WORKMAN. Are no tools here?

FIRST WORKMAN. We thought this was a time job, master. I will go back to the shop for the tools.

MASTER WORKMAN (*in a rage*). No tools, no boards, no anything, and you workmen doing nothing. By the dogs! And this work on contract.

SECOND WORKMAN. We can't build the platform, to-night, that's sure.

MASTER WORKMAN. I dismiss you, all, every one of you.

FIRST WORKMAN. Listen, master. Perhaps the king's dream won't come true.

MASTER WORKMAN. We could collect just the same, if the work was done.

FIRST WORKMAN. No man likes to be shown a fool. If the dream should not come true, the king might be exceedingly glad to have no reminders about in the shape of dance platforms.

MASTER WORKMAN. He, he! And would pay us better for having failed to build the platform, than for building it. That's a good idea.

SECOND WORKMAN. Well, since we can't build the platform, anyway, it's worth considering.

[*The Workmen take up their lanterns, and are about to pass out. Tolmid steps forward.*

TOLMID. My friends!

MASTER WORKMAN (*to his men*).   Wait, there.

[*The workmen pause.*

TOLMID.   In whose employ are you?

MASTER WORKMAN (*offended*).   I'm an independent contractor, sir.   These are my men.

WORKMEN (*bowing*).   Yes, sir.

TOLMID.   I beg your pardon.   My meaning was, for whom are you building the platform.

FIRST WORKMAN.   We're not building it, sir.

TOLMID.   Yes, yes.   I understand.   But for whom were you building it?

MASTER WORKMAN.   I've a contract with his majesty, the king.

TOLMID.   Come!   I've a job for you that will pay you better.

[*Displays a bag of money.*

MASTER WORKMAN.   At your service, my lord.

WORKMEN (*bowing*).   At your service.

TOLMID.   You are patriotic, I trust, like all good citizens, and ready to serve the state.   The state pays well for service.

MASTER WORKMAN.   We'll gladly serve the state.   Eh, men?

WORKMEN.   Yes, sire.

TOLMID.   I see I can rely on you.   Know you the king by sight?

ALL.   We do.

TOLMID.   And lord Leontes?

ALL.   We do.

TOLMID (*shakes the gold*).   Listen!   The king comes through the woods to-night in obedience to a fantastic dream.   This you know.   First, however, Leontes will come with a single companion.   This man resembles the king.   Indeed, you will scarcely know him from the king, but don't be deceived by that.   It's part of the plot.

ALL.   Plot?

TOLMID.   There's a dastardly plot on to-night to kill the king, when he comes to meet his bride.   The man with Leontes is responsible.   Would you save your king?

ALL.   We would, sire.

TOLMID. Then, my friends, with your clubs, there, strike
down Leontes' companion. Beat him to death. With
proof that you have done your work well, you will find
waiting for you in Corinth, three talents of gold.

FIRST WORKMAN. Three talents! That's a heap of money.

SECOND WORKMAN. But we're to kill a man to get it.

MASTER WORKMAN. My men, it's in the service of the state.
You save your king.

SECOND WORKMAN. But I couldn't kill anybody. It'd make
me sick.

MASTER WORKMAN. You can hold the other fellow.

TOLMID (*tosses the gold to the Master Workman*). So it's agreed.
There's to bind the contract.

MASTER WORKMAN (*pockets the money*). By which path comes
the murderer?

TOLMID. Direct from Corinth, as you came.

MASTER WORKMAN (*brandishes his club*). Kill the king,
would he? We'll see to that. Come, men!
[*The Workmen go out.*

TOLMID. So let him, if he will, believe in dreams.
I'll follow presently, and finding him,
Will say, "Dreamer, it were pity to awake."
Then Tolmid shall be king, and being so,
The Pleiad shall be mine. I'm glad she lives.
'Twere pity to have killed a thing so fair.
She weds the king, she says, so she weds me.
(*Walks about, impatient*)
By now, those fellows should have struck their blow.
(*Sees Sisyphus and Leontes approaching by boat*)
The king! Leontes! Coming here by boat!
The deadly deed must now be Tolmid's task.
[*Draws his sword, hides. Enter from the sea Sisyphus and
Leontes.*

SISYPHUS. I've never known you, friend, so timorous.
To please you I have stayed with you all night.
You conjure danger out of quietude,
Fancying the shadows, even, ambushed foe,

And flight of birds an enemy's approach.
This is the habit of a timid soul,
Not worthy you, Leontes.

LEONTES. 'Tis my love,
Which makes me fear for you, my lord. The things
In nature answer to our mood. To you
I owe all that I am, or have, and I,
Though you flout danger foolishly, would give
My life for you.

SISYPHUS (*with hand on Leontes' shoulder*). Dear friend, fear
not for me.

LEONTES. I beg that you return before ill comes.
I feel that it lies near. Stay not alone
In this strange place, which may but ambush prove.
Desire may urge, discretion whispers, "Nay."

SISYPHUS. Taut harnessing the winds that now sport wild,
You know how I would make these vacant seas
Alive with ships sailing to Araby;
You know how I desire that men should be
Not servitors of fear, nor couched in ease,
Chained to their ancient doubts and selfish aims,
But having, as is meant, dominion o'er
The earth, — and what is more, over themselves;
Yet should I fail to realize these aims,
Still would I fate fulfill, if wed to her
Whom heaven disclosed to me, my Pleiad bride;
And from the union, clear as this pure spring,
Which like a poet's inspiration flows
Forth to the day from some invisible source,
Be born a god-like child.

LEONTES. My lord, beware
Man cannot be a god.

SISYPHUS. There lies my fault.
You fear a foe without, I, one within.
Bearing within my breast the consciousness
Of power, I may be overproud, and claim
For self the glory.

LEONTES.   This is fault, my lord,
   Only as it is excess of virtue.
SISYPHUS.   Look!
   There breaks the dawn, a red streak in the east.
   The slumbering seas reflect the wizard beam;
   Afar arise the snow-capped peaks of song,
   Hymettus, and the far-famed Helicon.
   Though I have years, this moment is my birth.
   The womb of fate springs wide, and sends me forth.
   I search for Merope.   She must be near.
LEONTES   (attempts to hold Sisyphus back).   My lord wait
   here!
SISYPHUS.   Leontes, let me go!
   [Frees himself from Leontes' hold, and goes out to the right.
   Tolmid tries to slip past Leontes to follow Sisyphus.   Leontes
   grapples with Tolmid.
LEONTES.   'Tis as I thought.   It does not take much day
   For me to know you, Tolmid, or your will.
   You shall not pass to murder Sisyphus,
   Unless it be above Leontes' form.
TOLMID.   A slight youth, you, to mouth such braggart words.
   [Tolmid and Leontes fight.   Stabbed by Tolmid, Leontes falls.
LEONTES (calls, painfully).   My lord!
   (Reënter Sisyphus, running) I've fallen at his hand.
SISYPHUS (supports Leontes).   What's happened?
LEONTES (faintly).   Beware of Tolmid.   He doth mean you
   ill.
SISYPHUS (sees Tolmid).   This is your work, yours, Tolmid,
   whom I loved.
   (To Leontes) Leontes! my dear friend, — take courage,
   live!
LEONTES.   I am too heavy.   Lay me on the ground.
   [Leontes dies in Sisyphus' arms.   Sisyphus lays him on the
   ground, covers him with his cloak.   Tolmid approaches Sisy-
   phus stealthily, to stab him in the back, as he bends over
   Leontes.   Sisyphus quickly turns, faces Tolmid.
SISYPHUS.   Oh, base beyond belief!

TOLMID. Draw, Sisyphus!

And prove which is the better man of us.

SISYPHUS. Now I could strike you down, like some low worm,

But I'll not fight.

TOLMID. Do you refuse to draw?

SISYPHUS. I am the king.

TOLMID. Is kingship, then, a plea

For cowardice? By what right are you king?

SISYPHUS. My own.

TOLMID. Has heaven favorites, that it,

Like unfair mother, pets a certain child?

Why should one man be king, and not another?

SISYPHUS. In sight of heaven, all men are kings. Grant that,

The rest remains with us.

TOLMID. So be it, then!

All men are kings, but some do wear the crown,

While others serve.

SISYPHUS (*over the form of Leontes*). No crown could outshine that

Which rests now on the head of him you slew.

You, Tolmid, have met life with critic sneer,

Yet for our boyhood friendship I raised you

To place of minister. Leave Corinth! Go!

Before I strike you dead, as is my power.

TOLMID. You grant me life? I spurn your favors. Ha!

[*Rushes on Sisyphus with his sword. Sisyphus is compelled to defend himself. They fight fiercely.*

SISYPHUS. Trickster! coward!

TOLMID. Call what names you will!

[*Tolmid wounds Sisyphus, who falls.*

SISYPHUS. My faith was wrong. I am not king; — not king!

Or you would have no power over me.

[*Tolmid is about to slay Sisyphus. Enter Merope. She arrests Tolmid's sword.*

MEROPE. I heard the noise of battle. Tolmid, hold!

An armistice! What, would you murder him?
A fallen enemy? Lay down your sword.
Rise, Sisyphus! Your wound is naught.

SISYPHUS. Who speaks?

[Merope stands so that Sisyphus does not see her.

MEROPE. The voice of heaven!

(To Tolmid, indicating that he lay his sword down) Obey!

TOLMID. I keep my sword.
It is the only weapon that I have.

MEROPE. Then are you ignorant of true defense.
Rise, Sisyphus! Fight not as king,
But man, against your foe, since fight you must.

[Sisyphus rises. Merope retreats. The fight is renewed.

SISYPHUS. "Fight not as king, but man!" Aye, so I fight.
(Tolmid falls, mortally wounded) Thanks, heavenly voice,
that gave me strength to win.

[Tolmid forces himself to rise. Staggers to exit.

TOLMID. Thus has it ever been, you fortunate,
And I, whate'er my will, compelled to yield.

*[Exit Tolmid. Sisyphus sheathes his sword, kneels beside
Leontes, draws back the cloak from his face, weeps. Merope
advances, and stands beside Sisyphus.*

MEROPE. Loved you this man?

SISYPHUS *(deems Merope some peasant)*. As brother. Oh!
to undo this cruel deed!
How true it is, our victory too oft
Is built on other's woe. To this still friend
I owe my life. Leontes died for me.

MEROPE *(bends over Leontes. The white light becomes visible
about her)*. Such love of man for man is seldom met;
It bears within itself the seed of life.
Leontes is not dead. He lives! He lives!

[Leontes stirs, lifts his head. The light fades from Merope.

LEONTES *(dazed, stretches his hand to Sisyphus)*. My lord—

SISYPHUS *(astonished)*. What's this? He speaks, he moves,
he breathes!
Yet I could swear his heart had ceased to beat.

MEROPE. Speak to your friend.

[*Goes to the pool, takes water in a gourd, and returns to Leontes.*

SISYPHUS. Leontes!

LEONTES. Give me drink.

(*Drinks from the gourd, which Merope holds to his lips*)
Thanks, sister. You are kind. Enough, enough.

SISYPHUS. It is some miracle. I can't believe, —

MEROPE (*holds the gourd up, like an offering to heaven*).
Naught is death's power, but fear in minds of men.

[*Leontes rises; as if drawn by some irresistible power, approaches Merope.*

LEONTES. Whence came you? — who? —

[*Sisyphus rises. Merope turns, and looks into his eyes.*

SISYPHUS (*with joy*). The Pleiad! Merope!

[*Kneels before her.*

LEONTES. The dream come true. I'll never doubt again.

SISYPHUS. If now I dream, forever let me dream,
Lest no such visions feed my waking eyes.
My Merope! My bride! To me you've come,
The tissue of my thought made visible.

[*Merope, drops the gourd, holds out her hands to Sisyphus, who takes them in his, kissing them.*

MEROPE. You ask no sign from heaven to my truth?

SISYPHUS. You are yourself your own most heavenly proof.
Yours was the power that brought Leontes back.
Yours was the voice from heaven that gave me strength.

MEROPE. Not on the brawn of men, or sharpened steel
Rests true defense, but on a higher power.
The sword but symbol is; in righteousness
If drawn, it has resistless majesty.
Yet there is dawning for the earth a day
When swords shall be no more. 'Tis will of heaven.

[*Sisyphus unfastens his sword, and lays it on the ground.
Merope takes it up, passes to the rear, and symbolically flings it into the sea. Sisyphus rises, stands with bowed head.*

SISYPHUS. So be all swords!

LEONTES. Why, this were heaven on earth!

[*Merope returns from the rear; Sisyphus meets her, leading her forward. The sound of a brawl outside. Enter the Master Workman, beating the Fisherman, who is protesting loudly.*

FISHERMAN. By all the thunder and lightning of the universe, by all the rain in the bucket of Neptune, by everything under the sun, and above the moon, I never plotted to kill the king.

SISYPHUS (*parts the men*). What is this quarrel?

MASTER WORKMAN (*kneels to Sisyphus*). Sire, I've saved your life. This fellow, so Tolmid said, plotted to kill you.

FISHERMAN (*kneels to Sisyphus*). Sire, I'm naught but a poor fisherman. I never plotted to kill you, nor any man. My wife is sending you a fish for supper. (*Enter Bion, with a fish on a platter. Herse follows, with a wreath of daisies*)

Here is the fish! A god put it on my line for me. Therefore my wife said it was too good for us, and feared to eat it.

[*Herse runs to Merope, with the wreath.*

HERSE. Here is a wreath I made for you by moonlight.

LEONTES. Why, this is the fellow who's to build the platform for the dance, — a carpenter.

MASTER WORKMAN (*rises, pompously*). Contractor, sire.

SISYPHUS (*raises the Fisherman*). This fellow looks innocent.

MASTER WORKMAN. Tolmid bade us kill the man who walked with Leontes through the wood.

FISHERMAN. I never walked with Leontes.

LEONTES. That I swear.

MASTER WORKMAN. Contracts are contracts.

SISYPHUS. I see, you had to kill somebody, to get your money.

MEROPE (*comes forward with Herse and Bion*). My lord, these are the kind fisher folk who sheltered me last night. I know they mean you no harm.

[*Enter First and Second Workmen.*

FIRST WORKMAN. Murder! Master, he who promised us the bag of gold lies in the wood.

SECOND WORKMAN. Slain! Fallen into a hawthorn bush, the thorns catching his eyes.

FIRST WORKMAN. Who will pay us the gold?

MASTER WORKMAN. Ssh, — ssh! Say naught about the gold.

[*Draws the men back.*

SISYPHUS. Leontes, I appoint you minister.

LEONTES. My loyal thanks! I'll strive to serve you well.

SISYPHUS. The plot of Tolmid's done. Reward these men.

LEONTES (*to Merope*). Dear lady, you shall have such marriage feast,

As Corinth never saw before. Come, friends!

[*Exit Leontes, followed by the workmen, fisherman, Bion and Herse. The sun rises.*

MEROPE. Lo! Sisyphus, the day! The stars are gone.

I could not now return, e'en though I would.

SISYPHUS. You choose to stay with me?

MEROPE. Yes, Sisyphus.

Go where I would, I must return to you.

Love's arms are never loosed, but ever clasp

Invisibly the object of desire;

Love's lips are never far, but ever speak

Unvoiced words to ever listening ear.

SISYPHUS. Yet when I look on you, I would not keep

You here. Earth's ways are often dark. Too bright

You are for sorrow, and for toil too fair.

MEROPE. It is not toil to do what we desire.

Fear not for me, my king. All labor's sweet,

If 'tis a service born of a glad will,

And I would prove by all pure, simple things,

Children, and home, companionship, and you,

That earth, if mortals wish, can be as heaven.

SISYPHUS (*places the daisy wreath on Merope's head*). I crown you queen.

[Takes her in his arms, kisses her. A group of maidens dance in with garlands.

MEROPE. The sun-maids come! They raise
Each morn unto their lord, the sun, glad praise.

SUN-MAIDEN'S SONG.

Light and glory,
Rhythmic sun,
Lo! to greet thee,
Swift we come.
Ah! the night passed wearily;
Loath to sleep, oh! glad were we,
When thy heralds touched our eyes,
Bidding us awake, arise.
Breezes fresh sweep o'er the seas,
Tossing delicately the trees,
While the shadows flee away,
Chased by their bright enemy.

Now we bare our breasts, snow white,
To receive thy shafts of light;
Raise our arms in ecstasy,
We who serve thee, yet are free.
Were we blind, thy light we'd feel
Through our veinèd eyelids steal;
And thy warmth would cheer our bones,
Lay we chill and dull in tombs.
On whatsoe'er thy glad beams rest,
Is made glorified and blest.

Beauty of the earth and sky,
In our hearts increaseth joy;
Roses shimmering with dew,
Clover garlands gathered new,
Pearly cloudlets edged with gold,
All these do thy powers unfold.
Even the silence seems to shout
As the splendid sun bursts out.

Now the dawn blooms into day,
Slower moves our rhythmic sway;
Swallows darting here and there,
Almost touch our floating hair.
We the dawn and sun-rise sing,
Others praise to noon-time bring;
So we go, again to come,
When to-morrow is begun.

[*Tossing their garlands upon Sisyphus and Merope the Sun-Maidens run off. Sisyphus and Merope pass out left. Enter Isidore from the right, with basket freshly filled with wares.*

ISIDORE.   'Tis never well to be discouraged, friend,
For of beginning there is never an end.

CURTAIN

THE CHINA PIG

EVELYN EMIG

EVELYN EMIG was born May 29, 1895, at Washington, D. C. She was educated in private schools and at George Washington University, where, in 1919, her one-act play *The Old Order* won the University Prize.

In the spring of 1918 she joined a little group of Harvard Forty-Seveners in helping to found, and the following fall was elected Director of, *The Incubator Players*, a little theatre organization of about a hundred members, artists of all descriptions, who were marooned in Washington during the War.

Her one-act play *Wars of the Sea* won the Hollywood Community Theatre Prize in 1922.

THE CHINA PIG

A PLAY IN ONE ACT

By EVELYN EMIG

Characters

ELIZABETH MAYNARD, the mother.
ELSA, her elder daughter.
MURIEL, her younger.

THE CHINA PIG

The scene is the living room of a sixty-dollar per month apartment. It is filled with a rather heterogeneous collection of articles, some of which are reminiscent of a more prosperous period of the owner's career. The table in the center of the room is of beautiful mahogany. Two of the chairs are of the same; a third is a comfortable leather Morris, and the remaining one is of reed. A bookcase on the right is also of mahogany. The mantle on the left matches the oak doors, of which there are three: one, the entrance, in the back, left of a large window, with a small desk between, the other two beyond the bookcase on the right. The first of these last two leads into a hall; the second is a closet door.

The surroundings blend somewhat — it is a room much used — so that there is no clashing element to offend a cultivated nature, but neither is there any artistic effect. The whole atmosphere seems somewhat subdued and depressed; but it is an energetic depression; there is nothing lethargic about it. Perhaps it is the woman who conveys the impression; she seems somehow to dominate the room. One rather wonders why. She is no longer young: about forty-three, one should judge, and whatever charm she may have possessed — it probably lay in her quick black eyes and her young determination — has long lain dormant. She is badly dressed in an old brown skirt and a shabby waist. Her brown hair is lifeless and her mouth is faded, wistful at times, above all submissive; but her eyes are deep with a stubborn determination that no quantity of rebuffs can entirely subdue.

The doorbell has rung with the rising of the curtain and she is crossing from the hall to answer it. The caller is a messenger with a hatbox.

THE BOY. Mrs. Elizabeth Maynard?

THE MOTHER (*eagerly*). Yes. (*Taking the box*) Thank you.

[*She closes the door and carries the box quickly to the table, where she opens it and takes out the hat. She carries it to the mirror and tries it on diffidently. The result is eminently satisfactory. Reluctantly she removes it and takes it back to the box. In it she sees the sales slip. She opens it. The price, she realizes, is too high; but she does want the hat. Regretfully at last she decides that she cannot afford it. Then she returns to the mantel to try it on again.*

While she is standing there, Muriel enters.

MURIEL (*is eighteen, a slender, unformed young thing in inconspicuous attire; awkward, ambitious, with a boyish straightforwardness, but with all a girl's dreams and ambitions, and all a girl's needs. One can tell that from the word with which she enters. It is always the same*). Mother?—Say! Some hat!

MOTHER. Do you like it?

MURIEL (*enthusiastically*). It's a peach.

MOTHER. I'm afraid I can't keep it.

MURIEL. Why not?

MOTHER. Oh, I can't afford it. I saw it down town in a window, and it haunted me. So I telephoned them to send it up on approval.

MURIEL. Well — (*with an air of finality*) keep it. It's classy. How much is it?

MOTHER. Eight dollars.

MURIEL. Pshaw. We can spare that. You need a new hat, anyway. That old one's shabby. — Say, mother, you look spiffy in that. With a new coat now, and a set of furs —

MOTHER. Oh, Muriel!

MURIEL. Why not? You just wait until I start making money. Oh, say! What do you think I did? I went up to see Edith Gorman. The Red Cross woman, you know.

MOTHER. What for?

MURIEL. To see if I could go with them to Armenia next year. *You* remember; I read you the article the other day. About the school they are establishing?

MOTHER. They wouldn't take *you*, Muriel.

MURIEL. Why not? Of course she would. She *said* she would; (*qualifying*) said she *might.* — She was great to me, though.

MOTHER. What did she say?

MURIEL. Oh, she told me all about the mission. First thing, I asked her if she'd take me with her when she goes out next year. She said I'd need medical training. I asked if a year would do; she looked at me rather hard and said it would help. Then I said: If I study for a year will you take me? And she said perhaps she could. Gee, I was rattled. — She told me what subjects to take, and what to read up on.

MOTHER (*the hat in the box, has seated herself in the Morris chair and taken up her darning*). But, Muriel. Father expects you to go to business school.

MURIEL. Oh, he won't care.

MOTHER. Yes, he will care.

MURIEL. Well, I can't help it. I'm not going to do it. I guess I have a right to choose my own profession.

MOTHER. He's paying for it.

MURIEL (*annoyedly*). Oh, lord, he won't kick, will he?

MOTHER. You mustn't talk like that, Muriel.

MURIEL. Will you talk to him?

MOTHER. I'll try.

MURIEL. Do you think he'll be really sore?

MOTHER. I hope not. But he's been planning for years to have you in his office. Ever since you were small.

MURIEL. I can't help it. I'd like to do it — But I couldn't stand working in an office. I want to get out and see things.

MOTHER (*looks at her, the light of understanding in her eyes; but all she says is*). Red Cross work is a hazardous business, at best. It means hardships and bad climates, poor food, a life away from your own civilization, a life facing any sort of possibility. It isn't so wonderful as it sounds.

MURIEL. I know! I know what it is. But think of the value of it! Think of what it accomplishes! Think of what it means to help people, to uplift them, to change their whole

lives. Think of taking little heathen babies — naked
ignorant — and clothing them, teaching them, bringing
them up, and sending them out to teach others! Oh, you
can't understand — you're a home woman —

MOTHER (*half to herself*). Yes, I can —

MURIEL. Wait — (*diving down into her coat pocket*). Look
what she gave me. (*She brings out a photograph*) Isn't that
sweet! Those are three Kurdish children they cared for
last year. Aren't they darling? Look at their little dark
faces.

MOTHER (*taking it, with great interest*). Little Kurdish children.

MURIEL. That's in Armenia, you know.

MOTHER (*absorbed*). I know.

MURIEL. Oh, mother! It's just what I want to do. It's
the most important thing in life. (*She turns away restlessly*)
Father's got to let me.

MOTHER (*suggests timidly*). Just think, Muriel. Only a generation removed from fierce, wild, almost savage people.

MURIEL. I know.

MOTHER (*fingering it awkwardly*). What was she like, Muriel?

MURIEL (*absorbed*). Oh, sweet.

MOTHER. Nice looking?

MURIEL. No, not exactly. Like a school-teacher rather,
like a school principal. (*Pacing up and down*) Oh, I've got
to go with her. Father's got to let me. I wish he'd come
home. I can't stand waiting. (*The mother is fingering
the photograph, wistfully. Muriel turns decisively*) I think
I'll go down to the office and talk to him there.

MOTHER (*laying the picture on the table*). He may be busy.

MURIEL. I know, but — he — he'll be more polite down
there, with his clerks around. Besides, I can't wait. (*She
takes up her hat*) Good-by.

MOTHER. Good-by. (*Muriel comes back to kiss her*) Be
good, now.

MURIEL (*off again*). I will. (*She pauses at the door to remind
her*) And mother, you're to keep the hat.

MOTHER. We'll see.

[*She is gone. The mother darns slowly. The sock finished, she rolls the pair of them up in a little ball and starts on a long silk stocking. Once she stops to pick up the picture and gaze at it dreamily, but she lays it down again. After a moment, Elsa enters.*

ELSA (*is twenty-two; tall, slender, self-reliant, with a quick, decisive charm. She is an independent and fearless person, a girl who has weighed life in the balance and found thereby her own scale of philosophy by which she is satisfied to judge. She has little sense of humor. She thinks of herself as "serious" and worthwhile. To-day she is in an elated mood that she does not try to repress, although she is usually rather reserved. She speaks eagerly as she enters the door*). Mother — I'm going to New York! To-night! I've got an engagement with a theatrical company. I've been accepted! I met the manager down at the office. He came in, mind you! Mr. Burns had told him about me; about my acting for the Drama League. And after a little he offered me a part. Thirty dollars a week. Just imagine! And it's rather an important rôle.

[*She has removed her hat and taken a suit case from the closet while she finishes.*

MOTHER. But, Elsa — you can't go away like this.

ELSA (*withdraws into herself at this, and composedly opens the suit case*). Why not?

MOTHER. Why, you don't know the man.

ELSA (*decidedly*). Nonsense. I'm not going away with him.

[*She takes a coat from the closet and lays it on the table by the bag.*

MOTHER. But you can't go away to a strange city. Why, New York is an enormous place. You'd be lost. You have no place to go.

ELSA. I'll get a room from the Y. W.

MOTHER. You aren't a member.

ELSA (*impatiently*). Well, what of it? I guess they'll take me in.

MOTHER. But, Elsa, you *can't* go. You can't go away like this.

ELSA (*packing; politely, with forced patience*). Why not, mother?

MOTHER. You're too young and inexperienced. You've made no preparations.

ELSA (*calmly*). I'm going, mother.

MOTHER. Your father won't consent. He won't allow you to go.

ELSA. That's all the good it will do him.

MOTHER. You wouldn't go against his will?

ELSA (*politely*). Wouldn't I? (*Mother sighs injuredly and stands gazing at her beseechingly. Elsa looks up at the sigh. Stops packing and breaks out impatiently*) Mother, here's the biggest thing that ever came into my life. The chance I've been working toward for years; and when *it* comes to *me*, you ask me to give it up. I suppose you want me to be a stenographer all my life.

MOTHER (*breaking in*). No, I don't.

ELSA (*near tears of annoyance*). Yes, you do. You stand there and talk about father. Well, I suppose father *will* object. I expect him to. He'll storm around here as he always does, and then sulk for a month. Well, I don't care. Let him. I don't care what he does. I don't care if I never *see* him again!

MOTHER (*shocked*). Elsa! How can you talk like that?

ELSA. Why not? It's the truth. Why *shouldn't* we be truthful once in a while! What's the good of all this lying and pretending all the time? *You* know I don't care about him. (*After a breath, calmly*) Neither do you.

MOTHER (*pained*). Elsa, how can you *talk* like that?

ELSA (*melting*). I'm sorry, mother. (*Firing again*) But I just can't help it. It makes me wild when I think of how he tyrannizes over everybody.

MOTHER (*dutifully*). He's your father, Elsa.

ELSA. That's no reason why he should be disagreeable to me.

MOTHER. You don't understand him.

ELSA. Oh, yes, I do. That's why I despise him.

MOTHER (*righteously*). Elsa, you must not talk like that.

ELSA. Why not admit it, if it's true? *You* don't care for him any more than I do. Do you think I don't know you? If you had money of your own, you'd leave him to-morrow.

MOTHER (*dismissing her*). You don't know what you are talking about.

ELSA. Don't I? (*persisting*). Mother, tell me the truth. Do you love father?

MOTHER. Why, of course I do.

ELSA (*searchingly*). Honestly? Do you love him?

MOTHER (*coldly*). I don't care to discuss the subject.

ELSA (*looks at her wordlessly — what is the use of speaking? Then she does it*). Why do you stay with him? — Why don't you go away some place by yourself?

MOTHER (*arguing*). Where could I *go?*

ELSA. Why don't you come to New York with me?

MOTHER. Oh, Elsa, don't talk like that. You know it's impossible.

ELSA (*turning away gives it up, a little contemptuously*). Yes, I suppose it is.

MOTHER (*upset by it all, and hurt to the quick by her contempt, breaks suddenly through the restraint of their relationship*). Oh, it's not what you think. I'm not dead. You think I am, but I'm not. I'm as much alive as you are. I'm more alive. Much more! I — I want to go to New York as you never can want it. Until you've been put off for years and years as I have. (*Elsa is staring at her. Mother, gathering force*). Oh, I know what you think. You think I'm old and spiritless. You think I'm going to stick here till I die. But I'm not. *I'm* going to New York too. It won't be very long now, either. — You think it's just the money. But I *have* the money! I have almost a thousand dollars! Why do you think I've been wearing old shabby clothes? For fun? Why, I began saving before you were born.

ELSA. Mother —

MOTHER (*at the note of sympathy in her voice, the mother halts and stares at her, remembering. Then, almost whispering*). It's true.

ELSA. I never knew.

MOTHER (*carried away by the emotion of it all, she says poignantly something that means almost nothing — unless perhaps it means a great deal*). Sometimes I hardly knew myself.

ELSA. And all these years — ?

MOTHER. Ever since I was a girl. Look —
(*She goes down into the bottom drawer of the desk and brings up a little green china bank in the shape of a pig*) My grandfather gave me that china pig when I was sixteen, and the first thing I began to save for was a bicycle. My grandparents were old-fashioned; they didn't consider a bicycle was ladylike. But oh, how I did want it! I've wanted so many things I couldn't have. I was just supposed to stay at home, and I wanted to get out and study. I wanted to write. I've always wanted to write. Then I began to dream about college. I only spoke of it once at home. My grandfather was very angry. He said it wasn't womanly. *I* couldn't talk of a career to him. But I made up my mind I would have it. I began to save: for the time when I could go away and study. I saved up two hundred dollars. And then grandfather died and everything was just swallowed up. My money went to help pay the funeral expenses. The rest of it took grandmother and me to Pittsburgh, where I got a place in a factory. Oh, Elsa — how I hated that factory. How I hated all the sordidness, the petty jealousies — I couldn't stand it. My dreams were dying. I was too tired to dream. (*She looks down at the little green bank. She is speaking in a monotone now, jerkily*) So I began saving again. It meant more than just studying now. It meant freedom, living. — And then my grandmother died, and the money went again. But I started in again. My expenses were less now. I saved one hundred and six dollars in ten months. It wasn't very much. But I meant,

I had five hundred, to go to New York. To Colum-
niversity. All I was working for was one year of
. I don't know what I thought I'd do after I got
. I suppose I believed I could write at once and support
myself that way. Then I met your father. He was just
a young lawyer. He was different then; more gentle and
thoughtful. The first thing I knew, I told him what I
was saving for. Well — he, he encouraged me. He got
me night work to do. And I — we — well, one day he
proposed to me. And he promised, if I'd marry him, that
I should have my year of college anyway. As soon as we
could save the money, I was to go. But when the time
came you were here, and most of the money went for you.
(*More intensely*) You say I don't understand your wanting to go? Why, I gave you that longing. I lived it into
your little body before you were born. And you think
it's odd that Muriel wants to go to the East? How can she
help it? I've wanted to explore all my life. I've dreamed
of strange places, new environments. I — I — if a
strange man had come to me — and offered to take me
all those places, I'd have gone. Not loving him. I'd
have left my home and gone. But no one ever came.
I've just been chained here all these years.

ELSA. But, mother — why didn't you go?

MOTHER. How could I?

ELSA. Did you give it up then?

MOTHER. No. I meant to go when you were older. Your
aunt could have stayed with you. Your — your father
knew it. He never said much then, but he thought I
ought to give it up. One time — you were about six —
he had a chance to get in on a good business deal; and he
asked me to lend him the money. I had meant to go that
summer — and he knew it; but he said I might get it back
in time. I didn't. I never got it back. He couldn't spare
it at first, and afterwards — it made him angry when I
spoke of it. And the next money I saved — Do you remember that year when you got into so much trouble in

school? I had wanted to send you away for
You needed a change. But he couldn't afford
said you needed a strong hand.

ELSA. But I did go away.

MOTHER. Yes. I sent you. I had forty dollars then.
But I think I hated him then. I think I've hated him
ever since. When you were sixteen he made a lot of
money. (*Her voice becomes lower now, hard and even*) And
I stole six hundred dollars. He never knew. He never
even missed it. I changed the accounts. And then when
he failed I never said a word. I sat there, as hard as
steel, and watched him worry over those bills. I sat there
and thought about college. I have over a thousand dollars now.

ELSA. Mother, you're splendid —

MOTHER. No, I'm not. Sometimes I forget all about it.
Sometimes I think it's no use. I've had to give it up all
my life. Perhaps just in giving the desire to you and
Muriel I've fulfilled my mission.

ELSA. What nonsense!

MOTHER (*unhappily*). It's only occasionally that I think
of it now. Perhaps when the time comes I won't have the
courage to break away. I'm too old. (*Despairingly sinking into chair at table*) Oh, I *am* too old. I simply can't
bear to admit it.

ELSA (*suddenly*). Mother — come to New York with *me*.
You're *not* too old, yet. Break away to-day. You have
the money. What are you waiting for? There's nothing
to keep you now.

MOTHER. Muriel —

ELSA. Muriel doesn't need you. She's a woman herself.
(*Mother stares at her*) You said you didn't want me to go
alone. Come along and take care of me.

MOTHER. You don't need me, either.

ELSA. I want you. Can't you see? Isn't it splendid?
We've neither of us lived yet. We've both been waiting
and hoping. Now our chance has come. Let's take it

when her. What wonderful chums we could be now. bia U; you see it? Oh, *think* of New York! The lights, college the big streets. It means Fifth Avenue, and the :+ ..tropolitan Museum, and Broadway and the opera, and the shops and the theatres. All the theatres.

MOTHER. And the Statue of Liberty. I've always wanted to see that.

ELSA. Mother — won't you come? (*They stare at each other. There are tears in the Mother's eyes. Elsa takes her in her arms. Then, releasing her*) You will come, won't you? And you have the money. Can't you get it to-day? It isn't three yet. — Go down to the bank and draw it all out. Let's take it with us. [*They are tense with excitement.*

MOTHER (*breathlessly*). Yes. [*Goes to the closet for her old hat and coat.*

ELSA (*sees the hatbox*). No, wear your new hat. (*She puts it on her*) I'll pack your things for you. Now, hurry —

MOTHER (*turning at the door and coming back*). Oh, my check book —
[*She is getting it from her desk when Muriel enters.*

MURIEL (*is just recovering from a tempestuous scene in which she has been very angry. Her face is still set in fierce determined lines. She sees her mother and the girl in her calls out*) Mother — (*Then the woman in her comes to the fore. She speaks briefly*) I'm going away. Father won't let me study. He won't give me the money. So I'm going away somewhere and make it for myself.

MOTHER. But where will you go, Muriel?

MURIEL. Oh, I don't know. Out West somewhere. Or just in this city. I only know I'm going. He wants me to stay in a musty little office all my life and help him. But I won't do it. If he won't help me, I'll do it myself. I'm going to be a foreign missionary if it costs me my life. I —
[*She breaks off.*

MOTHER (*staring at her piteously*). But Muriel —

MURIEL. It's all right, mother. Don't you worry. I'll get through all right. (*Breaking*) But it would have been such a wonderful chance. To go with her next year.

[*She stares stiffly.*

MOTHER (*unwillingly*). How — how much would it cost?

MURIEL. Only about two thousand.

MOTHER. Would a thousand do?

MURIEL. I don't know. Why?

MOTHER (*quietly*). I can give you a thousand.

MURIEL. You?

MOTHER. I've been saving it for quite a while.

MURIEL. Oh, do you *mean* it? I'd pay it back. Oh, mother, could you?

ELSA. Mother —

MOTHER (*waving her aside*). Here. I have my check book. I'll write you out a check. You can cash it right away.

MURIEL (*while she is writing it*). Oh, mother. I can't believe it. It means so much to me. You can never understand how much it means.

MOTHER (*not answering that*). There! You can cash it to-day if you hurry.

MURIEL (*putting her young arms about her, kisses her quickly on the cheek*). Oh, mother! I do thank you. You wait — I'll do something for you some day.

MOTHER (*hurrying her unobtrusively*). It's all right, Muriel. Just be good; that's all I ask. (*Muriel kisses her again and starts out eagerly as she crosses the sill*). Hurry —

(*She is gone, slamming the door behind her. The mother stands silent a moment. Then, slowly she begins to take off her hat. Elsa, who has not moved, stands watching her. Elsa believes in not interfering. Mother puts the hat back in the box. Then slowly she sinks into the chair, left of table. Elsa is back, right of table. She twists her hands nervously. Then she looks at Elsa and looks away again*)

What could I do? I hadn't any choice. It was her life or mine. I couldn't have gone when it kept her back.

I couldn't — It's been the same thing all my life. Every time I've had to give it up.

ELSA. Come anyway, mother.

MOTHER. I can't.

ELSA. *Yes*, you can!

MOTHER. No. (*Resigned*) No; I've made my choice. Oh, it *wasn't* any choice. I've never had any. Every time it's been the same. Every time. It *can't* be right. It can't be. — And yet, it wouldn't have been right to go. I had to do it. It must have been right. *Wasn't* it right, Elsa? Why do you look so hard?

ELSA (*slowly*). I don't know —

~~MOTHER. The Bible says so.~~ *skip*

ELSA (*sure of this*). I can't quote Bible verses to you. But I know this — that a man's first duty is self-development.

MOTHER. Self-development? No. It can't be, Elsa. There are other things.

ELSA (*passionately*). It is. It is.

MOTHER. Then you think I should have gone? At the expense of Muriel's development?

ELSA. I can't decide for you.

MOTHER. What would you have done?

ELSA. I don't know.

MOTHER. You'd have done the same thing. Every time you'd have done it. And every time I've had to. All my life. (*Tears in her voice*) I've dreamed and dreamed. I've saved and saved until my heart was sick. And still I've kept on; saving and planning. And every time when it was within my reach I've had to give it up. I don't believe I was ever meant to go. I might just as well believe it. It's just been a game I've been deluding myself with all these years. This little china pig — (*She snatches it from the table and lifts it high above her head to dash it to the floor*) I'm going to break it! (*Then quickly she stops*) No! I won't! I won't give in! I won't! I'm going on. I'm going to start all over again. I won't give in! I won't!

ELSA. (*gladly*). *You'll come?*

MOTHER. No. I'm going to stay right here. I'm going to save again. (*Big*) And this time I'm going to *go!*

ELSA (*turns away wordlessly. Then she faces her again, and as she speaks the truth of what she is saying dawns on her*). I wish you had broken it. I wish you had smashed it to bits. Why do you wait for that? Why do you? That's been the trouble all along. All your life you've been wanting to grow. All your life. And every time you started, some other thing came and held you back. I don't say you were right in giving up the money. I don't say you were wrong. But why did you let it stop you? You had no right to do that. It's as if, each time you found yourself a stepping stone, some one else needed it, and you gave it up. But why did you wait to get another? Why didn't you wade across?

MOTHER. What do you mean?

ELSA (*more confidently now*). You asked me if you were right in giving up the money. And I say — it didn't matter. Whether you used it and went, or whether you gave it and stayed here. What does matter is that you've waited to save again. Don't you see? All your life you've been waiting and saving for an opportunity — when you should have been going on without it.

MOTHER. But I couldn't —

ELSA. Yes, you could. You can now. What have you done with your life? Saved. Saved money. When you should have been studying, working at home. When you should have been writing. Have you ever written anything? No. You've been waiting to learn. Well, why didn't you teach yourself? Don't you see? These years have been wasted; wasted in dreams. It didn't matter where you were. It didn't matter how busy. You could have grown somehow if you'd tried. But you've just saved.

MOTHER (*realizing it*). I've just saved. (*Slowly*) Saved and dreamed, instead of going ahead. You didn't do that. You've been working for years; getting ready. Now I've let my years slip by — and it's too late.

ELSA. *No*, it's not, mother.

MOTHER. Yes it is. No one else has been to blame. It hasn't even been circumstance. It's just been me. (*After a time*) A new environment would have helped —

ELSA. Yes.

MOTHER. But it wasn't necessary. I see it now. I see it all. Now that it doesn't matter. Now that I'm too old.

ELSA. You're not too old, mother. It's never too late if you can see it.

MOTHER. Do you believe that?

ELSA. I do. I do. Nothing matters, if you can see.

MOTHER (*deciding*). Then I'm going to begin.

ELSA. You'll come with me?

MOTHER. No. I'm going to do it here.

ELSA. — Are you afraid to go?

MOTHER. No. But I have no money. I'd hamper you. And besides — I don't need it now.

ELSA. Oh, mother!

[*She is not demonstrative, but she comes close to her and looks into her face.*

MOTHER (*wistfully*). Elsa — even it it's too late for writing — I can live.

CURTAIN

A PATRONESS
EVER YOUNG

ALICE GERSTENBERG

ALICE GERSTENBERG was born in Chicago and was educated there and at Bryn Mawr College. She is the author of two novels, "Unquenched Fire" (1912) and "The Conscience of Sarah Platt" (1915), and has dramatized Lewis Carroll's "Alice in Wonderland."

Miss Gerstenberg is best known for her contributions to the little theatre. Her plays have been collected in one volume under the title "Ten One-act Plays" (1921). The two plays from her pen appearing in this volume are not included in that collection.

A PATRONESS

A MONOLOGUE IN ONE ACT

By ALICE GERSTENBERG

Character

THE PATRONESS . . . . A Society Woman

A PATRONESS

(The Patroness is a society woman with much natural charm and some ability. In pantomime she pretends to sit up in the bed as she wakes in the morning, and yawns)

Oh, must I get up? Is it another day? What, Annie? My committee meeting! To be sure!

(She hurries out of bed and disappears behind a screen)

Where's my rubber cap? It has a hole. The water will ruin my marcel. John always turns off this shower knob so tight! I wonder if the water's cold. *(She shrieks)* Now my clothes.

(She looks over the screen and talks to her small daughter)

Yes, Dorothy, mother's here. Are you ready for school? You want another party dress? You are going to far too many parties. No, I won't promise anything until I have consulted other mothers at a Parents' meeting.

(To her small son, who is supposed to have entered)

What, Jimmie? Buy out the puppets for your birthday? Ask your Daddy! All my money's gone to charity. But I love you dearly. There's a kiss for you.

(Throws kiss to him)

But, son, look at your hair — *Oh, Mademoiselle, voyez! Il faut que vous* — Oh, I can't talk French and rush too! Take him to the barber's! *Oui, oui,* good-by dears, learn your lessons well — *look out* for Annie's tray!

(She comes from behind screen presumably wearing a dressing gown and sits down before her breakfast tray)

There's nothing so refreshing as orange juice! Oh, and the smell of coffee! No pancakes, Annie, I simply mustn't lose my figure.

(As she eats she reads the morning paper which came up with the tray)

What's the world been doing overnight? Another robbery!
Horrible!

(*Casually to her husband and without looking at him as he is
supposed to enter the room.*)

Hello, John!

(*She turns her cheek absent-mindedly for his kiss and puts
out her foot for Annie*)

Annie, my spats. What's Society doing to-day? Mrs.
Weather gives tea; I'm going to that. Mrs. Hemming
gives luncheon; I'm going to that. Mrs. Murray gives
dinner; we're going to that. Do get home early, John, and
send the car right back for me this morning. I've many
important engagements. Good-by. What?

(*Takes letters from him with nonchalant amazement*)

Bills to O K? Very well, as soon as I have time. I *didn't*
let them lie around last month. Don't be so particular!
They know you're good for it. I can't stop in the midst
of writing a paper for the Woman's Club to attend to bills.
My paper went off well too. You ought to be proud of
that. Yes, yes, yes, I'll look them over. Annie, my blue
serge; good morning, Miss Perkins, — sit there while I
dress my hair.

(*She sits before a table and in pantomime arranges her hair.*)

Look these bills over to-day, Miss Perkins, and O K them
if you can. Just open my letters.

(*She reads letters with eyes cocked sideways as she continues
to dress her hair and make up her cheeks and lips*)

Regret. Accept. Accept. No, no, regret, I couldn't be
seen in *her* house. Here's a list of names to be approached
for donations for the bazaar. Make copies of the letter I
outlined yesterday and send them to these people. And
just take this dictation. "My dear Sister: It is a long
time since your letter arrived, but this is a big city and we
are at the height of the season. I have been patroness
for countless affairs and am serving on every committee.
I am one of the women in this city who run things, who do
things, who start things, who manage things, but, thank

Heaven, we do not always finish things; we leave that to the climbers after we have taken the glory. You must come —

(*She starts*)

Oh, that telephone! Finish the letter to my sister yourself, Miss Perkins.

(*She crosses room to answer telephone*)

Good morning, Mrs. Hitchcock. You mean the voting at the Club? Yes, I think it was parliamentary. I *am* so sorry you lost out. (*While she is at the telephone she whispers orders to her servants*) Annie, my gloves. Don't forget to give me a handkerchief. No, Sarah, not at home for luncheon. But tell cook to plan a dinner for sixteen to-morrow night. Yes, I'm listening, Mrs. Hitchcock. Miss Perkins, you'd better plan the table decorations with Henderson. He's the best butler we've ever had for arranging flowers. Yes, Mrs. Hitchcock, I'll be glad to take the matter up with the Board. I'm far too good a friend of yours. Don't mention it, my dear.

(*She bangs up the receiver*)

I thought she'd never get through. Now, Annie, my dress! As late as that! Out of my way, everybody! Don't ask any more questions. Do the best you can. I'll be back at six.

(*She grabs hat, gloves, bag, and starts out, almost bumping into a nurse with a baby in her arms*)

Oh, Hannah, how's the baby? Mother's pet! Coo, coo, darling! Laugh at your sweet motherkins, sweetheart! That's the dear! By-by!

(*She turns, uses same stage space but gives in pantomime the impression that she runs down a winding flight of stairs, nods to a butler*)

Morning, Henderson.

(*She goes out of the house to her automobile*)

Morning, Jameson; to the Woman's Club as fast as you can.

(*As soon as she is seated in the car she takes a book out of one of its pockets and studies French*)

Vous avez beau dire, vous avez tort, say what you may you are wrong. *Il a beau dire, je ne le crois pas.* Let him say what he may, I do not believe him. Good morning.
(*She bows out of the car window*)

Je ne le crois pas, je ne le crois pas —
(*Her face distorts with fear as another automobile drives too closely*)

Oh, why do they drive so near; be careful, Jameson. *Il a beau dire, je ne le crois pas* — Oh, here we are —
(*She places the book back into the car pocket and hurries out. She enters a building, slips into a crowded elevator, looks at herself in its mirror, screws up her face as she adjusts her veil*)

Seventh, please.
(*She hurries out of the elevator and enters the Club*)

Sorry to be so late. In time for what — to come to the platform — in favor of prison reform? Certainly, if you will accept merely extemporaneous remarks.
(*She steps upon the platform and speaks fluently*)

Members of the Woman's Club, let us make a country-wide investigation of the expenditure made by our Government for the upkeep of prisons. Then let us prove that the same amount could be invested more profitably in farms where delinquents under guard could work in the open air and grow into more normal health. The sciences of physiology and psychology should be applied to criminals! We must enlist the services of our foremost educators. A reform so sweeping must be rightly started. I pledge myself to approach Doctors Maynard, Hill, Casper. Any suggestion from the floor? Yes, Mrs. Danby? Quite so. Next Wednesday here at this hour. Adjournment, Madam President? How do you do, how do you do —
(*She shakes hands cordially with the women who crowd around to greet her. Then she hastily retreats*)

So glad to see you, tell me more about it next time; I have to hurry to keep an appointment at Geraldine's.
(*She rushes out of the room, calling to the elevator man*)

Down, down, down!

(*She slips into the elevator, rides to the first floor, goes to automobile; she is impatient when Jameson is delayed by the
traffic*)

Jameson, to Geraldine's.

(*When seated in the car she takes a book from another pocket
of the limousine and begins to study Spanish with a far-away
look*)

Cierto lugareno estaba a punto de morir. Oh, I like Spanish.
No era muy rico. Solo tenia un perro y un caballo. No
tenio hijos pero tenia hi una mujer.

(*She alights from car*)

Wait, Jameson.

(*She hurries up the stairs of a house, opens the door and walks
right in*)

Good morning, I haven't much time. Can you hurry my
gown? Shall I take this room? Hello, Ursula, just had a
fitting? (*In whisper*) Are you satisfied? Do you think
Geraldine's the best in town? She's made mistakes for me
too, but then they all do. Glad to have seen you.

(*She steps into room*)

Morning, Madam, are you sure this is going to be the rage
down south? It's difficult to have a summer spirit with
snow outside. Really, two hundred and a quarter is outrageous for this wisp of chiffon. I'm doing so much for
charity, Madam, and I need so many clothes for the South.
Are you showing sport hats?

(*She criticizes the length of the skirt in the mirror*)

Too long? Are they? Well, if you say so, but it's ugly.
Smart, you think? Well, maybe; I suppose it is. I know,
I just have to carry it off with the *air* that it's smart!
What's that, Stella? A hat? The new shape? You call it
the casserole? Oh, it's awful on me! Much more suitable
for chorus squabs. What time is it? Oh, I'm late for Mrs.
Hemming's luncheon. Just put a pin in there. That's it,
now help me out. And into my dress — another hook
there, Stella. Next Tuesday? I'll try to make it by nine.

(She hurries out of the house, down the stairs to the curb)

Mrs. Hemming's, 347 Boulevard.

(She enters car; from its vanity case she takes powder, rouge, etc., to freshen herself, and from her bag a clean pair of gloves.)

Take care, Jameson. *(She speaks through the tube)* You lack calculation!

(She watches his progress with anxiety. She alights)

Get your luncheon and come back immediately.

(She enters house quickly, where a butler has been watching for her. She quickly lets him take her coat)

No, I'll not go upstairs. I suppose I am the last one.

(She turns to the left to enter the drawing-room)

How do you do, Mrs. Hemming? Waiting for me? So sorry! *(She leads guests with hostess into the dining room. She takes her place at the table and in pantomime unfolds napkin and begins to eat fruit cocktail out of a tall glass)*

Charming to be placed at your right, dear hostess. Now for a powwow over the bazaar. What are you collecting for your Arabian Booth? I have fifteen debutantes to look pretty at my French counters. I chose French because I am so well acquainted with the language and it's all so chic. *Oui, oui!*

(She is served a roll and eats chicken and mushrooms under glass)

By the way, I've a book of chances — no, excuse me, I mean shares; not at all the same thing. On a diamond bracelet. A dollar a share. Not one of you shall escape. What numbers will you take, Clara? Anywhere I open the book? There, 49, thanks! And you, Evelyn? Oh, my dear, you must! Yes, I'll take a chance from you in return — share, I mean — on your ice-box, although goodness knows what I'd do with it if I did win it. Let's give each other 23.

(She serves herself to salad)

Just send the book around, Mrs. Crosby, and don't dare to return it unfilled. That's what a bazaar is for, to force out of our pockets what we don't want to give. What delicious salad! Your own cook? What a time most of us have

acquiring cooks! Let's start a Cuisine Club for discussing
the most scientific ways of keeping house. When shall we
start it? My secretary can issue the cards calling a meeting at my house. Done! We were at the theater last night,
but truly we must uplift the Drama. I'm writing a play
myself. Oh, my share book!

(*She accepts the book returned to her*)

Not a delinquent at the table. Nobly done! Now, dear
hostess, while you are eating your ice cream—I'm on a diet
and don't take any — will you excuse me if I slip away? I
promised to appear at Mr. Pole's lecture on feminism;
I'm one of the patronesses — you know how it is. Are you
going too, Mrs. Crosby? Glad to take you in my car. You
too, Mrs. Winthrop? Any one else; my car holds six. I
hope I'm not breaking up the party. Such an enchanting
luncheon! Good-by, dear hostess; come, girls.

(*She leads the women out to her car*)

Jameson, the Ritz.

(*She makes the women comfortable in the car*)

Are you comfortable there, Mrs. Wright? You should have
taken the back seat. Do you want the robe? No, it wasn't
dreadful to hurry away. One can't give more time than
that for luncheon, and our hostess, no doubt, was relieved
not having to entertain us longer. One feels so helpless
when there are no more courses. My dear Grace, where
did you get that fetching veil? And hasn't Mrs. Clinch a
stunning bag? Made it yourself? Make me one. Put
it into Mrs. Canter's booth and I'll come and buy it.
That's the way to shop. My religion is economy in time
and effort. Here we are.

(*She alights from car and enters the hotel. She steps back*)

Just a moment. Let's go next door and see the new portrait
exhibit. How do you do, Mr. Dale? Fine collection, so I
was told.

(*She stands off and looks at pictures*)

I like that one. Don't know why. I just know how it makes
me feel. And that one—hasn't it color? And such perspec-

tive! That background — so unusual. And this — what technique. I must come in again at leisure for a real long look. We're on our way to a lecture. Good-day, Mr. Dale.

(*She hurries out with her friends*)

Glad we had a peek at the portraits — something to talk about to-night at dinner; sometimes it's difficult to know what to say.

(*As she enters the hotel ballroom where the lecture is being given*)

May we sit in the last row? Don't wish to remove our hats. Has he been talking long? Missed half of it? What a pity!

(*She pantomimes her attention to the lecturer, her reactions of interest, amusement, agreement, doubt. Finally she rises and whispers*)

Girls, you don't mind if I leave you. He's very clever, but now that I know his point of view, I can tell in advance what he is going to say and I really must go on my way. So glad to have seen you. Never mind moving, Grace, I'm not too fat; I can just slide by you.

(*She pushes her way out and hurries to the street*)

Jameson, as fast as you can to Mrs. Weather's.

(*She hurries into the car and takes calling cards from her purse*)

Cards — let me see — what did the invitation say — three, I think — one, two, three — Jameson, I'll get right out here; never mind driving up to the awning. Hello, hello, Mary!

(*She jumps from car and runs to meet a friend*)

Just the person I want to see. What do you mean by not taking an opera box this season? Where's your civic pride? Oh, I won't take "no"! I know it, I have a frightful time myself filling it every week — with handsome people — but — I'll tell them you've changed your mind — good for you — I said you would —

(*She has walked up the stairs of the house with Mary and now enters*)

Announce me right away, please.

(*She hands cards to butler and takes her place in the guest line*)

How do you do, Mrs. Caper; and this is your debutante daughter, the last one of the season. Isn't she sweet? Look at her gown, Mary. Geraldine must have made it. How do you do, how do you do?

(*She bows to left and right as she makes her way through the crush*)

Hello, this is the third time I've seen you to-day. Yes, I'm hurrying on now to another tea.

(*She hurries out to the car; taps her foot impatiently*)

Jameson, Jameson, right around the corner to Mrs. Hamilton's.

(*In the car she takes four cards out of her purse and holds them in her hand. She alights*)

No, I don't want a check. I'm coming right out again.

(*She hurries into a house*)

No, I do not wish to take my wraps off upstairs.

(*Gives cards to butler*)

Just announce me, please. How do you do, Mrs. Reid? And this is your new daughter-in-law; charming. And Mrs. Foster, her mother, and the grandmother too! How very touchingly sweet! No, I haven't time for tea. Hello, nicely decorated, yes. Music too loud! What did you say? Can't hear — the music — How do you do? Oh, I beg your pardon, what a crush! I must get out.

(*She jostles through the crowd and goes out to her car*)

Home, Jameson.

(*She sinks exhausted into the seat and closes her eyes. She alights from the car*)

Be back at seven, Jameson.

(*She rings the house bell*)

Henderson, has Mr. Clark come home? Bring me a glass of milk and a sandwich; I'm starved

(*She runs upstairs*)

Yes, Hannah, am I late again? He's fast asleep? Oh, dear, I did want to see him. I'll just take a peep.

(*She tiptoes into a room and approaches the baby's crib*)

Precious baby! Mother's lambkins! How sweet he looks!
Snookums, snookums!

(*She hurries out and calls aloud*)

Annie, quick, my blue and silver brocade.

(*She begins to undress*)

Miss Perkins, I haven't time to look at the letters. Just
sign them. The telephone numbers I am to call — as soon
as I come in? Well, pretend I'm not in. Let them catch
me if they can. There's a ring now.

(*She dashes into the hall and leaning over the banister calls
down*)

Henderson, answer that 'phone and say I have not come
home. Hello, John, I don't care what vest you wear. My
slippers, Miss Perkins. Dorothy, take my gold bag out
of the top drawer. Jimmie, run downstairs and see what
time it is. I think my clock is fast. Oh, Sarah, the milk,
yes — just a sip — Miss Perkins, my jewels. Annie, my
clothes into the bathroom —

(*She retires behind the screen but talks around and over it
from time to time*)

Run along, Dorothy. Now, Miss Perkins, the mail. Will I
be patroness for a revival of ancient chandeliers? I don't
know why they should be revived, but if Mrs. Cleverly
knows, I suppose I shall have to support her. By the way,
to-day at luncheon Mrs. Hemming had exquisite lace on
her table. Finer than mine. I wish you'd have some
pieces sent on approval the next time you go down to shop.
I can't let Mrs. Hemming have anything better than I have.
What next? They want me to be a patroness for the cam-
paign for new inkwells in the public schools? I wonder if
it wouldn't be better to raise a fund to provide fountain
pens. However, I haven't time to take up the matter and
I dare say they have canvassed the field. Yes, I'll be patroness.

(*She comes from behind the screen*)

I've had a hat on all day. Hasn't my hair kept beautifully?
Just give me the fillet.

(She sits before the dressing table, powders, etc.)

Two very personal letters to me? One from Mr. Forrest? He's sending me a book? How sweet of him! Quite a beau, Miss Perkins, quite a beau! Makes life worth while, a dash of romance now and then. Take your time to-morrow and compose a *billet doux* for me to send back to him. Something not too risque, just stimulating! Dear me, I had forgotten his existence, but it's wonderful even to have an admirer to forget!

(She rises to be helped into her evening gown)

Powder my back, Annie. I always like this brocade; don't you think it fits well, Miss Perkins? Yes, John, yes, I'm coming. How impatient men are! Nothing to do but their business all day and we are kept at such high speed. Quick, my opera cloak!

(She rushes into the hall)

Coming! Good night, children. Don't stay up too late. No, don't kiss me, you'll take off the powder.

(She runs down the stairs)

Good night, Henderson. Oh, it's snowing. John, tell Jameson to the Murrays'.

(She gets into the car)

Now, John, I hope you will be entertaining to-night and put Mr. Murray into good humor. I want to sell him a box for the benefit for Stray Cats. Now, that's not nice of you at all to make a pun about it! Stray cats are very pathetic and you needn't — no — I won't forgive you — no — I won't kiss you — you muss my hair — and, anyway, here we are.

(She alights from car)

Back at eight, Jameson.

(She hurries into house and drops her wraps)

We'll leave our things here.

(She enters the drawing room)

Oh, Mrs. Murray, forgive tardiness, but you know how much of my time and my strength this city claims! Oh, you flatter! Shall we go right in? Are you my partner, Mr. Boynton?

(*She takes his arm and walks into dining room, finds place card, thanks him for pushing her chair out for her, and sits*)

Well, Mr. Boynton, how have you been? You always accomplish so much that is wonderful! How proud your wife must be!

(*She begins to eat crab cocktail*)

We want you for our next mayor. With all your legal experience you are eminently suited. Indeed, I mean it. Of course you have had it as a secret ambition, but my intuition has found you out. Do I really give you inspiration? Isn't that lovely? How interesting life is! We meet, we eat a little crab together and then we part, — but that moment is mutual.

(*She is served a plate of soup*)

What have *I* been doing? Oh, at present I am selling boxes for the Stray Cat Benefit. By the way, won't you take a box? They're one hundred dollars. (*With languishing eyes*) So good of you, but then I knew you would. Oh, dear, I was so interested talking to you they took away my soup. I'd like to invent an anchor for plates at dinners.

(*She helps herself to the meat course and talks to the man at her left*)

What did you say, Mr. Tucker? You want to tell me a story? Ha, ha, very amusing. Where do you find all your clever jokes? How considerate of Mrs. Murray to place you next to me! How interesting life is! We meet, we eat a little lamb together, and then we part, but even that brief moment was freighted with — Ah, well, how is your wife? She wasn't very anxious to approach you about donating blankets to the hospital, but I said she misjudged you. I know you are generous and that two dozen blankets more or less won't cut into your finances very much — why, of course — certainly — I knew you would.

(*She talks across the table*)

What, Mr. Llewellyn? It's after eight and we'll miss the first act? Oh, I was cautioned particularly not to miss the first scene. Couldn't we go now? Who wants to go now? May we waive the conventions, Mrs. Murray, and desert before the salad? Ha, ha, that pun is due to your influence, Mr. Tucker. Mrs. Murray doesn't want to miss the first act either, — of course you don't. It just takes a daring person like myself to arrange matters satisfactorily for everybody. Let's go; delicious dinner, my dear, but let's go. We can take four more in our car. You and you and you and you!

(*She leaves the table, and hurries some of the guests to her car, and gets them into it*)

After you, after you; John, tell Jameson the Garrick Theater. Drive as fast as you can without spilling us. Delightful people, the Murrays. He's her second husband. She was a widow. Oh, Mr. Warren, are you sure she was divorced? Had you heard that before, Cora? Nor had I! But John dear, it doesn't matter which it was, widow or divorced, one simply wishes to be accurate. I never like to misquote. Do make inquiries, Mr. Warren, and set us right about it. Close the window, John, there's a draft.

(*She draws her cloak closer about her*)

I deeply regret, Mr. Orlopski, that there will be no opportunity this evening to hear you play, but we must arrange a concert for you. You should be more widely known. Such technique and what a soul! Here we are.

(*She alights from automobile, enters swinging doors of theater and whispers as they walk down the aisle to a box*)

You go in first and you and you. Who has the programmes? Ssh!

(*She watches the play. She applauds*)

Too bad we came so late. Missed most of it. There are the others in the box across the way. A packed house! How do you do? Why, I know any number of people in the audience; good evening. Have you seen the portrait exhibit at Dale's, Mr. Warren? Most charming. We dropped in a moment this afternoon — you really must go — ah, the curtain's going up again.

(She watches the play. She laughs, she weeps, uses her handkerchief furtively to her eyes, shudders with horror, applauds)

Oh, isn't it thrilling? I actually wept! Wasn't she superb! How does she keep her figure? Why, I thought she was grown up when I was a little girl. John, let's slip out ahead of the crowd before the last act is over. One catches cold waiting for the car.

(She watches the play and after a while pokes her husband and whispers)

Come, now that we know she's going to marry him after all there's no use to wait. Ssh, ssh!

(She tiptoes out of the dark theater to the street, where she stands shivering with cold)

Draw your fur over your chest, Mrs. Warren; you'll catch your worst! There's Jameson, John. Strong play! Get in, Cora, get in, don't wait to argue.

(She enters automobile)

Oh, it's cold! Give us the rug. What a jam of cars! Why so silent, Mr. Warren? The play? Yes, it makes one think. John, have Jamesom come back at one. We're going to take our coats off in the dressing room. We'll meet you at the head of the stairs.

(She alights from car, enters dressing room, gives coat to maid, accepts check for it, powders her nose, gives herself a glance in the mirror and goes out, walks up a short flight of stairs to join the others)

Here we are. Where's Mr. Llewellyn's table? Over there. Yes, let's dance to it.

(She dances with a partner and then sits at table)

Hello, everybody! How did you like the play? Oh, what good rarebit — nice and hot — how good it is when it's hot! Will I dance? Oh, yes!

(She leaves dish, dances around room, applauds, dances some more, comes back to the rarebit. By this time it is cold, stringy and tough. She has difficulty cutting it)

You know there's no dish so delicious as this when it's — will I dance — oh, yes!

(She dances, applauds, dances and comes back to table only to find that the waiter has removed the rarebit)

Oh, it's gone! Not through? Oh, yes, thank you, Mr. Llewellyn, the waiter was quite right! I had finished. But, John, it must be one o'clock. Will you excuse us? You know John is a hard-working business man and I have to look after him. I mustn't keep him up too late. Such a charming party. Mr. Llewellyn, thank you; good-by, every one!

(She hurries out, down the short stairs into the dressing room, exchanges her check for her coat, tips the maid, meets her husband outside and climbs into car)

wanted to hurry away so we wouldn't have to take any one home. I couldn't talk another word to anybody! I do wish, John, you wouldn't always dance with Mrs. Bailey; it forces me to dance with him and he can't. Oh, you *like* Mrs. Bailey; well, really, my dear, that's somewhat of a confession, isn't it, to tell your wife? You'd like to have me imitate her, I suppose! So quiet and has so much poise — isn't rushed! Oh, indeed, I should say she wasn't rushed. Her name doesn't count for a bag of beans in this city. She isn't asked to do anything. She has to be quiet because she hasn't the ability to be anything else. That's a horrid choice to put against me! You're an ungrateful husband, after all I've done to make your name count for something. There isn't a patroness list in town that hasn't your name on it, not an invitation list that counts but has your name! I haven't been making history for my maiden name. No, I do all the work and *your* name gets all the glory, and *your* children; that's why I'm doing it, for *your* children! *Your* children! And then after I've planned and worked to make this beautiful reputation, you dare to measure me against Mrs. Bailey. Oh, it is too cruel!

(She weeps)

No, you meant it, you can't apologize. Nothing you can

say can take away the sting! No, go away, I'm hurt, hurt! Let me alone, I can't let Jameson see me cry.

(*She wipes her eyes and alights from car*)

Good night, Jameson, to-morrow morning at ten. Hurry with your key, John, and don't keep me standing in the cold all night.

(*She enters the house, goes upstairs, undressing on the way*)

I'm so tired. No, you needn't help me up. Not after what you said. If I have to make my life alone, I suppose I can go up the stairs alone. Oh, to think that you — oh, why did I ever marry you! I'm not hysterical! Oh, do you love me? Do you really? As much as that? Of course I love you. Better than all the world. You do? You are proud? Oh, that's all I wanted to hear you say! And now I'll go and sleep peacefully, I am very tired.

(*She begins to lie down as she was at beginning of the sketch*)

Oh, how you startled me! What! You just remembered that there is to be a strange phenomenon to appear in the sky about this time? It only happens once in a thousand years? I don't care, I'd rather sleep. Oh, the children It's an education for the children! But they're asleep You insist! It's educational! Well, I suppose we have to

(*She gets out of bed with an effort, pushes open an adjoining door and calls*)

Jimmy! Dorothy! Come, dears, wake up! Father commands it! It's really cruel of you, John. Of course I want them educated. Wake up, Dorothy. Father wishes you to look at the sky. See the strange light! See! See Remember this always! How we showed you what some people never live to see! Isn't it marvelous? There Now you've seen it, run back to bed and don't ever accuse me of neglecting your education.

(*She pushes them out of the room and flings herself exhausted upon the bed*)

It happens once in a thousand years! They might have kept it for the next generation! Why pile it upon *me!*

CURTAIN

EVER YOUNG

A PLAY IN ONE ACT

By ALICE GERSTENBERG

The first performance of this play was given in the Anna Morgan Studios, Fine Arts Building, Chicago, Ill.

Characters

MRS. PHOEBE PAYNE-DEXTER
MRS. AGNES DORCHESTER
MRS. WILLIAM BLANCHARD
MRS. CAROLINE COURTNEY-PAGE

EVER YOUNG

SCENE. *These four distinguished women of some fifty and sixty years, but in spirit forever young, enjoy spending a few hours after dinner chatting in a corner of the lobby of the Poinciana Hotel, Palm Beach, at the height of the season, from which vantage ground they may view the passing show of fashionables.*

The lobby is furnished with wicker chairs (with cretonne cushions) sheltered by palms. From the distance come faint strains of an orchestra.

MRS. PAYNE-DEXTER (*enters from right as if looking for a comfortable chair. She pulls the chairs about until she has placed them to suit herself. Her face is wrinkled, but there is no sign of age in her worldly humorous eyes, her tightly corseted figure, her vibrant personality. She wears a lavender brocade evening gown and a dog collar of diamonds. Her white hair is perfectly marcelled and her well-manicured hands flash with rings. She uses a diamond-studded lorgnette and carries a large hotel room-key. She takes her chair with the authority of a leader*). There was no need to hurry through dinner, Agnes, there are plenty of chairs.

MRS. DORCHESTER (*follows Mrs. Payne-Dexter. She is a sweet, placid-faced woman with white hair, not marcelled, and she has the rosy complexion of one who has lived on a country estate. She wears eyeglasses. She is gowned in rich gold silk and is rather too overladen with old-fashioned jewelry, — earrings, bracelets, pendants, rings, mostly in amber, gold and black onyx. She carries a capacious bag of black and gold brocade which contains her wool, which she begins to knit as soon as she is comfortably seated. The ball of wool and the baby sock she is knitting are light blue*). We missed our chance last evening because you lingered over your coffee.

MRS. PAYNE-DEXTER (*dominatingly*). I always linger over my coffee. I always did when Thomas was alive. Our family always has lingered over the coffee.

MRS. DORCHESTER (*mildly*). In another moment there would not have been a chair vacant. Which one do you prefer?

MRS. PAYNE-DEXTER. Put one aside for Mrs. Blanchard. I nodded to her in this direction as we came out of the dining room.

MRS. DORCHESTER (*sits*). She will like this corner. We can see every one who crosses the lobby.

MRS. PAYNE-DEXTER (*using her lorgnettes*). How many sights and how many frights shall we see to-night? Really, Agnes, I wish *you* would give up wearing your old-fashioned onyx and amber. Why don't you turn in all that junk and get something new and fashionable?

MRS. DORCHESTER. Oh, I've never had any desire to buy jewelry since my husband died.

MRS. PAYNE-DEXTER. But that was ages ago. I've had all my diamonds reset since Thomas went, and I've had my wedding ring melted and molded again into an orange wreath.

MRS. DORCHESTER. There's the young bride who arrived to-day.

MRS. PAYNE-DEXTER. Where?

MRS. DORCHESTER. Over there near the fountain in a very low gown.

MRS. PAYNE-DEXTER. I don't see her.

MRS. DORCHESTER. She moved behind a column.

MRS. PAYNE-DEXTER (*rises and crosses*). I don't see her. Why didn't you tell me before the column got in the way?

MRS. DORCHESTER. If you were not so vain, Phoebe, you would wear decent glasses like mine.

MRS. PAYNE-DEXTER. Indeed, I can see perfectly well.

MRS. DORCHESTER. Well, I don't blame you for using your lorgnettes. It *does* add distinction to your Payne-Dexter manner.

MRS. PAYNE-DEXTER (*amused*). What! Are you still impressed by my manner?

MRS. DORCHESTER. I *have* been for forty years! Dear me, Phoebe, is it really forty years since you and I were debutantes?

MRS. PAYNE-DEXTER (*looking about cautiously*). Ssh! Don't let the hotel know I am sixty.

MRS. DORCHESTER. No one guesses it.

MRS. PAYNE-DEXTER (*rises and takes another chair which suits her better*). I certainly don't feel it, but let me tell you, these young debutantes to-day, with their supercilious airs, their sophisticated conversation, their smoking in public places, are not going to crowd me back into a grandmother's corner. No! I shall live another twenty years at least, if only to see these young things grow into the troubles of married life, and it will please me!

MRS. DORCHESTER. Why have you such animosity toward the debutantes? You terrorize them. Everywhere they side-step for you. In elevators, corridors, in the ballroom, on the beach, they put themselves out to be deferential to you. It is, "Good morning, Mrs. Payne-Dexter; good afternoon, Mrs. Payne-Dexter; good evening, Mrs. Payne-Dexter," but they never see me, even though we have been here since the opening of the season.

MRS. PAYNE-DEXTER. It is because you don't create the atmosphere which demands their attention. I am putting on all the Payne-Dexter airs I can invent in order to terrorize them. I want to make the debutantes and their smart young men side-step for me. Their youth and prettiness are no longer mine, but I hold over them the whip hand. I am a dowager, a member of a society that once ruled New York, and does still, to a certain extent, and they shall bow to me as long as I inhale one breath of life!

MRS. DORCHESTER. I do believe you are jealous of the present generation.

MRS. PAYNE-DEXTER (*rises and takes another chair which suits her better*). Agnes, you have kept your health living on your estate in Long Island, but you have watched the inevitable drying up of leaves in autumn and you have followed what seems to you the inevitable progress of autumn into winter; — well, my hair may be as white as snow, but my blood is still red!

MRS. DORCHESTER. Your vitality is a marvel to every one. Your club work, civic and social leadership make even the doctors amazed at you.

MRS. PAYNE-DEXTER. The doctors are my worst enemies. They tell me I must not do this nor that. They tell me I am getting old, that I must rest. I do not wish to rest. I simply won't grow old. When one has been a leader, one cannot let younger women usurp one's position.

MRS. DORCHESTER. You still have your leadership.

MRS. PAYNE-DEXTER. I still have it because I *will* to have it, because I will not let it go; but I have to strive harder for it every year; every year I must grow more imperious, more dominating, more terrorizing to hold supremacy over this new independent generation. (*Looks off left.*) There is that little presumptuous May Whigham. She is eighteen and so rude I should like to spank her.

MRS. DORCHESTER. They all fear you, Phoebe.

MRS. PAYNE-DEXTER (*with grim humor*). I hope so. I shall not be pushed into a corner as long as I still draw one breath of life.

MRS. DORCHESTER (*looking off right*). Good evening, Mrs. Blanchard.

MRS. PAYNE-DEXTER. We kept a chair for you.

MRS. BLANCHARD (*enters from right. She is thin, a trifle bent with age and needs a walking cane. It is gold-topped and suspended on it is a gold mesh bag. In her left hand she carries a book. She is exquisitely gowned in light blue chiffon and rare old lace. Her face is like a cameo, scarcely a wrinkle in it, and her smile is illuminatingly young. She wears a diamond necklace but no rings*). Good evening, Mrs. Payne-Dexter, Mrs. Dorchester.

MRS. DORCHESTER (*helping Mrs. Blanchard*). Sit down, Mrs. Blanchard.

MRS. BLANCHARD. No thank you, do not help me. I am about to throw it away.

MRS. PAYNE-DEXTER. Throw your cane away?

MRS. BLANCHARD (*with a light in her eyes*). Yes, I am not going to need it in a week or so.

MRS. DORCHESTER. I heard of a woman the other day who dispensed with her cane.

MRS. BLANCHARD. Who was it?

MRS. DORCHESTER (*nods straight ahead*). That golf champion over there, what's her name, — the one with the burnt V on her chest; she told me all about a case, but dear me, I never can remember names.

MRS. BLANCHARD. I shall have to ask her about it.

MRS. PAYNE-DEXTER. Are you getting stronger, Mrs. Blanchard?

MRS. BLANCHARD. I must get stronger. I am tired of depending upon a cane. Everywhere I go people are putting themselves out to be polite to me. Men help me; women send their men to help me; chauffeurs help me; bell boys, waiters, debutantes help me —

MRS. PAYNE-DEXTER. Debutantes! I can scarcely believe it!

MRS. BLANCHARD. The debutantes hop around me like so many sand-flies; I feel like swatting them with this (*shakes cane*); their politeness to my infirmity is an insult! If they would only be rude!

MRS. DORCHESTER. Mrs. Payne-Dexter was just complaining that they were too rude.

MRS. PAYNE-DEXTER. Rude! They are!

MRS. BLANCHARD. If they are rude to you, it is a compliment. They do not look upon you as old and decrepit. I resent their solicitude. In a day or two I shall throw this old thing away.

[*She tosses cane aside.*

MRS. PAYNE-DEXTER. Mrs. Blanchard!

MRS. BLANCHARD. It is no idle threat. I mean it!

MRS. DORCHESTER. But you told me you had used it fifteen years.

MRS. BLANCHARD. So I have and it is old enough to throw away. It is the oldest leg I have and it is going to be thrown away.

MRS. DORCHESTER. Oldest?

MRS. BLANCHARD. What are you doubting?

MRS. DORCHESTER. My dear Mrs. Blanchard, you just said your cane is the oldest leg you have —

MRS. BLANCHARD. So it is.

MRS. PAYNE-DEXTER (*humorously*). Mrs. Dorchester would like to know just exactly how old the others are.

MRS. BLANCHARD. The others are just exactly not more than nine months!

MRS. DORCHESTER. Nine months!

MRS. BLANCHARD. Do you think I should say ninety years?

MRS. PAYNE-DEXTER. Wouldn't that be a little nearer to the truth?

MRS. BLANCHARD (*triumphantly*). But it is not the truth! The wonderful truth is that my legs are not fifty years old, they are not more than nine months old. I have been reading an amazing book.

MRS. DORCHESTER. What is it?

MRS. PAYNE-DEXTER (*using her lorgnettes to read the title*). "Truth and Youth."

MRS. BLANCHARD. This book says that every cell in our body is completely new every nine months.

MRS. DORCHESTER. I heard about that. My daughter was reading a book about that. I forget what it was called.

MRS. BLANCHARD. Each cell reproduces itself according to the impression given to it by our subconscious mind. As we grow old we hold a thought of age and impress the cells with that thought, but if we rid ourselves of the illusion of old age we can remain ever young.

MRS. PAYNE-DEXTER. Let me have this book. I would pay a fortune for youth.

MRS. BLANCHARD. We do not have to *pay* for youth. We just have to *think* it and *be* it. It is very simple, they say, when one has faith.

MRS. DORCHESTER. What was that book my daughter was reading — dear, dear, I never can remember names and titles and numbers!

MRS. PAYNE-DEXTER. Too much wool, Agnes. Her mind is one hundred years old.

MRS. DORCHESTER (*good-naturedly*). Not quite. I have had too many financial matters to attend to since my husband died to let me slip too far behind the times, but I believe in accepting old age with as good a grace as possible.

MRS. BLANCHARD. Rubbish! That is antediluvian! I am just beginning to learn how to live. Do you know I have just obtained my divorce?

MRS. PAYNE-DEXTER. Have you divorced Mr. Blanchard after all these years?

MRS. BLANCHARD. Yes, after all these years. I suppose you know the story of my life. It was commented upon nationally when my daughter married the Duke of Cau-breigh.

MRS. PAYNE-DEXTER. My St. Louis friends often mentioned you; that is why I was so interested meeting you here this season. When my husband was alive he used to *hear* things at the clubs.

MRS. BLANCHARD. No doubt he did. My husband has been notoriously unfaithful to me and I never had the sense to get rid of him. Never had the courage, until now; but now it is all as clear as day to me, — if I have been a fool for forty years, must I stay a fool forever? No, I kicked over the traces with my wooden leg — and I am a free woman.

MRS. DORCHESTER. How odd, to think of your willingly giving up your husband when we widows so wish ours back again!

MRS. PAYNE-DEXTER. Did your husband contest it?

MRS. BLANCHARD. My husband was amazed, indignant;

he writes me imploring letters. He is old now and ready to settle down. Now, when he is ready to sit before the fireplace and watch me knit, I have played a trick on him. I am not ready to sit before the fireplace and I would rather play roulette than knit. By the way, I gambled three hundred dollars away last night.

MRS. DORCHESTER. We left early.

MRS. PAYNE-DEXTER. That is, at midnight.

MRS. DORCHESTER. We rode around a bit before coming in. It was so balmy and I just love to ride in the wheel-chairs.

MRS. PAYNE-DEXTER. I suppose it was not quite the thing for two lone women to be riding around in the moonlight, at midnight, but the colored boy said *every one* does it at Palm Beach.

MRS. DORCHESTER. It was very romantic.

MRS. PAYNE-DEXTER. There is romance in every breeze through the palm trees.

MRS. BLANCHARD (*gaily*). I didn't come back to the hotel until morning. I stayed on and played, had breakfast there — came home without a ring on my finger — handed them over as security to a friend who thought it amusing to take them.

MRS. DORCHESTER. We missed you on the beach this morning.

MRS. BLANCHARD. I slept until luncheon. I am going back to-night to win my rings again. (*She dangles her gold bag stuffed with bills*) Starting with five hundred to-night.

MRS. PAYNE-DEXTER. Before you know it, you will have gambled a fortune away.

MRS. BLANCHARD (*laughs*). I'm not worrying. I receive an amazingly high alimony. The court figured that I would not live long and that I needed much medical care. Well, I am not paying out any money for medical care and when it comes to having a good time I am making up for thirty years. I found only one man in my whole life whom I really loved and he was not my husband.

MRS. PAYNE-DEXTER. What happened?

MRS. BLANCHARD. I have never known what became of him.

MRS. DORCHESTER. I can't imagine what it must be not to love one's husband. I miss mine so.

MRS. BLANCHARD. I had been married only four months when I heard of my husband's infatuation for a married woman in our own set. He had married me only, it seems, to allay suspicion. Of course, I see now that I should have divorced him then and there, but I was very young and it wasn't being done in those days. In those hours of my disillusion, a dashing young lieutenant understood my despair and planned to arouse my husband's jealousy and so bring him back to me —

MRS. DORCHESTER. Phoebe, stop fuddling with your door-key. It gets on my nerves.

MRS. BLANCHARD. He succeeded in arousing my husband's jealousy, but meanwhile I had fallen in love with the lieutenant.

MRS. PAYNE-DEXTER. And he with you, no doubt?

MRS. BLANCHARD. Yes.

MRS. DORCHESTER. Mrs. Blanchard, it is a life tragedy, but not a line of it shows in your face.

MRS. BLANCHARD. I wouldn't let it show in my face. I harbored a secret thought — a terrible thought — that my husband might die, that I might be free to find the other again, that then he should not see an old wrinkled face after he had cherished the memory of my youth.

MRS. PAYNE-DEXTER. Think of living like that all these years when you might have had a divorce long ago.

MRS. BLANCHARD. It's humorous in a way, isn't it? That when women like you and Mrs. Dorchester are widowed, I had to put up with a husband who just *wouldn't* die.

MRS. PAYNE-DEXTER. What became of the lieutenant?

MRS. BLANCHARD. He asked to be transferred to another post. He wanted to go as far away from me as possible — no distance seemed far enough to break the magnetic attraction between us. Finally he was sent as far away as China and there we lost track of him in the Boxer Rebellion.

MRS. DORCHESTER. And you never heard from him again?

MRS. BLANCHARD. No. The Government reported him as missing. No doubt the Chinese took him prisoner. If he died — and I think he must have died — all these years I have imagined that he died — I have felt his spirit near me — guiding me — watching over me.

MRS. DORCHESTER (*shakes her head*). Do you believe he could be near you? I don't believe that my husband is. I sit and knit and think of him, but the beyond seems nothing but void and silence.

MRS. PAYNE-DEXTER (*practically*). Well, I believe in believing anything that helps you.

MRS. DORCHESTER (*shakes her head*). I can't get into communication.

MRS. BLANCHARD (*hopefully*). Oh, I know Oliver Trent has never forgotten me. If he had lived or escaped, Oliver would have found me. I know Oliver died and that his spirit has been lovingly near me these twenty odd years!

MRS. DORCHESTER. My husband and I loved each other deeply. That love, it seems to me, should hold us together even after he has gone, but I can't believe that it does.

MRS. BLANCHARD. It does and it will, if you have faith. There is nothing but love — I am beginning to *feel* it. For a long while I tried to make myself believe it — for a long while I could only *think*, but now I am beginning to *feel*, deep within me to realize it — and I feel warm all through. Oh, I shall put aside my ancient leg!

MRS. PAYNE-DEXTER. Of course he loved you — I am sure he did.

MRS. DORCHESTER. If he were alive, now that you have your divorce —

MRS. BLANCHARD. So you see my romance is only a shadow. I never dared keep a letter from him, not a token — I have only my thoughts —

MRS. PAYNE-DEXTER. And the thoughts have kept your face young.

MRS. BLANCHARD. I would not let my face change — if by some miracle he should see me again — but I couldn't control my body as well — it grew wearier and wearier until I needed a cane to lean on.

MRS. DORCHESTER. And here you are threatening to walk without it.

MRS. BLANCHARD (*brightening*). I will, too! I only get blue when I begin to think of the past. It's a bad habit. I shall not do it any more. Only, if I could be sure that he died with just me in his heart, I wouldn't mind so much his not being alive — if I could but know —

MRS. PAYNE-DEXTER. I should certainly continue to believe that he remembered.

MRS. DORCHESTER (*consolingly*). I am sure he did.

MRS. BLANCHARD. I built my life upon my faith in him — if I should be robbed of this belief in his love for me — I think it would — kill me.

MRS. PAYNE-DEXTER. But if you could have proof of his love —

MRS. BLANCHARD (*with shining eyes*). If I could have proof!

MRS. PAYNE-DEXTER (*looking off stage through lorgnette*). There's that beautiful Mrs. Courtney-Page. I should ike to know her better. Shall we invite her to sit with us?

MRS. BLANCHARD. Who is she?

MRS. PAYNE-DEXTER. The white-haired woman in white velvet carrying a black feather fan. She is just coming out of mourning for her last husband.

MRS. DORCHESTER. *Last!* How many has she had?

MRS. PAYNE-DEXTER. The manicurist told me she had three — and the clerk in the jewel shop told me only one; they were appraising her pearls — she has such marvelous pearls — I'd love to see her pearls close by, wouldn't you?

MRS. BLANCHARD. Oh, do invite her over; I'd like to exchange data about husbands. Is she down here alone?

MRS. PAYNE-DEXTER. They say she came alone, but I noticed her on the beach with one man and in a wheelchair with another — she's alone now though and looking for a place to sit — call her over, Agnes.

MRS. DORCHESTER (*timidly*). Oh, *I* don't know her, Phoebe; *you* call her.

MRS. BLANCHARD. Don't *you* know her, Mrs. Payne-Dexter?

MRS. PAYNE-DEXTER. I might pretend to. How do you do? [*She bows.*

MRS. COURTNEY-PAGE (*enters from right. She is white-haired and about fifty-five, but she has dash in her manner and her figure is stunning in a white velvet gown with long sleeves, but very low at the throat. She is the type that can be a vampire at any age. Her jewels are pearls, ropes of pearls. She carries a black fan and a batch of mail, among which is a black-rimmed letter*). How — do — you — do? I don't recall the name.

MRS. PAYNE-DEXTER. Mrs. Payne-Dexter of New York. Don't tell me, Mrs. Courtney-Page, that you have forgotten me.

MRS. COURTNEY-PAGE (*with poise*). Mrs. Payne-Dexter, a name so well known? I remember exactly — five years ago at the opera — your box was next to the Carrolls. We were their guests one evening when my late husband and I were in New York on a wedding trip.

MRS. PAYNE-DEXTER. Why, yes, yes, of course, I remember — My friends, Mrs. Dorchester, Mrs. Blanchard.

MRS. BLANCHARD. How — do — you — do? Won't you sit down?

MRS. COURTNEY-PAGE. Yes, thank you. (*She sits*) I have noticed you, Mrs. Blanchard. Your cane? [*She picks it up courteously and hands it to Mrs. Blanchard.*

MRS. BLANCHARD (*courteously appreciative*). Thank you.

MRS. PAYNE-DEXTER. Mrs. Dorchester and I have been spending the season in Palm Beach.

MRS. BLANCHARD. And I came down from St. Louis and had the good fortune to become acquainted with them.

MRS. COURTNEY-PAGE. Blanchard of St. Louis. The name is very familiar.

MRS. BLANCHARD. My daughter married the Duke of Caubreigh.

MRS. COURTNEY-PAGE. Oh, yes, yes, but just lately — it seems to me I saw that name just lately.

MRS. BLANCHARD. No doubt you did. I am celebrating my divorce.

MRS. DORCHESTER. I think she has a great deal of courage to face the world alone voluntarily.

MRS. BLANCHARD. It is rejuvenating to feel so marvelously free!

MRS. COURTNEY-PAGE. She is quite right. Why should a woman remain in bondage when there is at every turn a new chance for a better alliance.

MRS. BLANCHARD. Good gracious! Do you believe me capable of marrying again at my age?

MRS. COURTNEY-PAGE. Why not? A woman can marry any man she wants.

MRS. DORCHESTER (*mildly*). Oh, the *man* may get the woman he wants; Henry kept insisting until I married him, but I don't think it's the other way round, do *you*, Phoebe?

MRS. PAYNE-DEXTER (*dominating manner*). I don't know. I worked hard for Thomas, but I got him.

MRS. BLANCHARD. I haven't an opinion. The one *I* wanted I met only when it was too late.

MRS. COURTNEY-PAGE. What do you mean by too late?

MRS. BLANCHARD. After I was married to some one else.

MRS. COURTNEY-PAGE. But now that you are divorced —

MRS. BLANCHARD. Oh, it's too late now. My romance was over twenty years ago.

MRS. DORCHESTER. Do you really think a woman can marry any man she wants?

MRS. COURTNEY-PAGE. I've proved it. I was engaged three times, married once, once widowed, and now I have another fiancé. Isn't that proof?

MRS. BLANCHARD. You are, if you will pardon my frankness, a very handsome woman, Mrs. Courtney-Page; such attractions would not require much further effort on your part.

MRS. COURTNEY-PAGE. Thank you, but there is a science about attracting love as there is about everything else. There hasn't been a moment of my life when I haven't been in love.

MRS. PAYNE-DEXTER (*rather snortingly*). That's impossible! There aren't enough people in the world for that!

MRS. COURTNEY-PAGE (*with real tenderness*). Oh, yes, there are. As long as you hold the thought of love you will find that you *can* love — and as long as you love you will attract it in return.

MRS. PAYNE-DEXTER. Where is your home now, Mrs. Courtney-Page?

MRS. COURTNEY-PAGE. Chicago, but I was born in San Francisco. I was Emily Tarden.

MRS. PAYNE-DEXTER. Emily Tarden! Were you indeed!

MRS. BLANCHARD. Why, it just seems yesterday when all the magazines were full of your photographs.

MRS. DORCHESTER. The most beautiful debutante on the Western coast!

MRS. COURTNEY-PAGE. They did make a fuss about it when I became engaged to Harlow Bingham — I was only eighteen then. When I look back and think what a brilliant career I might have had with Harlow — well — you know he died — (*she sighs*) before we were married — an accident — steeple-chase — poor Harlow (*she unconsciously fondles a strand of her pearls*), he gave me my first pearls.

MRS. BLANCHARD. Magnificent pearls!

MRS. PAYNE-DEXTER (*using lorgnettes*). I have scarcely been able to keep my eyes off them.

MRS. COURTNEY-PAGE. This strand — the shortest and smallest — was given to me by Harlow upon our engagement. He gave me a solitaire too, but the pearls were a thank-offering because I had given up the desire to go on the stage to marry him.

MRS. DORCHESTER. Oh, did you want to be an actress?

MRS. COURTNEY-PAGE. I have wanted nothing more all my life.

MRS. BLANCHARD. You would have made a good one too.

MRS. COURTNEY-PAGE. My family opposed me, as all families do.

MRS. PAYNE-DEXTER. They did in those days.

MRS. COURTNEY-PAGE. So I had to give up the idea of acting — on the stage.

[*But it is evident that she has been acting in real life ever since.*

MRS. PAYNE-DEXTER (*in a whisper, looking out front*). Look, look, that's the man who tried to flirt with me the other day at the tea dance in the Cocoanut Grove.

MRS. COURTNEY-PAGE. Don't you know who that is?

MRS. PAYNE-DEXTER. No.

MRS. COURTNEY-PAGE. That's Beverly Strawn, our best-seller novelist.

MRS. PAYNE-DEXTER. Mercy! Hide me! He must have been picking me out as the dowager mother-in-law for his next novel.

MRS. DORCHESTER. Did you marry Mr. Courtney-Page after Mr. — what's his name died, your first fiancé?

MRS. COURTNEY-PAGE. No, I became engaged to Philip Craw, an Englishman I met in Egypt. He was on his way to South Africa. He had been in diplomatic service in India and had been transferred. He brought me this second strand — the second largest and longest — from India. He went ahead to South Africa to prepare a home, intending to come back for me — but he died of fever.

MRS. BLANCHARD. How thrillingly tragic!

MRS. DORCHESTER. I could not have endured it.

MRS. PAYNE-DEXTER. And the other strands — you have two more —

MRS. COURTNEY-PAGE. This third one was the gift of my husband, Mr. Courtney-Page. I would not let him give them to me until after we were married.

MRS. DORCHESTER. That was a wise precaution. They say pearls mean tears.

MRS. PAYNE-DEXTER. It is surprising that he risked giving you pearls at all.

MRS. COURTNEY-PAGE. He was jealous of the others. Of course, I couldn't throw the others away — they were so costly.

MRS. PAYNE-DEXTER. Naturally not!

MRS. COURTNEY-PAGE. So he finally purchased a strand in Vienna — larger and longer than the others.

MRS. BLANCHARD. Then did he die too?

MRS. COURTNEY-PAGE. Oh, no, Mr. Courtney-Page was the third man I was engaged to, but the only one I married. He died scarcely a year ago.

MRS. DORCHESTER (*takes some digestive tablets out of her bag and offers them*). Will you have a life-preserver? I ate something to-night that didn't agree with me.

MRS. PAYNE-DEXTER (*takes one*). Thank you.

MRS. DORCHESTER (*offering*). Mrs. Blanchard?

MRS. BLANCHARD. No, thanks, I don't need them any more since I am taking the new diet.

MRS. PAYNE-DEXTER. What is your new diet?

[*Mrs. Dorchester offers Mrs. Courtney-Page a tablet. She takes one. Mrs. Dorchester takes one.*

MRS. BLANCHARD. Nuts, fruit, no meat, no bread, no hot vegetables, no coffee, no tea.

MRS. DORCHESTER. Have you stopped eating altogether?

MRS. BLANCHARD. Only fruit and nuts. I feel as light as a feather — in another day I shall walk and throw away this stick!

MRS. DORCHESTER. You said in another week you would throw it away.

MRS. PAYNE-DEXTER. Now be careful, don't take risks!

MRS. BLANCHARD. The book says we must not have negatives in our mind. I tell you that if I can have enough faith, I shall walk alone!

MRS. PAYNE-DEXTER. Oh, the book.

MRS. BLANCHARD (*handing book to Mrs. Payne-Dexter*). "Truth and Youth."

MRS. PAYNE-DEXTER (*reads*). "The average man and woman of middle age chooses a comfortable chair and settles down into it with the thought that life is finished and it is necessary to await the end. When women see their little children grown to manhood and independent of them, they feel that their use in life is over. Nothing is more untrue. The grandmother is a free —"

MRS. DORCHESTER (*interrupting as she glances out front*). Just a moment, Phoebe, excuse me, but what did you say was the name of the woman in jet — walking with the aviator — did she fly down with him from New York?

MRS. COURTNEY-PAGE. That's Hilda Dane, one of the Follies. They say she has her skin insured when she's on the beach.

MRS. BLANCHARD. I have never seen her skin. She white-washes it and her lips are thick with paint. Yesterday on the beach she wore a lemon-colored woolen cape with a big sable collar and every diamond that has ever been given to her.

MRS. DORCHESTER. Is she married to the aviator?

MRS. PAYNE-DEXTER. Don't ask absurd questions, Agnes.

MRS. DORCHESTER. Oh!

MRS. PAYNE-DEXTER (*reading*). "The grandmother is a free woman, she has a new youth. She has the wisdom of experience with which to experiment for greater wisdom." Agnes, you must read this book; it will stir you up — your very mind is turning to wool.

MRS. DORCHESTER. I have always been more domestic than you, Phoebe.

MRS. PAYNE-DEXTER. Domestic! Haven't I done my share? Haven't I run a house in New York, a house in Newport, a house in London, an apartment in Paris; I even had a palace one season in Venice. No, it is not domesticity that is making you old; it is mental lethargy.

MRS. COURTNEY-PAYNE. That is an enemy to youth, mental lethargy. I refuse to have it!

MRS. PAYNE-DEXTER. Mrs. Dorchester doesn't live for herself any more. When she is at home she is a slave to her grandchildren; when she is away she scarcely can take time from the wool to look at a palm tree.

MRS. DORCHESTER (*looking away*). I can knit without looking.

MRS. PAYNE-DEXTER. I am more selfish. I let my children and grandchildren alone. I do not spend my evenings knitting baby socks. I have my opera box, I entertain distinguished foreign visitors. I have my club committees, my charities and I am studying to add to my husband's collection of paintings — as a memorial to him — and I am taking up Spanish so that I may spend next season in Buenos Aires. But you, Agnes, you make your children dependent upon you — you are always nursing some grandchild through something.

MRS. DORCHESTER. But when they are ill, I *must* help them.

MRS. PAYNE-DEXTER. You think you must and they let you think it because they don't want to hurt your feelings by letting you know they don't need you. You take care of a grandchild so its own mother can go and play bridge; you save your son a nurse's bill while he spends the money playing polo at the country club.

MRS. DORCHESTER. But it isn't a happy thought not to be needed.

MRS. BLANCHARD. You were telling us about your pearls, Mrs. Courtney-Page. Where did you get the fourth strand?

MRS. COURTNEY-PAGE. The fourth, the largest and longest, is the gift of my new fiancé. I am down here waiting for time to pass; we shall be married as soon as it seems correct.

MRS. PAYNE-DEXTER (*looking out front*). Dear me, there's Mrs. Wallace Morton in another gown and as usual no petticoat.

MRS. COURTNEY-PAGE. I think she does wear *one!*

MRS. BLANCHARD. Aren't you lucky to find a fiancé again? I am afraid I couldn't bring myself to care for any man as much as I have cared for one in the past.

MRS. DORCHESTER. Nor I.

MRS. PAYNE-DEXTER. Hump! Men aren't worth bothering about.

MRS. COURTNEY-PAGE. I was so lost without marriage companionship that when I was in Paris last autumn I picked out the most eligible man I could find. He is quite old but very nice and has valuable mines in Australia.

MRS. PAYNE-DEXTER. Is he a Frenchman?

MRS. COURTNEY-PAGE. No, an American, but he hasn't been in this country since he was sent to the American legation in China. He has had an exciting life. He was taken prisoner in the Boxer Rebellion and was reported missing for years, but a faithful Chinese servant smuggled him to Australia.

MRS. BLANCHARD (*begins to tremble; her hands quiver as they clutch her cane*). Your fiancé — his name?

MRS. COURTNEY-PAGE. Oliver Trent — president of the Australian Mining Company of —

MRS. BLANCHARD (*with a gasp of anguish loosens her hold upon her cane; it falls unheeded*). Oliver Trent — you said Oliver Trent?

MRS. DORCHESTER (*blandly*). Why, wasn't that the name of the man you loved — wasn't that the name, Phoebe?

MRS. COURTNEY-PAGE. The man, Mrs. Blanchard — I do not understand.

MRS. PAYNE-DEXTER (*trying to relieve the situation*). Mrs. Blanchard has been telling us about a friend of hers who had been lost in the Boxer Rebellion. She thought he had died. No doubt it is a consolation to her to know that he still lives.

MRS. BLANCHARD (*wilted, old-looking and speaking with an effort*). No, Mrs. Courtney-Page, I scarcely can bear it that he lives. I have held him in my heart as one dead for twenty years. I have lived on the thought that he loved me. He loved me once, but I know now that men cannot be true. When he went to China he put me out of his mind forever. He has forgotten me for younger and handsomer women.

MRS. PAYNE-DEXTER. Hump! I wouldn't let it worry me! Men aren't worth such lifelong adoration. You look about and find some one else.

MRS. DORCHESTER. Perhaps Mrs. Courtney-Page will give him up if we tell her what he means to you.

MRS. BLANCHARD (*fiercely*). I want my own — not what is cast off.

MRS. COURTNEY-PAGE (*drawing her chair closer to Mrs. Blanchard and speaking gently*). You want me to give him up? (*She fondles the largest strand of pearls reluctantly*) That would be difficult to do. It wasn't easy to win him. I had to use all the art I have learned in past experiences to get him. He has never been married and is a little afraid. If I gave him up, are you sure he would remember you?

MRS. BLANCHARD (*in anguish of spirit but under control*). No, do not trouble. I shall have to bear it. I feel quite blind — as if I had been struck on the head — but maybe it is just my heart. You see, he and I were very much in love, but I was married and he had to go away. He promised not to forget, but he was young; I shouldn't have believed him. That last day before he went I met him clandestinely in the Park. I cut off a bit of my hair that day. It was golden then, like golden amber, he said, and he put it into an amber locket he wore on his watch charm.

MRS. DORCHESTER (*throws her knitting aside and lets the wool roll to the floor*). I remember, I remember, amber locket, from a watch charm — I have it here — I've had it twenty years! made into a bracelet — (*she takes off the bracelet*)

My son brought it home from the Philippines — it was given to him by a Chinese servant —

MRS. BLANCHARD (*in extreme excitement*). The locket —

MRS. COURTNEY-PAGE. A Chinese servant —

MRS. DORCHESTER (*excitedly*). Yes, the very one you said rescued him! I remember it all now. How stupid of me not to think of it before, but as Phoebe says, my mind's all wool — that Chinese servant —

MRS. BLANCHARD. Yes, yes, go on —

MRS. DORCHESTER (*speedily*). You know the Boxers stormed the Legation. He fought desperately and valiantly — the Chinese servant described all that — how he was taken prisoner and tortured so he almost lost his mind. At night he raved in delirium. He called a woman's name but there was no one of that name in the legation — my son told me but I have such a wretched memory for names — but it wasn't a real name that one could identify — it must have been a nickname —

MRS. BLANCHARD. Was it Dee-Dee?

MRS. DORCHESTER (*pouncingly*). Dee-Dee, Dee-Dee! That's what it was! Oh, my stupid head!

MRS. BLANCHARD (*pathetically*). It meant "dear."

MRS. PAYNE-DEXTER (*to Mrs. Dorchester*). Why have you kept this from us all this time?

MRS. DORCHESTER (*gaining assurance*). How could I know my son's story was about Mrs. Blanchard until she mentioned the watch charm? But now it all comes back to me. At night in delirium he called this name — how he loved this woman. he took the amber locket and opened it and kissed the blond lock of hair and he treasured it as nothing else he had. He treasured it so highly that he gave it to his Chinese servant to keep for him — for fear they would rob him of it. They took his money and everything else he had, but the servant kept the amber safely, but — but —

MRS. BLANCHARD (*in rapt attention*). But then how did *you* get it?

MRS. DORCHESTER. That's just it — I'll tell you how — oh, my stupid memory! Phoebe, stop fuddling with your door-key — you distract me! The amber — the Chinese servant smuggled him into a boat —

MRS. BLANCHARD. Who was smuggled into the boat?

MRS. DORCHESTER. Mr. What's his name — your —

MRS. BLANCHARD. Oliver Trent.

MRS. DORCHESTER. Yes, into the boat — and in the excitement of concealing him behind some kegs — the ship began to move and the Chinese servant had to run to get off, and in running he forgot to give up the amber locket — and so he kept it — he kept it as a talisman and a few years later when he served my son in the Philippines he gave it to him as a talisman when my son was very ill with fever — and my son became superstitious about it and had it set in a bracelet for me as my protection, and now I shall give it to you — for it is *your* talisman, Mrs. Blanchard, a talisman of his undying love!

[*Mrs. Blanchard takes the bracelet but is incapable of speech. She raises it to her lips and a light of inspiration comes into her eyes.*

MRS. COURTNEY-PAGE (*going on with the fabrication*). And that is why I had such difficulty making him care for me. He told me about his first love — he spoke of her as Dee-dee and he told me that when he lost the amber he felt that she had gone out of his life forever. He said that she was married and it was unlawful for him to think of her — but he has never forgotten — he told me he would love her always — and when I tell him of you, Mrs. Blanchard, he will come to you at once, for you have been right — his love has been yours and is yours still. I think you ought to have these pearls!

MRS. BLANCHARD (*her eyes illumined, her body stronger*). No, no, thank you — I don't want them — I — I — have this — (*She holds the locket in her hands and rises, forgetting her cane*) Excuse me, ladies, if I go to my room — I —

I — have had my answer out of the silence — and I'm a little — unstrung.

[*She walks out right with great dignity and composure, and the light in her eyes is a triumph of youth.*

MRS. PAYNE-DEXTER (*looking after in awe*). *Without* her cane!

MRS. COURTNEY-PAGE. Don't remind her!

MRS. DORCHESTER (*sighing*). Poor dear, poor dear!

MRS. PAYNE-DEXTER. Was that all true what you said, Agnes? I never heard you talk so fast in all your life — and how you suddenly got such a memory — you never told me anything about the amber locket and you've worn it forever, it seems to me!

MRS. DORCHESTER. Father gave it to me on my twenty-first birthday to save a lock of my blond hair. I risked the chance that mine was a duplicate of hers.

MRS. PAYNE-DEXTER. And all you said was a *lie?*

MRS. COURTNEY-PAGE. It doesn't matter. We shall make it true.

MRS. PAYNE-DEXTER. But when she finds out that you have deceived her —

MRS. COURTNEY-PAGE. She will never find out. I shall warn him to hide away his amber locket on his watch charm.

MRS. DORCHESTER. Does he still wear it?

MRS. COURTNEY-PAGE. Yes, and many other trophies from other loves; they say he has been a great beau —

MRS. PAYNE-DEXTER. The outrageous flirt!

MRS. DORCHESTER. Poor dear Mrs. Blanchard! I thought she would die — I was afraid she was dying. I *had* to say something to bring her to.

MRS. PAYNE-DEXTER. But what have you gained by these lies?

MRS. COURTNEY-PAGE. Does she not walk?

MRS. PAYNE-DEXTER (*with awe*). Yes, it is a miracle!

MRS. COURTNEY-PAGE. Merely a miracle of the realization of love!

MRS. PAYNE-DEXTER. But it is built on a false belief! He has not been true to her.

MRS. COURTNEY-PAGE. Mrs. Payne-Dexter, I have never questioned the depth of any one's love for me. That which counts is, after all, only that which is in our own hearts. If Mrs. Blanchard is convinced of his love — that is all that is really necessary.

MRS. PAYNE-DEXTER. But when you marry him —

MRS. COURTNEY-PAGE. I shall not marry him — I shall only keep the pearls —

MRS. BLANCHARD. But if *you* love him —

MRS. COURTNEY-PAGE. As for that — *I*, *always*, can find some one else.

MRS. DORCHESTER. Gracious! My wool is a mess!

MRS. PAYNE-DEXTER. You'd better give up knitting, Agnes, and turn to story telling — you've quite surprised me with your sudden brilliancy. (*She beckons off stage left*) Bell boy, you may have these glasses —

MRS. DORCHESTER. Your diamond platinum lorgnettes!

MRS. PAYNE-DEXTER. Hump! Do you think that *I* have to manufacture a love affair to get rid of *my* crutches?

MRS. DORCHESTER (*scarcely able to grasp the idea*). She walked without her cane!

MRS. COURTNEY-PAGE (*with a romantic smile*). Oh, to stay young, one must *love!*

CURTAIN

FOR DISTINGUISHED SERVICE

FLORENCE CLAY KNOX

FLORENCE CLAY KNOX was born in Cedar Falls, Iowa, and was educated at the Stanly Hall Finishing School and the University of Minnesota.

She is an amateur actress of ability and was one of the founders of the Waterloo Little Theatre. Her play "The China Guinea Pig" won the Drama League Prize.

/

FOR DISTINGUISHED SERVICE

A COMEDY IN ONE ACT

By FLORENCE CLAY KNOX

Characters

MISS KATHARINE BURTON,
            a young woman of the "smart set"

MRS. JIM HARDING (otherwise Ethel) . . . her friend

MARY . . . . her maid

FOR DISTINGUISHED SERVICE

SCENE. *The exquisitely appointed, rose and ivory boudoir of Miss Katharine Burton. In the center stands a long narrow reading table. A scarf of rose brocade, draped across it, with one end trailing gracefully to the floor, offsets the severity suggested by the tall twin candlesticks. At the left of the table, and a little in front, is a gossipy little rocking chair, with cushions and arms. At the right, a chaise longue. At the further side of the chaise longue, convenient to the occupant's elbow, is a desk 'phone. A huge bunch of violets, whose basket container and gauze bow proclaim the fashionable florist, stands upon a small table or pedestal at the extreme right. An entrance at the right — back, another chair, extreme left, are among the essential furnishings.*

The curtain, rising, discloses Miss Katharine Burton, attired in adorable négligé, comfortably and gracefully ensconced among the rose-colored cushions of the chaise longue, reading. Miss Burton is still young — which means not too young — and beautiful. An ease of manner, just touched with weariness, bespeaks the woman of the world, but fails to disguise the fact that Miss Burton is a very genuine sort of person, preserving, among the frivolities of her set, her own ideals, and independence of thought and action. She possesses a fine sense of humor and a dauntless spirit that asks no quarter.

A bell rings off stage, and Mary, the trimmest of little maids, enters, bearing a huge confectioner's box, tied with a crimson ribbon, and a note. She comes around the table, and stands at Miss Burton's side, holding out the box for inspection.

KATHARINE. Oh — Oh — Mary — One fine little box — (*She admires it without rising. Mary places the box on the table and waits expectantly for further developments*) I'm too busy now, but there will be a grand opening soon and then I'll send for you.

MARY. Oh, thank you. (*She gazes wistfully at the box*) Don't you just love chocolates?

KATHARINE. Yes, I do. Especially when a very nice person sends them to me.

MARY. Yes'm. I suppose that is nice.

[*She lingers, looking first at the box and then at the note in Miss Burton's hand, but receiving no encouragement, heaves a sigh and leaves.*

Katharine watches her go — rises — listens — and waits till certain that Mary has quite entirely disappeared. She takes a precautionary survey of the room, then curls up in the chaise longue and opens the note in the manner of one handing herself a great treat.

KATHARINE (*reading out loud*). "Dear Katharine: — Of course I know it would be highly improper to write you a note — out of a clear sky, so I'm sending the sweetmeats for an excuse. I believe this is what you call tossing a bone to Mrs. Grundy. And the reason I write to you is a purely selfish one. I know the sympathetic, soul-satisfying little note I will receive in reply. Of course you may scold a little, but one learns to take the bitter with the sweet, and you wouldn't have the heart to make it all bitter. I will see you, of course, at the Martin's house party?

Till then —

Jim."

(*She kisses the note shyly and holds it as if afraid its contents might escape*) "Till then —" Thursday, Friday — Two whole days — Oh, whatever are we coming to? (*She dreams for a moment and then shrugs her shoulders*) Oh, well, it's no more than his wife does all the time. Why should I care? (*The desk 'phone beside her rings. She takes down the receiver*) Hello — Yes, this is Miss — Oh, hello, Jim. . . . Fine, thank you. I'm just about to open the chocolates. Really, Jim, throw bones to Mrs. Grundy if you must, but you needn't

throw such big ones. You're liable to kill the poor
woman. . . . What? Oh, I wish she were dead too.
Thank you, anyway. . . . You insist on written thanks?
. . . Very well. But I shall wait till I've eaten the chocolates. I intend to scold and I can't be severe when my
mouth is watering. . . . Yes, of course I'm going. Won't
it be splendid? Ideal place for a house party and such
grand weather. . . . Ride over with you? Oh, I'd love to.
How far is it? . . . Really? . . . Does it appeal to me?
A sixty-mile ride in the moonlight with you and Ethel?
Why Jim, you know I'd love it. . . . What? . . . You
say Ethel is going earlier? . . . I see. . . . Just you and
I. . . . Why, wait a minute, let me think. . . . Yes, it
appeals just as much, but . . . No, I'm not prim. Don't
call me that. . . . Listen — I'll prove it to you. I'd
rather take that ride with you than — than anything I
ever did in all my life. Does that sound prim? (*She listens
to a reply that pleases her and yet makes her shake her head*)
Jim, hush. You don't mean a thing you're saying. . . .
Jim, please. I won't listen. I can't go with you. . . . No,
this is final. No use to call again. . . . Very well, if I do
change my mind, I'll let you know. Good-by. (*She
hangs up the receiver but continues talking to the phone*)
And maybe I will, maybe I will. Who cares, anyway?
(*A bell rings off stage and a moment later Mary enters with
a visiting card, which she hands to Miss Burton*) Ethel —
Mercy me — (*She hesitates a moment*) Tell Mrs. Harding
to come right up. (*Exit Mary. Katharine conceals the
note in her dress. She picks up the box of chocolates
nervously, as if to remove it, and then puts it down again,
smiling*)
Feeding Mrs. Harding on Mr. Harding's chocolates strikes
me funny. I must be depraved.
[*Enter Mrs. Jim Harding. She is also still young, and
making a very evident effort to remain so. She is dressed in
the height of fashion, groomed to the point of hardness, and
daringly rouged. She wears long earrings, carries a "Vanity*

Box," and her voice has the nervous tension of a woman who is breaking all the speed laws in her mad rush through life.

ETHEL. Well, my dear, for goodness sakes — Are you ill or lazy?

KATHARINE. Lazy — blissfully lazy. Throw off that perfectly stunning wrap and make yourself comfy.

ETHEL. Thanks, I will, but I mustn't stay long. (*She crosses stage, throws her coat over chair at extreme left, and seats herself in the little rocking chair. Suddenly she spies the chocolates*) My word — What do I see? Is it a steamer trunk?

KATHARINE. You see a box of chocolates, my dear, a regular box.

ETHEL. Oh, regular — Dear me, how regular?

KATHARINE. Well, that all depends. Some people would even call it slightly irregular, I suppose. Anyway, you're in luck, for I was just about to open them. We'll have a gorgeous time, gorging chocholates and gossiping. Don't you love to gossip and gorge?

ETHEL. Do I? Let's pretend we're sixteen. Talk about our beaux and tell all our secrets.

KATHARINE. Very well.

[*She proceeds to the opening of the box.*

ETHEL. To begin with, who sent you that box of chocolates?

KATHARINE. Don't you wish you knew?

ETHEL. Well, I'll say he's either very young, very old, or very much in love.

KATHARINE. Really, how interesting! Because he's certainly not young, and he's not old. So he must be very much in love. I haven't been at all sure before.

ETHEL. Come, come, who is he? Don't be a clam.

KATHARINE. Maybe I bought them myself. I do sometimes.

ETHEL. Doesn't look like a box you'd buy yourself. Somehow or other, it smacks of Romance.

[*Katharine passes the chocolates, helps herself, and places the box on the table between them. Ethel exhibits a deep love for chocolates, helps herself often and eats with keen relish.*

KATHARINE. Chocolates are romantic, aren't they? Now

there's nothing romantic about gumdrops, or licorice sticks. You'd never ask me who sent those. But chocolates — Ah — Mystery and Romance!

ETHEL. That's right. Chocolates and violets. The violet stage of an affair really succeeds the chocolate stage and is more violent. Violent violets — how's that for a — Why — Katharine Burton — there are violets. Now I sniff something interesting. Out with it at once. Who is he?

KATHARINE. Who is he? Oh, anybody — nobody. (*She pauses a moment and gives Ethel a look of keenest scrutiny*) But I have a secret. I've half a mind to tell you. Do you want to hear it?

ETHEL. Do I? Well, you know me. Wait till I find a big one with gummy insides. (*She searches the box industriously*) Here we are. Proceed. Isn't this bliss?

KATHARINE. Ethel, I believe I'm in love.

ETHEL. In love? Not you? After all these years? Well, I never.

KATHARINE. Of course, if I'm going to have my advanced age thrown at my head you can't expect me to be very eloquent. Besides, I'm not joking.

ETHEL. My dear, a thousand pardons. If you'll move that box nearer, I won't talk so much. (*She draws the box nearer, and selects a fresh piece*) Tell me more. It isn't Melville Shaw, is it? After all these ye—

[*She hurriedly plunges a chocolate in her mouth and smothers the last word.*

KATHARINE. No, it isn't Mel — after all — these — years. I wish it were. This man is already married.

ETHEL. Katharine — not you? In love with a married man? Oh, this is the funniest thing I ever heard. (*She throws back her head and laughs with unfeigned amusement*) Why, my dear, there's hope for you yet.

KATHARINE (*still observing Ethel closely*). He's married, and his wife is a friend of mine.

ETHEL. Wait a minute. Can't you see I'm gasping? (*She composes herself with an effort and shakes her head in mock solemnity*.) Katharine, Katharine, my poor young friend. When we Puritans decide to step down off our little pedestals we certainly come off with both feet.

KATHARINE. I haven't come off my pedestal at all. I'm just squirming a little.

ETHEL. Squirming? You are hopping around. And you can't do that on one small pedestal. Better step down gracefully before you tumble off and mess things up. Does his wife suspect you? Is she jealous?

KATHARINE. No, not yet. She is too taken up with her own affairs to notice or care what her husband is doing, and she has the modern viewpoint, like you.

ETHEL. Good. And isn't that an argument in favor of it? I'll take another gummy one on that. Well, how about him? Is he likely to want to get a divorce and stir things up, man fashion?

KATHARINE. Oh, Ethel, how heartless you are about it! It hasn't gone nearly so far as that — but it terrifies me to hear you talk so plainly about such awfulness. Does marriage mean so little to you?

ETHEL. Little nothing. It means this — and this — and this. (*She points to various expensive items of her costume*) It means a bank account and an unassailable position in society, where I can do as I please, and nobody dares say a word. And besides all that — Jim and I are excellent friends. We get along better than most. Only we make no pretenses. We each live our own lives comfortably.

KATHARINE. But, Ethel, are you sure Jim is so comfortable? Of course I know he is head over ears in all sorts of men's affairs. But he does not flirt with other women. But look at you. You know very well that Jim nearly came to blows with Dick Farwell over you, not more than six months ago. And here you are, acting scandalously with Tommy Andrews, if I do say so.

ETHEL. Oh, Katharine, Tommy is a darling! He's a darling. Why, Jim himself hasn't the heart to ask me to give up Tommy. He just said, "Have a good time, Ethel, only don't bring disgrace upon an old and honored name." And of course I don't intend to. Have you seen Tom's new car?

KATHARINE. No, I haven't.

ETHEL. It's wonderful. He designed it himself and no one has ever ridden in it — but he and I. You know that's what appeals to me in him. Sweet little romantic things, you know, and so — so respectful. You know I'm awfully romantic.

[*She sighs and takes a huge bite of chocolate.*

KATHARINE. I see.

ETHEL. And Jim isn't. There isn't a romantic molecule in his whole system. And my nature craves that sort of thing. I must have it. I — I wish you wouldn't look at me in that tone of voice.

KATHARINE. I didn't even know I was looking at you. I'm just bewildered. I'm really trying to see it your way.

ETHEL. It's all in your point of view. Now listen. Your idea of marriage is the old-fashioned one. Two people marry, and after that they own each other. Each must give the other a strict account for everything he says, or does, or thinks, forever and ever, till Death them do — do separate. Isn't that horrible? Why is it all married people don't hate each other? Now my idea of marriage is this. Two people agree to live together and be jolly good pals, and each says to the other, "Now we'll pool our interests, but we'll neither of us infringe on the other's personal liberty in any way." So Jim goes off on his precious excursions — goodness knows where — I don't — and I certainly don't pout about it. And when I go riding with Tommy every day, Jim buys me a stunning new auto coat, and never even says "Boo —"when Tommy runs into the street car and breaks my rib. See how much saner and broader this is.

KATHARINE. It doesn't sound so bad, but it looks like the Dickens.

ETHEL. Let's stop talking about me, and talk about you. Tell me every little juicy bit from the beginning.

KATHARINE. Well, his wife has your idea of marriage exactly, and like you she always has at least one dangler — to satisfy that craving for Romance, I suppose. Her husband is too big a man to curtail his wife's personal liberty, and she takes unfair advantage of it. In fact, she sees so little of him that I doubt if she'd remember who he is if she didn't need him to pay her bills. I've always admired him because he is big and splendid, and because he has been so chivalrous to her. Nobody has suspected that he cared, but as I've seen more of him, I found out that at heart he is dead lonesome and forlorn. He has come to me for sympathy, although he doesn't suspect that I know it — and perhaps he doesn't know it himself. I've had lunch with him a few times, and —

ETHEL (*covering a yawn*). Is that all?

KATHARINE. Oh, it isn't nearly so tame as you think. I told you he needs sympathy, and I've given it to him, and sympathy is a wonderful thing. He's really sore at his wife, and he thinks he's rather crazy about me.

ETHEL (*with keen relish*). Can't you keep him thinking so?

KATHARINE. Yes, I can. What's more, I can make him really crazy about me if I want to. If I could only forget his wife.

ETHEL. Wife fiddlesticks! Why worry about her? She would probably be grateful to you for taking him off her hands, anyway.

KATHARINE. Do you suppose so? (*Looking straight into Ethel's eyes*) Would you feel that way about Jim?

ETHEL. Jim? Heavens — Fancy blessed old Jim with an affinity! That's too absurd to consider seriously.

KATHARINE. Well, it's all over, Ethel. I've decided. Perish my last scruple. His happiness means so much to me that if his wife can't stay on the job, I'm going to take it away from her. She's forefeited it — absolutely — And he's going to be mine.

ETHEL. Good for you. I admire your spunk. Katharine, you're a regular person, after all.

KATHARINE (*sighing*). I'd rather that his wife were not a friend of mine.

ETHEL. It should make no difference in your friendship. If she's a broad-minded, progressive woman, like me, it won't. Not a bit.

KATHARINE. Ethel, listen. Our affair is just at that fascinating stage, where one glance, one touch, will turn it into a full-fledged love affair. But on the other hand, I can veer off, and he will never know how close he came to the abyss. Men are like that, you know.

ETHEL. Well, don't veer off. I'm going to get some excitement out of this, and I'm betting on you. Only — don't back down. I'm so afraid you'll get weak-kneed about this everlasting wife.

KATHARINE. You needn't worry. He's mine, now, and no one can take him from me. Ethel, would you mind if I 'phone him? He asked me to ride over to Glenwood with him to the Martin's house party, and I hesitated, because I felt, somehow, that would settle it, one way or the other. But now, I've no more scruples. I'm going to go, wouldn't you?

ETHEL. By all means. I'm riding over with Tommy.

KATHARINE. Oh, Ethel, how glad I am that you have helped me to this clearer vision of things! Isn't it wonderful? My heart almost stops beating to think of it. We're to have dinner at Stanley's road house and drive over by moonlight. It will be the longest time we have ever had alone together.

ETHEL. Well, telephone him while I put on my wraps. I must be going.

[*Ethel walks over to the chair where her wraps are lying Katharine picks up the receiver, carefully holding down the bracket.*

KATHARINE. Trenton 6258. (*Ethel starts, and stands motionless with her coat half on*) Hello — Jim? . . . Yes, I'll go. . . . No, it's all right, and I'll never hesitate again. . . . Did it really mean so much to you? I'm glad. Be-

cause it does to me too. I'll call you later. Good-by. (*She hangs up the receiver. Ethel throws off her coat like a warrior preparing for the fray and comes slowly back toward Katharine. Katharine appears engrossed with the chocolate box and pretends not to see her*)
I suppose you think it is funny for me to be crazy about your blessed old Jim. You see, he's not my blessed old Jim. He's my Romance — just as Tommy Andrews is yours. (*She continues to explore the chocolate box*) I never would have had the courage to do it, if it hadn't been for you. Oh, here's one of your gummy ones.

[*She hands a chocolate to Ethel without looking at her. Ethel throws it back into the box angrily.*

ETHEL. What under the sun are you talking about? Is this a joke? If so, I fail to see the humor in it.

KATHARINE. It is not a joke. The facts are just as you heard them. Jim asked me to ride over with him. He said that he couldn't get away until six, and that you were going with Tommy earlier in the day.

ETHEL (*still unable to grasp the situation*). Indeed! Well, how far do you intend to let this pleasant little affair go?

KATHARINE. I don't know. (*Smiling brightly*) But that will settle itself nicely, now that all three of us have this broader, saner outlook on life. Jim and I will probably marry as soon as possible — we're both just that old-fashioned and prosy — and I want him to be generous and pay you all the alimony you want, so you will still have all the money you want, but be scot-free in the bargain. How much happier we'll all be!

ETHEL. Have you gone plum crazy?

KATHARINE (*appearing to notice her for the first time*). Why, Ethel dear, surely this isn't going to make any difference in our friendship?

[*She rises and attempts to embrace Ethel.*

ETHEL (*pushing her away*). Don't you dare touch me. I hate you. That's always the way with you people who pretend to be so good. In their hearts they're a thousand times wickeder than anybody else.

KATHARINE. Why, Ethel, it's silly for you to be miffed about this. You have forfeited your claim to Jim, if ever a wife did. You know it. You admitted you did.

ETHEL. He never seemed to care.

KATHARINE. Did you want him to whine around? How much good would it have done him if he had?

ETHEL. At least I didn't suppose my friends were conniving for him behind my back.

KATHARINE. You shouldn't have kept your back turned so much.

ETHEL. I don't know how much of this you really mean, but I'll tell you right here — if you ride over to Glenwood with Jim Harding, I shall not go one step.

KATHARINE. Not even with Tommy?

ETHEL. Oh — damn Tommy!

[*She stamps her foot and bursts out crying. Katharine looks down at her, smiling.*

KATHARINE. So you do care for him after all? (*No answer*) I'll tell you. Jim cares more than you think, but he will never ask for quarter, and he won't care for always. He needs sympathy, and he will just naturally cling to the person that gives it to him. Now if you don't want him to cling to me, you know how to prevent it. There is still time.

ETHEL. I can see I've been an awful fool. Of course, I've loved Jim all the time, but — but I've kind of taken him for granted — just thought he was mine forever — like my right hand. I — I couldn't live without him. I never thought of anybody taking him away from me — and whoever does — will do it over my dead body — that's all.

KATHARINE. Don't leave him lying around loose then. Next time somebody may offer him sympathy who has the modern viewpoint, and she won't signal you when she gets to the turning point, like I did.

ETHEL. Katharine, you're a brick. Are you quite sure Jim doesn't care for you? For if he does, I would try — I would try — to give him up, but —

KATHARINE (*after a brief moment of preparation for the sacrifice*). My dear girl, don't worry. He — has never cared for me — a single moment.

ETHEL (*with suddenly renewed suspicion*). How do you account for that telephone message then?

KATHARINE. Sure enough. That conversation was for your benefit only. I was holding down the receiver bracket.

[*Ethel, who has succumbed to a fresh avalanche of sobs, turns a tear-stained face to Katharine, which gradually becomes radiant as the truth dawns on her. She fairly gasps with joy.*

ETHEL. Oh, Katharine, I feel awfully humble and grateful to you! I feel like a drowning person just pulled out in time. I'm going right down to the office now, to tell Jim he has a wife again — if he wants one, and to ride home with him just like we used to.

KATHARINE. Splendid. Put some powder on your nose, honey, and here's another gummy one to go on.

[*Ethel dabs on some powder from her vanity box and puts on her coat. Katharine watches her silently.*

ETHEL (*somewhat embarrassed*). Katharine, you'll ride over to Glenwood with Jim and me, anyway, won't you, dear?

KATHARINE. I'll see. Why don't you will me Tommy?

ETHEL. You can have him. Good-by.

[*Ethel waves her hand merrily and dashes out. Katharine stands looking after her for a moment, then she heaves a little sigh and shrugs her shoulders. Her eye falls on the box of chocolates and she seems suddenly to come to a determination. She presses a button and Mary appears.*

KATHARINE. You may have the rest of these, Mary. (*She holds out the box*) The ground floor is still intact, I think.

MARY. Oh, thank you, Miss Burton, thank you.

[*She gathers up the box joyfully. Katharine looks around and suddenly notices the violets. She picks up the basket.*

KATHARINE. And you may have these too. The smell of violets is — makes me a little sick, sometimes.

MARY. Oh, thank you, Miss Burton. These are perfectly grand.

[*She takes the violets from Katharine and turns to go.*

KATHARINE. I believe I'll keep the ribbon, Mary. (*Mary returns and hands her the crimson ribbon which has been tied around the box, and goes out. Katharine dreamily loops the ribbon into a bow and holds it to her breast, smiling a whimsical little smile, — the warrior who may have lost a limb in battle, but has won a Decoration*) For Distinguished Service under Fire.

CURTAIN

ROCKING CHAIRS
MANIKIN AND MINIKIN

ALFRED KREYMBORG

ALFRED KREYMBORG was born in New York City December 10, 1883, and was educated in the city schools. He has earned his living as a clerk, a teacher of chess, and as a reporter for a musical weekly. He has been editor of several artistic and literary periodicals, among them "The Glebe", "Others", and "Broom". He now resides in Vallallo, Italy. His published plays are contained in two volumes: "Plays for Poem-Mimes" and "Plays for Merry Andrews".

ROCKING CHAIRS

A CONCERTINO FOR KATYDIDS

By ALFRED KREYMBORG

Characters

MRS. BOYLE
MRS. ALMS
MRS. BERRY
KATYDID VOICES

ROCKING CHAIRS

SCENE. *The dining room of a fairly prosperous home in the township of Jasmine Way, New Jersey. Looking out on the street, a broad French window, draped by portraits of Washington, Lincoln and Wilson. There is nothing unusual in the furnishings: it is sufficient that rocking chairs are visible to the number of three; and a child's hobbyhorse. Doors open to the left and right. Two of the rockers are in action, occupied respectively by Mrs. Boyle, the hostess of the present occasion, and Mrs. Alms, a neighboring visitor, facts to be deduced solely by the presence of a hat on the head of the latter. They are sober-looking ladies in middle life. The single peculiarity of the proceedings (to a foreigner, that is) rises from a dual happening: while the one lady speaks, the other rocks in tempo, the speech and rocking alternating with the given mood; and so, too, in rotation, the one has a habit of interrupting or of taking up or concluding the speech of the other, so that a dialogue really sounds (which it is) like a continuous monologue: a gift acquired only after heated apprenticeship in the school of gossip. The voices of the ladies and their inflections are pretty much of a piece, and their method of delivery, or rather of recitation, a nimble staccato rattled off in a monotone of nasal impersonality derived from the strictest adherence to the curriculum of the alma mater. The prosaic lines of the transcription are broken, not so much to conform to some sacred ethic of free verse as to indicate or adumbrate the metronomic beat of the rockers.*

MRS. ALMS.   A woman should not
    have ideas until after
    she weds, when the law,
    stamping her moral,
    gives her the privilege —

MRS. BOYLE.   within, of course,
   the circumscribed boundary,
   hermetically sealed.

MRS. ALMS.   Her views being legal,
   sacrosanct and free
   from anarchic tendencies
   of an individual turn,
   are certain to partake
   of assertions no more

MRS. BOYLE.   dangerous to the welfare
   of surrounding society

MRS. ALMS.   than is involved
   in discussions of,
   let us say,

MRS. BOYLE.   the price of corn and butter,
   and the shape and shade
   of new frocks for one
   goodman's further aesthetic
   as well as athletic
   maintenance, and as
   licentious spice,

MRS. ALMS.   the pepper of trifling comment,
   on the inferiority of all
   women not similarly disposed,
   as being, — don't you agree, Mrs. Boyle? —

MRS. BOYLE.   I do, Mrs. Alms —

MRS. ALMS.   A wee bit unmoral —

MRS. BOYLE.   if not immoral.

MRS. ALMS.   Exactly, precisely!

   [*They rock together in momentary silence. A woman passes
   the French window, right to left, and is immediately spied.*

MRS. BOYLE.   There now!

MRS. ALMS.   There now!

MRS. BOYLE.   What did I say?

MRS. ALMS.   What did we say?

MRS. BOYLE.   Just look at that creature
   go by my window again

with that brazen, scarlet
symbol on her head —

MRS. ALMS.   Mrs. Berry once again.

MRS. BOYLE.   One can be certain now,
if one was doubtful before.
I call you to witness,
Mrs. Alms, it's the fourth,
fully the fifth time
since twilight descended.

MRS. ALMS.   I'm only too glad to testify
she has evil in her heart
and some man in her eye.

MRS. BOYLE.   She'd do that, she would —
she with her husband
fresh in the cemetery,

MRS. ALMS.   and the pretty white stone
marking her indelible devotion
scarcely dry of the dew

MRS. BOYLE.   she and the rest of us women
shed only five, only four,

MRS. ALMS.   only three months ago,

MRS. BOYLE.   in honest, open sight

MRS. ALMS.   of our whole community.

MRS. BOYLE.   I'm sure you agree, my dear —

MRS. ALMS.   and so would any other woman —

MRS. BOYLE.   who isn't a —

MRS. ALMS.   isn't likely to be a —

MRS. BOYLE.   doesn't happen to be —

MRS. ALMS.   the creature we mean.

MRS. BOYLE.   Precisely, exactly!

(*Mrs. Boyle steals from her rocker, and is followed by Mrs. Alms, to the window. Their heads create a parallel profile, prying leftwards. Slower tempo.*)

I wonder who he is.

MRS. ALMS.   Must be a rendezvous.

MRS. BOYLE.   Does anybody know?

MRS. ALMS.   Nobody knows.

MRS. BOYLE.   Has anybody heard?

MRS. ALMS.   Nobody's heard.

MRS. BOYLE.   You've asked?

MRS. ALMS.   I've inquired. .

MRS. BOYLE.   And nobody's told?

MRS. ALMS.   How could they?

MRS. BOYLE.   It's disgraceful.

MRS. ALMS.   Just like her.

MRS. BOYLE.   She ought to be
run out of town —

MRS. ALMS.   to the town-pump,
the sewer, the river.

MRS. BOYLE.   Our river's too good
for such as her.

MRS. ALMS.   Can you see her any longer?

MRS. BOYLE.   She's too slippery for that.

MRS. ALMS.   She'd do that, she would —

MRS. BOYLE.   must have slid
behind that building
my husband claims
breaks the building law —

MRS. ALMS.   stuck out so far, it's

MRS. BOYLE.   outlandish, criminal!

MRS. ALMS.   Ah!

MRS. BOYLE.   Oh!
(*They steal most reluctantly back to their rockers.   Former
tempo.*)
Our river would be much too good
for the like of her and her ways —

MRS. ALMS.   though it's muddy enough as it is
without such a scandal as this.

MRS. BOYLE.   It's a job for the town council
which has trouble enough
keeping our streets clean
without having to keep

MRS. ALMS.   our society scrubbed.
But that, my dear —

MRS. BOYLE.   that little job, my dear —

MRS. ALMS.   is ours —

MRS. BOYLE.   always has been —

MRS. ALMS.   always will be.

MRS. BOYLE.   Thank God for that.

MRS. ALMS.   No, pardon me,
  thank us women!

MRS. BOYLE.   Yes, pardon me!

MRS. ALMS.   We'll show her

MRS. BOYLE.   and her paramour!

[*They smile and wag their heads.*

MRS. ALMS.   If it hadn't been for us —

MRS. BOYLE.   and it weren't for us —

MRS. ALMS.   always and ever —

MRS. BOYLE.   ours wouldn't be
  the community it is —

MRS. ALMS.   the best in New Jersey —

MRS. BOYLE.   best in America —

MRS. ALMS.   best in Christendom!

[*Mutual sighs in satisfaction — which only a recurrent
thought ruffles again.*

MRS. BOYLE.   I wonder who the man is.

MRS. ALMS.   The scoundrel, you mean.

MRS. BOYLE.   I know one thing for certain —

MRS. ALMS.   he isn't, can't be
  a native or citizen of
  Jasmine Way —

MRS. BOYLE.   not one of ours —
  but some heathen
  hinterlander, some
  traveling man,
  drummer or salesman.
  Ugh!

MRS. ALMS.   Ugh!

[*They rock silently and muse.*

MRS. BOYLE.   One should wear black

MRS. ALMS.   from head to heels
a whole year thereafter.

MRS. BOYLE.   Though it's not in the statutes,
nor in the decrees —
it's a custom —

MRS. ALMS.   a time-honored custom —

MRS. BOYLE.   introduced and tested
by the best families
in our American history;

MRS. ALMS.   and for the matter of that,
in the British we came from;

MRS. BOYLE.   or for that matter,
in any other civilized race —

MRS. ALMS.   and especially, particularly so

MRS. BOYLE.   in our own Jasmine Way,

MRS. ALMS.   as good a place, you'll agree,

MRS. BOYLE.   I'll agree, as any anywhere —

MRS. ALMS.   as good as Boston itself —

MRS. BOYLE.   as Plymouth itself —

MRS. ALMS.   where the *Mayflower* landed —

MRS. BOYLE.   our *Mayflower!*

MRS. ALMS.   Though Jasmine Way
is generations removed
from that good ship and landing-place,
that which was good enough
for one's forefathers
is good enough and better
for one's grandchildren —
so I say —

MRS. BOYLE.   I say black, not red,
should be worn
all the way from head to heels

MRS. ALMS.   a whole year thereafter —

MRS. BOYLE.   or, for the matter of that,
two, three, five, ten years,
the rest of one's lifetime.

MRS. ALMS.   A good woman,

MRS. BOYLE. real woman,
MRS. ALMS. moral woman would —
MRS. BOYLE. utterly —
MRS. ALMS. absolutely!
MRS. BOYLE. Not that I'd gossip about it —
MRS. ALMS. nor I —
MRS. BOYLE. but that I know what I know,
sure that I simply quote
the blood that flows in me —
MRS. ALMS. like the Mississippi
down the backbone of America.
MRS. BOYLE. It isn't gossip —
MRS. ALMS. it's gospel!

*[Another pause. Mrs. Alms, obviously, wants to introduce
a new variation. She appeals to Mrs. Boyle with a look
and falters. A discrepancy arises in the ensuing rhythm
of words and accompaniment of rockers — a condition which
prevails whenever uncertainty intervenes: a rubato or syncopa-
tion interrupting the customary flow.*

MRS. BOYLE. What is it, my dear?
MRS. ALMS. Has she ever —
no offense, my dear —
what I want to ask is —
does she ever call on you?
MRS. BOYLE. *Who*, Mrs. Alms?
MRS. ALMS. I said, no offense, dear.
I don't mean, do you invite her —
of course, she's not on your list —
such a creature — but —
has she the audacity
ever to visit you?
MRS. BOYLE. Holy horrors, dear —
holy judgment, holy doom —
do you think,
do you suppose,
do you imagine —

MRS. ALMS. I neither think,
suppose nor imagine.
I know, happen to know
you wouldn't let her in;
you'd show her the door.

MRS. BOYLE. I almost wish she would —
I'd show her the street.

MRS. ALMS. Of course, you would —
so would I —

MRS. BOYLE. and so would the rest
of our women, unless
they've lost their self-respect —

MRS. ALMS. every woman in Jasmine Way.
But what I mean is —
what I'd insinuate —
how *are* we going to find out —
if for instance we *should*
happen to meet her —
just accidentally —
how are we going to learn
if whoever happens to be
the victim of her call
shows her the street —
before we actually —
somehow or other —
one never knows how —
it's never the same —
usually accidentally —

MRS. BOYLE. What *are* you
trying to find out?
Who *he* is?

MRS. ALMS. Yes, and what *they* intend!

MRS. BOYLE. H'm!

MRS. ALMS. H'm!

MRS. BOYLE. That's a poser —

MRS. ALMS. a puzzle!

MRS. BOYLE.   As you say —
  I wouldn't have her here;
  you wouldn't have her at
  Woodlawn Villa.
  Nobody'd have her —
  and one wouldn't,
  simply couldn't, be seen
  conversing with her like
  anywhere else —
  nowhere, anywhere else —
  surely not a woman
  who respects herself —
  which I hope we do.
MRS. ALMS.   There's no need hoping —
  we do, you and I.
MRS. BOYLE.   One would merely
  not be seen where she's seen —
  and as for that,
  the Wiggins wouldn't have her,
  the Frys wouldn't tolerate her,
  the Bisons would ostracize her,
  the Dalrymples, the Mackinaws,
  the Websters, the Lovells —
MRS. ALMS.   the Jenkinses, the Hotchkisses —
MRS. BOYLE.   the Kirkpatricks, the Perkinses —
MRS. ALMS.   the Wayland Smythes, the Ossip Brownes —
MRS. BOYLE.   every solitary one of them —
  simply and collectively —
  with one voice and in chorus —
  would cry out upon her like —
MRS. ALMS.   would silently point out —
MRS. BOYLE.   with the scornful forefinger
  more eloquent than speech —
MRS. ALMS.   the lofty little stare
  more powerful than blows —
MRS. BOYLE.   with just that oblique tilt
  of one's chin more accurate

in directing the wayfarer
than any cross-road sign —

MRS. ALMS.   as to whither she should go —

MRS. BOYLE.   as to where she belongs!

MRS. ALMS.   However —

MRS. BOYLE.   nevertheless —

MRS. ALMS.   notwithstanding which —

MRS. BOYLE.   admitting the painful certainty —

MRS. ALMS.   that one must see to be able to hear —

[*The woman with the red hat appears at the left of the window
— stops and looks in without being seen.*

MRS. BOYLE.   and that one must hear to be able to learn —

MRS. ALMS.   who he is and what they intend —

[*The woman smiles mischievously and nods and wags her
head in roguish change of character.*

MRS. BOYLE.   and deducing from this
that to clean city streets
or dust city homes —

MRS. ALMS.   one must find out
where the dust lies —

MRS. BOYLE.   it is our paramount duty
in the interests of our own
civic welfare, as women
who have made and kept
our society spotless —

MRS. ALMS.   whiter than lamb's wool,
white as driven snow —

MRS. BOYLE.   to find out —
even at the expense of
temporarily soiling oneself
what a woman, who should
in all righteousness
be wearing black
from head to heels —

MRS. ALMS.   means by flaunting
such an insulting red symbol —

MRS. BOYLE.   red bird, red feather —

MRS. ALMS.   red something or other —

MRS. BOYLE.   and what she means
by parading back and forth
right under our noses —

[*The woman disappears — slightly nodding and wagging —
to the right.*

MRS. ALMS.   with evil in her heart —

MRS. BOYLE.   and some man in her eye.

MRS. ALMS.   But how, my dear?

MRS. BOYLE.   Yes, how, my dear —

MRS. ALMS.   will we find out?

MRS. BOYLE.   Would *you* have her?

MRS. ALMS.   Would you?

MRS. BOYLE.   H'm.

MRS. ALMS.   H'm.

[*A distant door bell rings.   The women start.*

MRS. BOYLE.   Good gracious.

MRS. ALMS.   What's that?

MRS. BOYLE.   It gave me such a scare.

MRS. ALMS.   Sounded like a summons.

MRS. BOYLE.   Only my door bell!

MRS. ALMS.   Heaven be praised!

[*They listen.   The bell rings again.   Mrs. Boyle rises with
annoyance.*

MRS. BOYLE.   Pardon me, dear.

MRS. ALMS.   Certainly, dear.

MRS. BOYLE.   Cook must be busy cooking.

MRS. ALMS.   By all means.

MRS. BOYLE.   Awfully stupid of her
to be so hard of hearing.

MRS. ALMS.   She's only conscientious —

MRS. BOYLE.   deaf to all but the present duty —

MRS. ALMS.   which can't help but absorb her
to the extinction of all other sound.

MRS. BOYLE.   How you do understand —
thank you, dear.

MRS. ALMS.   Not at all, run along!

(*Mrs. Boyle leaves by the door to the right. Mrs. Alms indulges a soft, droning monologue, the while she looks about inquisitively*)   "Cook must be busy cooking" —
h'm —
What's become of her maid?
Does she expect a cook
to be a centipede,
with legs for a kitchen
and legs for a door bell?
h'm —
it was only last night
I was asking Mr. Alms:
"How is it the Boyles
no longer afford a maid?
The last time I called
Mrs. Boyle answered my ring?"
And he said, the innocent:
"Mr. Boyle's upholstery trade
is just a little slack now;
besides, it's none of our affair —"
of course it isn't —
"and it's not for us to pry into theirs —"
of course it isn't.
But what I'd like to know
and have a right to know is:
Why should such a woman
set herself up as a leader in society,
a censor of other folks' conduct —
an authority in civic betterment —
when she hasn't even a maid
to answer her bell —
and has the effrontery,
the throw-dust-in-your-eye
obviousness to resort to
"Cook must be busy cooking"?
H'm —
Washington — Lincoln — Wilson?

What are they to her,
or she to them?
Does she fancy herself of their breed —
qualified to live with them —
such awful chromos of them —
just because she's better.
Fancies herself superior —
to a woman *passing* her window?
French, of course, what else would it be?
What's that hobbyhorse doing here?
It doesn't belong in a drawing-room —
but in the children's room.
I suppose they can't afford
a children's room —
this house is a wee bit too small —
they can't quite afford
a house just a wee bit larger.
H'm.
It just serves you right, Mrs. Alms.
Don't blame Mrs. Boyle, blame yourself.
If you must be visiting folk,
you might be more careful
of some folk you visit —
and don't blame them
for your own indiscriminate
lack of discretion.
Last week,
it was that Vandusen woman
and her bridge party —
unmentionable —
and the week before,
that lawn party at the Ossip Brownes —
unspeakable.
What'll it be next week?
Will you ever, ever learn?
[*She hears footsteps and hurried voices — and sits up prim
and straight — like a picture in a family album. The door*

is opened. Mrs. Berry — the lady in the red hat — a pictur-esque figure withal, some, or a few, years younger than the others — is ceremoniously ushered in by Mrs. Boyle, in a hectic flutter. They are in the midst of a discussion, excited on Mrs. Boyle's part, quiet on Mrs. Berry's, and do not greet Mrs. Alms, who rises in temporary horror and backs away from her rocker, her eyes on the symbol.

MRS. BOYLE. This is most overwhelming, my dear.

MRS. BERRY. Not at all,
it's you who overwhelm me.

MRS. BOYLE. But fancy you selecting me —
picking me out first —
among all your many friends —
surely you have older,
much older friends than I?

MRS. BERRY. Older, yes, but not dearer.

MRS. BOYLE. Even so,
your visiting me first of all,
right out in front,
leaves me speechless,
breathless, without a word.

MRS. BERRY. Then don't say it, dear —

[*Nudges Mrs. Boyle, indicating Mrs. Alms, whose horror melted down to curiosity, now broadens to a stereotyped smile Mrs. Boyle reverts to Mrs. Alms with a suspicion of intro-ductory condescension.*

MRS. BOYLE. Oh — pardon me — dear Mrs. Alms —
I'm so agitated!
Just imagine —
do pardon me —
you're acquainted, aren't you,
with Mrs. Berry?

MRS. ALMS (*a little uncertain*). Why, yes —
to be sure, most assuredly.
What makes you ask such a question?

[*Mrs. Berry shakes her part-way outstretched hand cordiall*

Mrs. Alms, apparently, in the dilemma of not knowing how far to respond, but anxious not to err.

MRS. BERRY.   Indeed —
what should cause Mrs. Boyle
to put such a question to you —
and to me — such firm friends?

MRS. ALMS.   None better.

MRS. BOYLE.   My fault entirely —
but what else could I do?
I'm really so overwhelmed —
wait till you hear; you'll understand.

MRS. ALMS.   Understand what?

MRS. BOYLE.   Just fancy, my dear —
Mrs. Berry —
it's absolutely incredible,
delightful, intriguing —
so like her —
only *she* would do such a thing!

MRS. ALMS.   What thing?

MRS. BOYLE.   Mrs. Berry —

MRS. BERRY.   Mrs. Berry no longer.

MRS. ALMS.   Eh?

MRS. BOYLE.   You may well say, "eh."
I said more than "eh" when I heard the tale.

MRS. ALMS.   What tale?

MRS. BERRY.   Don't keep Mrs. Alms in suspense —
I'm not worth so much flattery.

MRS. BOYLE.   Oh, but you are, Mrs. —
if Mrs. Alms knew,
if she could even guess!

MRS. ALMS.   Of course I know —
of course I can guess —
and I congratulate you
from the bottom of my heart, Mrs. —?

MRS. BERRY.   Mrs. —

MRS. BOYLE.   Don't say the name —
that would spoil all.

It's too dumfounding
to tell all at once.

MRS. ALMS.   What is, what is?

MRS. BERRY.   Nothing, my dear.

MRS. BOYLE.   It is, it is —
and don't you dare give it away —
let me tell the whole story.

MRS. BERRY.   You tell it then —
but no embellishments, please —
none of your exaggerated feelings —

[*Mrs. Alms is obviously chagrined at having to receive the
tale from an intermediary.*

MRS. ALMS.   Do be calm, Mrs. Boyle.

MRS. BERRY.   Are you calm now, dear —

MRS. BOYLE.   Perfectly, thank you —

MRS. BERRY.   as a story-teller should be?

MRS. BOYLE.   Heaven knows you were calm —
I can't understand with your fortune
how you could be so cold.

MRS. ALMS.   Fortune?

MRS. BERRY.   Mrs. Boyle's off again.

MRS. BOYLE.   No, my dear —
you watch me —
and if I leave anything out,
you caution me.

MRS. BERRY.   Yes, but be careful you don't
put anything in.

MRS. BOYLE.   I won't, I couldn't —
there's nothing to add.

MRS. ALMS.   Mrs. Boyle, Mrs. — !

MRS. BOYLE.   There, dear friend —
forgive me — I'm really
beside myself —
come — let us sit down
in these rockers —
they'll bring me back to my senses.

MRS. BERRY.   The same gentle rockers of yore —

MRS. BOYLE.   freshly upholstered in the new style —
MRS. BERRY.   but still capable of lulling one —
MRS. ALMS.   as only Mr. Boyle's rockers can.
MRS. BOYLE.   Bless the dear man! Thank you, friends!
   [*They sit down and begin rocking — slowly, at first, but later,
   in accordance with the varying moods. Mrs. Alms and Mrs.
   Berry and Mrs. Boyle, the former not without secret resent-
   ment, the latter not without delight.*
MRS. ALMS.   Pray, Mrs. Boyle, may I ask — ?
MRS. BOYLE.   Thank you for reminding me —
this chair was for sending me off —
into a dream, an Oriental trance,
almost like the Arabian Nights!
MRS. BERRY.   Hurry back to Jasmine Way!
MRS. BOYLE.   Yes, but not the way you did —
went off in a quiet cloud —
and came back in a thunder storm.
MRS. ALMS.   What's wrong with her now?
MRS. BOYLE (*rocking suddenly*). No, it's impossible!
MRS. ALMS.   The saints protect us!
MRS. BOYLE.   I can't hold it in —
no dam could stay such a flood.
I'd like to tell it
from start to finish —
but I'm no story-teller —
nor ice like you, dear Mrs. —
MRS. BERRY.   Say it.
MRS. BOYLE.   All at once?
MRS. BERRY.   Altogether!
MRS. BOYLE.   You won't mind?
MRS. BERRY.   Not at all.
MRS. BOYLE.   And you, Mrs. Alms,
won't be disappointed
that I tell the climax first?
MRS. ALMS.   No, but I'll go
clean daft with the fidgets
if you don't return to reason, Mrs. Boyle!

MRS. BOYLE (*leaning forward provocatively*).   It's —

MRS. ALMS.   Yes — yes?

MRS. BOYLE.   Mr. — Wellington!

MRS. ALMS.   Mr. — Wellington?
not *the* —

MRS. BOYLE.   Yes, the Mr. Ambrose Wellington —

MRS. ALMS.   The multi-millionaire?

MRS. BOYLE.   Manufacturer of farm implements —

MRS. ALMS.   harrows, hoes, rakes —

MRS. BOYLE.   tractors, engines, plows —

MRS. ALMS.   himself?

MRS. BOYLE.   Himself and no other!

[*Mrs. Alms turns on Mrs. Wellington with round eyes.*

MRS. ALMS.   Is it the truth,
the gospel truth?

MRS. WELLINGTON.   The simple truth, so help me.

MRS. ALMS.   Dear, dear Mrs. Wellington!

[*She fairly pounces on Mrs. Wellington; the latter ha*
difficulty extricating herself.

MRS. ALMS.   Let me be the very first
to congratulate you,
you angelic creature!

MRS. BOYLE.   The second, Mrs. Alms.

[*Mrs. Alms is forced back to her rocker.*

MRS. ALMS.   The second, third, fourth,
tenth, hundredth, thousandth —
what difference would it be
were I the last in line,
the least and most humble —
this is miraculous.

MRS. WELLINGTON.   You're as mad as the other.

MRS. ALMS.   No woman begins to deserve
such an event as you do.
Ambrose Wellington —
the Wellington agricultural interests —
advertised on every other billboard —
way out on the prairies,

high up in the mountains,
the Rockies themselves —
known from the Atlantic to the Pacific,
all around the globe itself —
and the Wellington mansion —
with that sunset view —
I do hope you won't
forsake Jasmine Way.
There's no such view
in the whole wide world!

MRS. WELLINGTON. How about Naples, Rio, Frisco?

MRS. ALMS. Mere bird views —
microscopic by comparison.
I'm speechless —

MRS. BOYLE. So was I —

MRS. ALMS. There are no such grounds
In the whole of Christendom.
Will I ever forget to my dying day
that magnificent lawn party
the Wellingtons —
oh, I do beg your pardon!

MRS. WELLINGTON. On the contrary,
we both honor *her* memory.

MRS. ALMS. To be sure —
why shouldn't you —
who would blame you for it —
who would do other than praise you?

MRS. BOYLE. That's what I said —

MRS. ALMS. I distinctly recall the sumptuous funeral —

MRS. WELLINGTON. The one painful detail —

MRS. ALMS. Of course — pardon me —
just as painful to *him*,
as we all realize only too well —

MRS. WELLINGTON. as Mr. Berry's was to me — but —

MRS. ALMS. On the contrary —
excuse me for insisting —
these are gladsome events.

I mean —
they aren't happenings
to cry one's eyes completely out
the rest of one's lifetime.
They make way for healing
compensations — Emerson's compensations —
you've set an immortal example!

MRS. WELLINGTON.   How so?

MRS. ALMS.   Mrs. Boyle can tell you.

MRS. BOYLE.   Yes, let me tell.

MRS. ALMS.   Mrs. Boyle can tell you
I was saying only this very afternoon,
how wonderful it was,
how courageous of you,
what a superlative precedent
of you not to
enter mourning,
complete mourning —

MRS. BOYLE.   from head to heels —

MRS. ALMS.   when dear Mr. Berry departed this life.

MRS. WELLINGTON.   Let me explain —

MRS. ALMS.   You don't have to —

MRS. BOYLE.   There's no explanation in order —

MRS. ALMS.   It would sound like an apology —

MRS. BOYLE.   an insult to our broad-mindedness.

MRS. ALMS.   I apprehend you fully —

MRS. BOYLE.   so do I.

MRS. ALMS.   You have laid that barbarous custom —
relic of the last bulwarks of heathenism —

MRS. BOYLE.   deep down the grave of the past
where all things black or dark belong.

MRS. ALMS.   You have shown the stupid folk of this town —
the Wiggins, the Frys —

MRS. BOYLE.   the Bisons, the Dalrymples —

MRS. ALMS.   the Mackinaws, the Websters —

MRS. WELLINGTON.   Spare me, ladies.

MRS. ALMS.   Spare them, you mean.

MRS. BOYLE. I'd like to examine
the whole telephone directory —
ferret each and every one. —

MRS. WELLINGTON. Don't, don't!

MRS. ALMS. Don't, don't!

MRS. BOYLE. Haven't I heard them
refer to you in doubtful terms?

MRS. ALMS. Haven't I heard them
sneer at you —

MRS. BOYLE. gossip about you?

MRS. ALMS. Yes, and why —

MRS. BOYLE. yes, why?

MRS. ALMS. Because you refused
to advertise your grief
so they might glory in it —

MRS. BOYLE. because you preferred
to hold your head above sorrow
like — is it the Chinese
when a relative departs?

MRS. WELLINGTON. Chinese?

MRS. ALMS. You're like them in that —

MRS. BOYLE. though white in every other way.

MRS. WELLINGTON. Ever so many thanks to you both.

MRS. BOYLE. You're much too good for Jasmine Way.

MRS. ALMS. Yes, but don't leave us —

MRS. BOYLE. it'd be a living, crawling
cemetery if you did.

MRS. WELLINGTON. Leave dear old Jasmine?

MRS. ALMS. It isn't so bad, the rest of it —

MRS. BOYLE. though it does need cleaning
in more ways than our street
department sweeps it.

MRS. ALMS. Turning on hydrants
is only part of the job; —

MRS. BOYLE. the whole smelly river
ought to be turned loose
for the benefit of some folk.

MRS. WELLINGTON.   Dear old river —
    you wouldn't ask that of it?
    So peaceful, so serene —
    so like a lizard
    spreading in the sun —
    so particularly dear
    in the twilight.
MRS. BOYLE.   In the twilight!
    Just think, Mrs. Alms —
    you recall we saw Mrs. Wellington —
    once or twice —
MRS. ALMS.   passing your window?   Yes!
MRS. BOYLE.   And I wanted to rush out
    and ask her in to tea?
MRS. ALMS.   Yes, and you said —
MRS. BOYLE.   Yes, and I said,
    maybe she's strolling back and forth
    with some purpose in her mind
    I had better not disturb?
MRS. ALMS.   Yes, and I said —
MRS. BOYLE.   Yes, and we were absolutely
    both of us wrong.
MRS. ALMS.   Indeed?
MRS. BOYLE.   Tell Mrs. Alms —
    do, Mrs. Wellington!
MRS. WELLINGTON.   I was only renewing my memories —
    refreshing myself with sights
    one never entirely forgets
    but always likes to recall.
MRS. ALMS.   Of course.
MRS. BOYLE.   Isn't that lovely?
MRS. ALMS.   Who else would be so romantic?
MRS. BOYLE.   so truly sensible!
MRS. ALMS.   Who else would see the least
    thing in our town worth seeing twice?
MRS. WELLINGTON.   You malign it, my dears —
    consider old High Street —
    with its grave, baronial homes —

MRS. BOYLE.   yes, and its majestic emerald lawns —

MRS. ALMS.   and the elms and oaks eternally shading it —

MRS. WELLINGTON.   and the graceful, faithful churches
  so straight in their aspiration —

MRS. BOYLE.   their spires so poignant —

MRS. ALMS.   their genuine stained glass —
  (Mr. Alms says it is —
  glass is his trade, he knows) —
  so like bleeding, devout hearts —

MRS. WELLINGTON.   and the quaint country stores
  so redolent of our past,
  of our upright forefathers,
  our honest pioneers —

MRS. BOYLE.   their simple diligence —

MRS. ALMS.   and hardy perseverance —

MRS. WELLINGTON.   and the squat town hall
  where the mayor lives
  and our wise town council,
  watching over us
  like hens over chicks —

MRS. BOYLE.   That isn't so bad —

MRS. ALMS.   Nor he, nor they —

MRS. WELLINGTON.   and the place where we all go,
  where we all lie, where we all stay,
  guardian spirits over those yet to come —

MRS. BOYLE.   The cemetery?

MRS. WELLINGTON.   Our dear, sacred, white cemetery.

MRS. BOYLE.   Spare yourself that detail.

MRS. ALMS.   Yes, why drag that in?

MRS. WELLINGTON.   On the contrary —

MRS. BOYLE.   No, why shouldn't you?

MRS. ALMS.   Yes, why shouldn't you?

MRS. WELLINGTON.   He's happy —

MRS. BOYLE.   Yes, because you made him so.

MRS. ALMS.   No, because she keeps him so.

MRS. WELLINGTON.   Thank you, dear friend.

MRS. BOYLE.   Not at all, my dear —

MRS. ALMS.   no thanks are due us.

MRS. WELLINGTON.   Oh, yes, they are.
  Let me ask
  one simple question, may I?

MRS. BOYLE.   Ask two —

MRS. ALMS.   a dozen.

MRS. WELLINGTON.   Who, during my absence,
  short though it was —
  who were the only ladies
  in the entire Jasmine Way
  who didn't —
  I hate to use the word —

MRS. BOYLE.   say it, dear —

MRS. ALMS.   out with it: gossip!

MRS. WELLINGTON.   Can you perchance tell me
  how many ladies didn't?
  (*Mrs. Boyle and Mrs. Alms examine each other evasively*)
  You don't have to tell me —
  nor look so sheepish and modest.

MRS. BOYLE.   Dear, dear —

MRS. ALMS.   Mrs. Wellington!

MRS. BOYLE (*excitedly*).   Is that why —
  can that be the reason?

MRS. WELLINGTON.   I rang your door bell?
  Yes — but I was also
  on my way to one other.

MRS. ALMS.   You exquisite creature!

MRS. WELLINGTON: And now —

MRS. BOYLE.   Yes?

MRS. ALMS.   Yes?
  [*They lean forward.*

MRS. WELLINGTON.   Mr. Wellington and I —
  in the nature of a quiet celebration —

MRS. BOYLE.   yes?

MRS. ALMS.   yes? —

MRS. WELLINGTON.   are planning
  an old-fashioned house-warming —

MRS. BOYLE.   ah! —

MRS. ALMS.   ah? —

MRS. WELLINGTON.   for —

MRS. BOYLE.   Us?

MRS. ALMS.   Us?

MRS. WELLINGTON.   Not you two alone.

MRS. BOYLE.   Oh!

MRS. ALMS.   Oh!

[*They lean back.*

MRS. WELLINGTON.   You don't comprehend.
    It isn't our intention —
    quite to ostracize the community.
    That'd be ostracizing ourselves —
    shutting us off from the spectacle —
    and the amusement of the spectacle;
    besides, it'd be in poor taste —
    undemocratic, un-American —

MRS. BOYLE.   and would be showing your cards —

MRS. ALMS.   most undiplomatic!

MRS. WELLINGTON.   What we want you ladies for —

MRS. BOYLE.   yes?

MRS. ALMS.   yes?

[*They lean forward again.*

MRS. WELLINGTON.   is to act as a
    sort of committee with me —
    to send out the invitations.

MRS. BOYLE.   You adroit little schemer!

MRS. ALMS.   Tiny bag of mischief!

MRS. BOYLE.   How thoughtful of such a man —

MRS. ALMS.   typical of such a woman —

MRS. BOYLE.   to light on two such —
    may I say, practised —

MRS. ALMS.   hardened campaigners?

MRS. WELLINGTON.   God send you His blessing.

MRS. BOYLE.   Amen!

MRS. ALMS.   Amen!

MRS. WELLINGTON.   Now, I'd like you angels
to draw up a list
of the eligibles, so to speak.

MRS. BOYLE.   The Wiggins, the Frys —

MRS. ALMS.   the Bisons, the Dalrymples?

MRS. WELLINGTON.   Each and every eligible —

MRS. BOYLE.   say no more —

MRS. ALMS.   don't tell me —

MRS. WELLINGTON.   for next Sunday at four.

MRS. BOYLE.   Next Sunday —

MRS. ALMS.   at four —

MRS. BOYLE.   couldn't be a better day —

MRS. ALMS.   nor a better hour.

MRS. BOYLE.   They'll be able to see the sunset —

MRS. ALMS.   and think of the sunrise —

MRS. BOYLE.   of a new home —

MRS. ALMS.   a new harmony —

MRS. BOYLE.   nobler than any heretofore —

MRS. ALMS.   higher than any hereafter.

MRS. WELLINGTON.   Thank you, conspirators —
that will do!

MRS. BOYLE.   Ah!

MRS. ALMS.   Ah!

[*They rock in meditation.   Mrs. Alms rises suddenly.*

MRS. WELLINGTON.   What are you up to now?

MRS. ALMS.   I must be going —
I must be telling Mr. Alms —
the dear man will be so overwhelmed —
and may I tell —
I wonder would you mind?

MRS. WELLINGTON.   why should I? —

MRS. ALMS.   just one or two in advance?

MRS. WELLINGTON.   Certainly, three or four,
as many as you like.

MRS. ALMS.   Thank you kindly —
one or two will do —
that sweet Mrs. Wiley

and that cute Mrs. Carey —
they'll be ample.

MRS. BOYLE. Why them in particular?

MRS. ALMS (*laughing*). That would be telling.

MRS. WELLINGTON. I know why, dear.

MRS. ALMS. You're so clairvoyant!

[*The three chuckle. Mrs. Boyle rises. Mrs. Wellington tries to imitate her, but is detained.*

MRS. BOYLE. I beg of you —
stay just one moment longer —
one delicious moment?

MRS. WELLINGTON. I never decline delicacies!

[*Mrs. Alms cannot conceal her disappointment, but manages to blurt forth —*

MRS. ALMS. The katydids are beginning —
I really must run along.

[*The katydids are indeed beginning their nasal choral.*

MRS. BOYLE. Shall I show you out, dear?

MRS. ALMS. Not at all necessary, dear —
I know the way by myself.
Au revoir, Mrs. Ambrose Wellington.

MRS. WELLINGTON. *Au plaisir!*

MRS. ALMS. Until —

MRS. WELLINGTON. Let me calculate —
this is Tuesday —
let us meet —
let me say, Thursday at four.

MRS. ALMS (*eagerly*). Where?

MRS. BOYLE (*eagerly*). Here again?

MRS. WELLINGTON. At Mrs. Alms' this time, don't you think?

MRS. BOYLE. Oh!

MRS. ALMS. Ah!

MRS. WELLINGTON. And we'll confer finally
on the select choice of names
and send out the invitations.

MRS. ALMS. Exactly!

MRS. BOYLE. Precisely!

MRS. ALMS.   Good-by, Mrs. Boyle.

MRS. BOYLE.   Good-by, Mrs. Alms.

MRS. ALMS.   I can't begin to thank you
for the pleasant afternoon.
I can't begin to remember
when I spent a pleasanter.

MRS. BOYLE.   Don't mention it, dear!
[*They kiss ever so affectionately with a historic, short, sharp
sound.   Mrs. Alms nods several times in departing — mainly
to Mrs. Wellington — and leaves.   Mrs. Boyle returns to
her chair with a sigh.*

MRS. BOYLE.   Thank God, that's over!

MRS. WELLINGTON.   What's over?

MRS. BOYLE.   Now that that woman's gone,
we can have such a tête-à-tête.

MRS. WELLINGTON.   It'll have to be brief, my dear —
even though it concern Mrs. Alms.

MRS. BOYLE.   How you *do* understand!

MRS. WELLINGTON.   You credit me with virtues
I'm totally innocent of.

MRS. BOYLE.   Innocent?
A woman who's caught a second man —
such a lion, a dragon?

MRS. WELLINGTON.   Thanks awfully —
but we're done with him.
And you began with —

MRS. BOYLE.   that woman, yes.
You see —
I didn't want to say anything about her —
I'm not the kind to talk about friends.

MRS. WELLINGTON.   Obviously.

MRS. BOYLE.   Mrs. Alms *is* a dear soul —
none dearer anywhere —
but you see —
when a woman pretends,
even though she's a bosom friend —
don't you think it just a little wrong —

don't you think it the duty,
however painful,
of another friend —
if friendship means more than words —
to take her down a trifle —
bring her down from her false height?

MRS. WELLINGTON. Did she reach too high?

MRS. BOYLE. Didn't you notice?

MRS. WELLINGTON. I? — no!

MRS. BOYLE. You angel —
you know very well you did.

MRS. WELLINGTON. When — where — how?

MRS. BOYLE. You want *me* to tell!

MRS. WELLINGTON. No, I'd tell if I knew —
but I've been away from Jasmine
just the least while too long.
I've lost track of —

MRS. BOYLE. Jasmine ways.
You're like a person
who's been away from the piano —

MRS. WELLINGTON. who forgets even the elementary exercises.

MRS. BOYLE. That excuses you.

MRS. WELLINGTON. Thanks — now hurry —
the katydids are growing
thicker, louder,
nearer to the dinner bell.

MRS. BOYLE. You noticed, did you?

MRS. WELLINGTON. What?

MRS. BOYLE. How the women referred to your
not wearing black?

MRS. WELLINGTON. Yes, but you said that too? —

MRS. BOYLE. But it was I, not she,
who said this very afternoon,
before you came — I alone.

MRS. WELLINGTON. It was? — Then how noble of you
to let her take the credit she did!

MRS. BOYLE.   Nothing noble about it —
  it was simply my duty —
  not alone as a friend —
  but still more as a hostess —
  not to contradict her.

MRS. WELLINGTON.   Contradict?

MRS. BOYLE.   You'd make me tell all?

MRS. WELLINGTON.   Don't I deserve the confidence?

MRS. BOYLE.   Indeed you do — well —
  will you believe me when I state
  that that woman —
  I know you'll say, incredible! —

MRS. WELLINGTON (*simulating surprise*).   No, I won't — I
  can promise you
  I can believe almost anything now.

MRS. BOYLE.   You can?

MRS. WELLINGTON.   Try me!

MRS. BOYLE.   Well, would you believe
  that that creature
  sat here this very afternoon,
  sipping my tea,
  there in that very rocker,
  so still now,
  and said things behind your back
  she didn't say to your face?

MRS. WELLINGTON.   Impossible!

MRS. BOYLE.   She said things even I
  don't dare repeat!

MRS. WELLINGTON.   For instance?

MRS. BOYLE.   I do so hate to tell them —
  the woman tries her best,
  but she's a little unfortunate —
  not as successfully married as we are —
  Mr. Alms' glass works
  not what they used to be —
  and that sort of thing —
  so it's hard for her to keep up appearances —

to stand the gaff of competition —
climbing's not so easy as it was —
and so —

MRS. WELLINGTON. and so —

MRS. BOYLE. she's the more liable to make missteps —
prone to miss a rung or two —
in her eagerness, her illusion,
her self-delusion —
quite laudable in any woman,
but so grievous in its failures —
pretensions — poor woman —
you know what I mean —

MRS. WELLINGTON. Yes, poor dear.

MRS. BOYLE. Your pity shows the heart you have.

MRS. WELLINGTON. And yours shows yours.

MRS. BOYLE. But that's no reason, is it,
why I should shirk my duty
to you — as a friend?

MRS. WELLINGTON. And a hostess, no —
but don't mind me —
don't tell if it hurts you.

MRS. BOYLE. The need of self-surgery
is supreme where others are involved.

MRS. WELLINGTON. How I envy you the courage!

MRS. BOYLE. You have it too.

MRS. WELLINGTON. On the contrary.

MRS. BOYLE. Didn't you wear red —
that wild, thrilling bonnet —
when everybody expected, demanded
that you wear black?

MRS. WELLINGTON. How else could I interest a man
sad with feeling black all day long?

MRS. BOYLE. Artless child!
But think of the enemies you faced,
the unanimous malice you courted.

MRS. WELLINGTON. We've been through that.

MRS. BOYLE. But we haven't been through *all* —
notice, I said, unanimous.

MRS. WELLINGTON. Ah — I begin to see.

MRS. BOYLE. Are you positive?

MRS. WELLINGTON. Oh — what a treasure you are —
how rare — what a rhinestone! —
how can I ever repay you?

MRS. BOYLE. Spare me — I don't deserve it!

MRS. WELLINGTON. You do — think of you —
a saint in behalf of a sinner —
you alone — against so many —
against even your closest friend⌋

MRS. BOYLE. Yes, Mrs. Alms!
She called it a brazen, scarlet symbol —
think of that —
this guileless red bonnet.

MRS. WELLINGTON. Enough.

MRS. BOYLE. She called you for flaunting it —
flaunting was her expression —

MRS. WELLINGTON. enough, enough —

MRS. BOYLE. she insinuated that your
parading — as she termed it —
back and forth past my window —

MRS. WELLINGTON. You have told me all
in confiding this last,
single, solitary detail.

MRS. BOYLE. One detail is sufficient?

MRS. WELLINGTON. Among friends, yes, indeed!
[*She rises, so does Mrs. Boyle.*

MRS. BOYLE (*apprehensive*). Well?

MRS. WELLINGTON. I don't feel —

MRS. BOYLE. Yes? —

MRS. WELLINGTON. I don't feel it would be wise —
do you — for me to betray what I feel?

MRS. BOYLE (*disappointed*). No?

MRS. WELLINGTON. I mean —
that would be showing my cards —
her expression, wasn't it?

MRS. BOYLE. Just like her.

MRS. WELLINGTON. I suggest the committee
should go on as it started —
as though no disturbing,
foreign element were present.

MRS. BOYLE. Oh?

MRS. WELLINGTON. I mean — the two of us —

MRS. BOYLE (*eagerly*). us two? —

MRS. WELLINGTON. will have the additional pleasure
of watching the antics in our midst
of an additional person.
There's never enough merriment
on God's sad earth, is there, dear?

MRS. BOYLE (*gratefully*). No, no!
Never half enough!
You dear, dear, dear —

MRS. WELLINGTON. One dear will do, sweet ally!
[*She stretches out her hand.*

MRS. BOYLE. Oh, but let me see you to the door! (*She
bends forward to kiss Mrs. Wellington, who submits gracefully*) How can I begin?

MRS. WELLINGTON. Don't begin, dear —
it's so late —

MRS. BOYLE. and I feel so much —

MRS. WELLINGTON. you'd never reach the end
till midnight or dawn.

MRS. BOYLE. Until Thursday then?

MRS. WELLINGTON. At four —

MRS. BOYLE. at Mrs. Alms?
In the mouse's
own little mouse-trap?

MRS. WELLINGTON. With crackers and cheese on the side!

MRS. BOYLE. You incorrigible! (*Mrs. Wellington starts for
the door, adjusting her hat on the way. Mrs. Boyle bustles close
behind*) Adorable brazen symbol!
It looks like a headlight —
a danger signal!

MRS. WELLINGTON. How you imagine everything!

MRS. BOYLE. Like the flag of a general
leading his army single-handed! —

MRS. WELLINGTON. double-handed, my dear!

MRS. BOYLE. Your standard-bearer!

MRS. WELLINGTON. My ensign, dear.

MRS. BOYLE. Call me Arabella!

MRS. WELLINGTON. And you must call me Katherine!

MRS. BOYLE. Katherine!!

[*They disappear. The stage is empty. But not the world just outside the French window. Presently, two katydids, or a myriad of twos, swinging on leaves or grass blades, begin a high, nasal, mysterious colloquy.*

Katy did — Katy didn't —

Katy did — Katy didn't —

she did — she didn't —

she did so — she did not —

I say she did — I say she didn't —

I know she did — I know she didn't —

she told me — she did not —

she did so — she told me —

she did not — she did —

Katy didn't — Katy did —

Katy didn't — Katy did —

she didn't — she did —

she did not — she did so —

I say she didn't — I say she did —

you're a liar — you're another —

Katy did — Katy didn't —

Katy did — Katy didn't —

Katy did — Katy didn't —

[*The curtain falls ever so sleepily.*

MANIKIN AND MINIKIN

A BISQUE PLAY

By ALFRED KREYMBORG

"Manikin and Minikin" was originally produced by the St. Louis Players.

Original Cast

MANIKIN	Susan Cost
MINIKIN	Cornelia McNair

MANIKIN AND MINIKIN

Seen through an oval frame, one of the walls of a parlor. The wall paper is a conventionalized pattern. Only the shelf of the mantelpiece shows. At each end, seated on pedestals turned slightly away from one another, two aristocratic bisque figures, a boy in delicate cerise and a girl in cornflower blue. Their shadows join in a grotesque silhouette. In the center, an ancient clock whose tick acts as the metronome for the sound of their high voices. Presently, the mouths of the figures open and shut after the mode of ordinary conversation.

SHE. Manikin!

HE. Minikin?

SHE. That fool of a servant has done it again.

HE. I should say, she's more than a fool.

SHE. A meddlesome busybody —

HE. A brittle-fingered noddy!

SHE. Which way are you looking? What do you see?

HE. The everlasting armchair,
the everlasting tiger skin,
the everlasting yellow, green and purple books,
the everlasting portrait of milord.

SHE. Oh, these Yankees! — and I see
the everlasting rattan rocker,
the everlasting samovar,
the everlasting noisy piano,
the everlasting portrait of milady.

HE. Simpering spectacle!

SHE. What does she want, always dusting?

HE. I should say —
that is, I'd consider the thought —

SHE. You'd consider a lie —
oh, Manikin!
You're trying to defend her!

HE.　I'm not defending her!

SHE.　You're trying to.

HE.　I'm not trying to.

SHE.　Then what are you trying to — ?

HE.　Well, I'd venture to say,
　　if she'd only stay away some morning —

SHE.　That's what I say in my dreams!

HE.　She and her broom —

SHE.　Her everlasting broom —

HE.　She wouldn't be sweeping —

SHE.　Every corner, every cranny, every crevice.

HE.　And the dust wouldn't move —

SHE.　Wouldn't crawl, wouldn't rise, wouldn't fly —

HE.　And cover us all over —

SHE.　Like a spider-web — ugh!

HE.　Everlasting dust has been most of our life —

SHE.　Everlasting years and years of dust!

HE.　You on your lovely blue gown —

SHE.　And you on your manly pink cloak.

HE.　If she didn't sweep, we wouldn't need dusting.

SHE.　Nor need taking down, I should say —

HE.　With her stupid, clumsy hands —

SHE.　Her crooked, monkey paws.

HE.　And we wouldn't need putting back —

SHE.　I with my back to you —

HE.　I with my back to you.

SHE.　It's been hours, days, weeks —
　　by the sound of that everlasting clock —
　　and the coming of day and the going of day —
　　since I saw you last!

HE.　What's the use of the sun
　　with its butterfly wings of light —
　　what's the use of a sun made to see by —
　　if I can't see you!

SHE.　Manikin!

HE.　Minikin?

SHE.　Say that again!

HE.   Why should I say it again — don't you know?

SHE.   I know — but sometimes I doubt.

HE.   Why do you, what do you doubt?

SHE.   Please say it again!

HE.   What's the use of a sun —

SHE.   What's the use of a sun?

HE.   That was made to see by —

SHE.   That was made to see by?

HE.   If I can't see you!

SHE.   Oh, Manikin!

HE.   Minikin?

SHE.   If you hadn't said that again,
my doubt would have filled a balloon.

HE.   Your doubt, — which doubt, what doubt?

SHE.   And although I can't move,
although I can't move unless somebody shoves me,
one of these days when the sun isn't here,
I would have slipped over the edge
of this everlasting shelf —

HE.   Minikin!

SHE.   And fallen to that everlasting floor
into so many fragments,
they'd never paste Minikin together again!

HE.   Minikin, Minikin!

SHE.   They'd have to set another here —
some Ninikin, I'm assured!

HE.   Why do you chatter so, prattle so?

SHE.   Because of my doubt —
because I'm as positive as I am
that I sit here with my knees in a knot —
that that human creature — loves you.

HE.   Loves me?

SHE.   And you her!

HE.   Minikin!

SHE.   When she takes us down she holds you much longer.

HE.   Minikin!

SHE. I'm sufficiently feminine —
and certainly old enough —
I and my hundred and seventy years —
I can see, I can feel
by her manner of touching me
and her flicking me with her mop —
the creature hates me.
She'd like to drop me, that's what she would!

HE. Minikin!

SHE. Don't you venture defending her!
Booby — you don't know live women!
When I'm in the right position
I can note how she fondles you;
pets you like a parrot with her finger tip;
blows a pinch of dust from your eye
with her softest breath;
holds you off at arm's length
and fixes you with that spider look;
actually holds you against her cheek —
before she releases you!
If she didn't turn us apart so often,
I wouldn't charge her with insinuation;
but now I know she loves you —
she's as jealous as I am —
and poor dead me in her love power!
Manikin?

HE. Minikin?

SHE. If you could see me —
the way you see her —

HE. But I see you —
see you always — see only you!

SHE. If you could see me,
the way you see her,
you'd still love me,
you'd love me the way you do her!
Who made me what I am?
Who dreamed me in motionless clay?

HE. Minikin?

SHE. Manikin?

HE. Will you listen to me?

SHE. No!

HE. Will you listen to me?

SHE. No!

HE. Will you listen to me?

SHE. Yes.

HE. I love you —

SHE. No!

HE. I've always loved you —

SHE. No.

HE. You doubt that?

SHE. Yes!

HE. You doubt that? *leave in!*

SHE. Yes!

HE. You doubt that?

SHE. No.

You've always loved me —

yes —

but you don't love me now —

no —

not since that rose-face encountered your glance.

No!

HE. Minikin!

SHE. If I could only move about the way she can —

if I had feet —

dainty white feet which could twinkle and twirl —

I'd dance you so prettily

you'd think me a sun butterfly.

If I could let down my hair

And prove you it's longer than larch hair —

if I could raise my black brows,

or shrug my narrow shoulders

like a queen or a countess —

if I could turn my head, tilt my head

this way and that, like a swan —

Ogle

ogle my eyes, like a peacock,
till you'd marvel,
they're green, nay, violet, nay, yellow, nay, gold —
If I could move, only move
just the moment of an inch —
you would see what I could be!
It's a change, it's a change,
you men ask of women!

HE.   A change?

SHE.   You're eyesick, heartsick
of seeing the same foolish porcelain thing,
a hundred years old,
a hundred and fifty,
and sixty and seventy —
I don't know how old I am!

HE.   Not an exhalation older than I —
not an exhalation younger!
Minikin?

SHE.   Manikin?

HE.   Will you listen to me?

SHE.   No!

HE.   Will you listen to me?

SHE.   No.

HE.   Will you listen to me?

SHE.   Yes.

HE.   I don't love that creature.

SHE.   You do.

HE.   I can't love that creature.

SHE.   You can.

HE.   Will you listen to me?

SHE.   Yes —
if you'll tell me —
if you'll prove me —
so my last particle of dust —
the tiniest speck of a molecule —
the merest electron —

HE.   Are you listening?

SHE. Yes!

HE. To begin with —
  I dislike, suspect, deplore —
  I had best say, feel compassion
  for what is called humanity —
  or the animate, as opposed to the inanimate.

SHE. You say that so wisely —
  you're such a philosopher —
  Say it again!

HE. That which is able to move
  can never be steadfast, you understand?
  Let us consider the creature at hand
  to whom you have referred
  with an undue excess of admiration
  adulterated with an undue excess of envy.

SHE. Say that again!

HE. To begin with —
  I can only see part of her at once.
  She moves into my vision;
  she moves out of my vision;
  she is doomed to be wayward.

SHE. Yes, but that which you can see of her —

HE. Is ugly, commonplace, unsightly.
  Her face a rose-face?
  It's veined with blood and the skin of it wrinkles;
  her eyes are ever so near to a hen's;
  her movements —
  if one would pay such a gait with regard —
  her gait is unspeakably ungainly;
  her hair —

SHE. Her hair?

HE. Luckily I've never seen it down.
  I daresay it comes down in the dark;
  when it looks, most assuredly, like tangled weeds.

SHE. Again, Manikin, that dulcet phrase!

HE. Even were she beautiful,
  she were never so beautiful as thou!

SHE.   Now you're a poet, Manikin!

HE.   Even were she so beautiful as thou —
lending her your eyes, and
the exquisite head which holds them
like a cup two last beads of wine,
like a stone two last drops of rain,
green, nay, violet, nay, yellow, nay, gold —

SHE.   Faster, Manikin!

HE.   I can't, Minikin!
Words were never given to man
to phrase such a one as you are.
Inanimate symbols
can never embrace, embody, hold
the animate dream that you are.
I must cease.

SHE.   Manikin!

HE.   And even were she so beautiful as thou,
she couldn't stay beautiful.

SHE.   Stay beautiful?

HE.   Humans change with each going moment.
That is a gray-haired platitude.
Just as I can see that creature
only when she touches my vision,
so I could only see her once, were she beautiful —
at best, twice or thrice.
You're more precious than when you came!

SHE.   And you!

HE.   Human pathos penetrates still deeper
when one determines their inner life,
as we've pondered their outer.
Their inner changes far more desperately.

SHE.   How so, wise Manikin?

HE.   They have what philosophy terms moods,
and moods are more pervious to modulation
than pools to idle breezes.
These people may say — to begin with —
I love you.

This may be true, I'm assured —
as true as when *we* say, I love you.
But they can only say,
I love you,
so long as the mood breathes,
so long as the breezes blow,
so long as water remains wet.
They are honest —
they mean what they say —
passionately, tenaciously, tragically —
but when the mood languishes,
they have to say,
if it be they are honest —
I do not love you.
Or they have to say,
I love you,
to somebody else.

SHE.   To somebody else?

HE.   Now, you and I —
we've said that to each other —
we've had to say it
for a hundred and seventy years —
and we'll have to say it always.

SHE.   Say "always" again!

HE.   The life of an animate —

SHE.   Say "always" again!

HE.   Always!
The life of an animate
is a procession of deaths,
with but a secret sorrowing candle,
guttering lower and lower,
on the path to the grave.
The life of an inanimate
is as serenely enduring
as all things are.

SHE.   Still things?

HE.   Recall our childhood in the English museum —
ere we were moved,

from place to place,
to this dreadful Yankee salon.
Do you remember
that little old Greek tanagra
of the girl with a head like a bud —
that little old Roman medallion
of the girl with a head like a —

SHE.   Manikin, Manikin —
were they so beautiful as I?
Did you love them, too?
Why do you bring them back?

HE.   They were not so beautiful as thou.
I spoke of them —
recalled, designated them —
well, because they were ages old —
and — and —

SHE.   And — and?

HE.   And we might live as long as they —
as they did and do!
I hinted their existence
because they're not so beautiful as thou,
so that by contrast and deduction —

SHE.   And deduction?

HE.   You know what I'd say.

SHE.   But say it again!

HE.   I love you!

SHE.   Manikin?

HE.   Minikin?

SHE.   Then, even though that creature has turned us apart,
can you see me?

HE.   I can see you.

SHE.   Even though you haven't seen me
for hours, days, weeks —
with your dear blue eyes —
you can see me
with your hidden ones?

HE.   I can see you.

SHE. Even though you are still,
and calm, and smooth,
and lovely outside —
you aren't still and calm
and smooth and lovely inside?

HE. Lovely — yes —
but not still and calm and smooth!

SHE. Which way are you looking? What do you see?

HE. I look at you.
I see you.

SHE. And if that fool of a servant —
oh, Manikin —
suppose she should break the future —
our great, happy centuries ahead —
by dropping me, throwing me down?

HE. I should take an immediate step
off this everlasting shelf —

SHE. But you cannot move!

HE. The good wind would give me a blow!

HE. Now you're a punster!
And what would your fragments do?

HE. They'd do what Manikin did.

HE. Say that again!

HE. They'd do what Manikin did.

HE. Manikin?

HE. Minikin?

HE. Shall I tell you something?

HE. Tell me something.

HE. Are you listening?

HE. With my inner ears.

HE. I wasn't jealous of that woman.

HE. You weren't jealous?

HE. I wanted to hear you talk.

HE. You wanted to hear me talk?

HE. You talk so wonderfully!

HE. Do I, indeed? What a booby I am!

HE. And I wanted to hear you say —

HE. You cheat, you idler, you —

SHE. Woman —

HE. Dissembler!

SHE. Manikin?

HE. Minikin?

SHE. Everlastingly?

HE. Everlastingly.

SHE. Say it again!

HE. I refuse.

SHE. You refuse?

HE. Well —

SHE. Well?

HE. You have ears outside your head —
I'll say that for you —
but they'll never hear —
what your other ears heard!

SHE. Say it —
down one of my ears —
outside my head?

HE. I refuse.

SHE. You refuse?

HE. Leave me alone.

SHE. Manikin?

HE. I can't say it!

SHE. Manikin!

[*The clock goes on ticking for a moment. Its mellow chime*
strike the hour. Curtain.

THE DEATH OF TINTAGILES

MAURICE MAETERLINCK

MAURICE MAETERLINCK was born August 29, 1862, at Brussels, Belgium. He is famous as a poet, naturalist, philosopher and playwright. "La Mort de Tintagiles" was originally published in 1894, but was not produced until 1899. The best study of Maeterlinck is by Una Taylor. In "Prophets of Dissent", O. Heller has an illuminating chapter entitled Maeterlinck, the Mystic.

THE DEATH OF TINTAGILES

A PLAY IN FIVE ACTS

BY MAURICE MAETERLINCK

Characters

TINTAGILES
YGRAINE
BELLANGERE } Sisters of Tintagiles
AGLOVALE
THREE SERVANTS OF THE QUEEN

THE DEATH OF TINTAGILES

ACT I

SCENE. *On the top of a hill overlooking the castle. Enter Ygraine, holding Tintagiles by the hand.*

YGRAINE. Your first night will be sad, Tintagiles. The roar of the sea is already about us; and the trees are moaning. It is late. The moon is sinking behind the poplars that stifle the palace. We are alone, perhaps; but here, one has ever to be on one's guard. They seem to watch lest the smallest happiness come near. I said to myself one day, right down in the depths of my soul — and God himself could scarcely hear — I said to myself one day that I was feeling almost happy. There needed nothing more; and very soon after, our old father died, and our two brothers disappeared, and not a living creature can tell us where they are. I am here all alone, with my poor sister and you, my little Tintagiles; and I have no confidence in the future. Come to me; let me take you on my knees. First kiss me; and put your little arms — there — right around my neck; perhaps they will not be able to unfasten them. Do you remember the time when it was I who carried you in the evening, when the hour had come; and how frightened you were at the shadows of my lamp in the corridors, those long corridors with not a single window? I felt my soul tremble on my lips when I saw you again, suddenly, this morning. I thought you were so far away, and in safety. Who made you come here?

TINTAGILES. I do not know, little sister.

YGRAINE. Do you remember what they said?

TINTAGILES. They said I must go away.

YGRAINE. But why had you to go away?

TINTAGILES. Because the Queen wished it.

YGRAINE. Did they not say why she wished it? — I am sure they must have said many things.

TINTAGILES. Little sister, I did not hear.

YGRAINE. When they spoke among themselves, what was it they said?

TINTAGILES. Little sister, they dropped their voices when they spoke.

YGRAINE. All the time?

TINTAGILES. All the time, sister Ygraine; except when they looked at me.

YGRAINE. Did they say nothing about the Queen?

TINTAGILES. They said, sister Ygraine, that no one ever saw her.

YGRAINE. And the people who were with you on the ship, did they say nothing?

TINTAGILES. They gave all their time to the wind and the sails, sister Ygraine.

YGRAINE. Ah! That does not surprise me, my child.

TINTAGILES. They left me all alone, little sister.

YGRAINE. Listen to me, Tintagiles. I will tell you what I know.

TINTAGILES. What do you know, sister Ygraine?

YGRAINE. Very little, my child. My sister and I have gone on living here ever since we were born, not daring to understand the things that happened. I have lived a long time on this island, and I might as well have been blind; yet it all seemed natural to me. A bird that flew, a leaf that trembled, a rose that opened — these were events to me. Such silence has always reigned here that a ripe fruit falling in the park would draw faces to the window. And no one seemed to have any suspicion; but one night I learned that there must be something besides. I wished to escape and I could not. Have you understood what I am telling you?

TINTAGILES. Yes, yes, little sister; I can understand anything.

YGRAINE. Then let us not talk any more of these things; one does not know. Do you see, behind the dead trees which poison the horizon, do you see the castle, there, right down in the valley?

TINTAGILES. I see something very black — is that the castle, sister Ygraine?

YGRAINE. Yes, it is very black. It lies far down amid a mass of gloomy shadows. It is there that we have to live. They might have built it on the top of the great mountains that surround it. The mountains are blue in the day-time. One could have breathed; one could have looked down on the sea and on the plains beyond the cliffs. But they preferred to build it deep down in the valley; too low even for the air to come. It is falling in ruins, and no one troubles. The walls are crumbling; it might be fading away in the gloom. There is only one tower which time does not touch. It is enormous; and its shadow is always on the house.

TINTAGILES. They are lighting something, sister Ygraine. See, see, the great red windows!

YGRAINE. They are the windows of the tower, Tintagiles; they are the only ones in which you will ever see light; it is there that the Queen has her throne.

TINTAGILES. Shall I not see the Queen?

YGRAINE. No one can see her.

TINTAGILES. Why can no one see her?

YGRAINE. Come closer, Tintagiles. Not even a bird or a blade of grass must hear us.

TINTAGILES. There is no grass, little sister. (*A moment's silence*) What does the Queen do?

YGRAINE. That no one knows, my child. She is never seen. She lives there, all alone in the tower; and those who wait on her do not go out by daylight. She is very old; she is the mother of our mother, and she wishes to reign alone. She is suspicious and jealous, and they say she is mad. She is afraid lest some one should raise himself to her place; and it is probably because of this fear of hers that you have been brought hither. Her orders are carried out; but no one knows how. She never leaves the tower, and all the gates are closed night and day. I have never seen her, but it seems others have, long ago, when she was young.

TINTAGILES. Is she very ugly, sister Ygraine?

YGRAINE. They say she is not beautiful and that her form is strange. But those who have seen her dare not speak to her. And who knows whether they have seen her? She has a power which we do not understand, and we live here with a terrible weight on our soul. You must not be unduly frightened, or have bad dreams; we will watch over you, little Tintagiles, and no harm can come to you; but do not stray far from me, or your sister Bellangere, or our old master Aglovale.

TINTAGILES. Aglovale too, sister Ygraine?

YGRAINE. Aglovale too, — he loves us.

TINTAGILES. He is so old, little sister!

YGRAINE. He is old, but very wise. He is the only friend we have left; and he knows many things. It is strange; she made you come here, and no one was told of it. I do not know what is in my heart. I was sorrowful and glad to know that you were far away, beyond the sea. And now — I was taken by surprise. I went out this morning to see whether the sun was rising over the mountains; and I saw you on the threshold. I knew you at once.

TINTAGILES. No, no, little sister; it was I who laughed first.

YGRAINE. I could not laugh — just then. You will understand. It is time, Tintagiles, and the wind is becoming black on the sea. Kiss me before getting up; kiss me, harder — again, again. You do not know how one loves. Give me your little hand. I will keep it in mine and we will go back to the old sick castle.

[*They go out.*

ACT II

SCENE.   *A room in the castle, in which Aglovale and Ygraine are seated.   Enter Bellangere.*

BELLANGERE.   Where is Tintagiles?

YGRAINE.   He is here; do not speak too loud.   He is asleep in the other room.   He was a little pale, he did not seem well.   The journey had tired him — he was a long time on the sea.   Or perhaps it is the atmosphere of the castle which has alarmed his little soul.   He was crying, and did not know why he cried.   I nursed him on my knees; come, look at him.   He is asleep in our bed.   He sleeps very gravely, with one hand on his brow, like a little sorrowful king.

BELLANGERE (*suddenly bursting into tears*).   Sister! Sister! my poor sister!

YGRAINE.   Why are you crying?

BELLANGERE.   I dare not tell what I know; and I am not sure that I know anything.   But yet I have heard — that which one could not hear.

YGRAINE.   What have you heard?

BELLANGERE.   I was passing close to the corridors of the tower —

YGRAINE.   Ah!

BELLANGERE.   One of the doors was ajar.   I pushed it very gently.   I went in.

YGRAINE.   Where?

BELLANGERE.   I had never seen.   There were other corridors lighted with lamps; and then low galleries, which seemed to have no end.   I knew it was forbidden to go farther. I was afraid and was about to turn back, but there was a sound of voices — though one could scarcely hear.

YGRAINE.   It must have been the servants of the Queen; they live at the foot of the tower.

BELLANGERE.   I do not know quite what it was.   There must have been more than one door between; and the voices came to me like the voices of some one who is being strangled. I went as near as I could. I am not sure of anything; but I believe they were speaking of a child who had arrived to-day, and of a crown of gold. They seemed to be laughing.

YGRAINE. They were laughing?

BELLANGERE. Yes, I think they were laughing; unless it was that they were crying, or that it was something I did not understand; for one heard badly, and their voices were low. There seemed to be a great many of them moving about in the vault. They were speaking of the child that the Queen wished to see. They will probably come here this evening.

YGRAINE. What? This evening?

BELLANGERE. Yes, yes; I think so, yes.

YGRAINE. Did they not mention any name?

BELLANGERE. They spoke of a child — a little, little child.

YGRAINE. There is no other child here.

BELLANGERE. Just then they raised their voices a little, for one of them had doubted whether the day was come.

YGRAINE. I know what that means, and it will not be the first time that they have left the tower. I knew only too well why she made him come, but I could not think she would show such haste as this! We shall see; there are three of us, and we have time.

BELLANGERE. What do you mean to do?

YGRAINE. I do not know yet what I shall do, but I shall surprise her. Do you know what that means, you who can only tremble? I will tell you.

BELLANGERE. What?

YGRAINE. She shall not take him without a struggle.

BELLANGERE. We are alone, sister Ygraine.

YGRAINE. Ah! it is true we are alone! There is only one thing to be done, and it never fails us! Let us wait on our knees as we did before. Perhaps she will have pity! She allows herself to be moved by tears. We must grant her everything she asks; she will smile, perhaps; and it is her habit to spare all who kneel. All these years she has been there in her enormous tower, devouring those we love, and not a single one has dared strike her in the face. She lies on our soul like the stone of a tomb, and no one dares stretch out his arm. In the times when there were men here, they too were afraid, and fell upon their faces. To-day it is the woman's turn; we shall see. It is time that some one should dare to rise. No one knows on what her power rests, and I will no longer live in the shadow of her tower. Go away, if you two can only tremble like this — go away, both of you, and leave me still more alone. I will wait for her.

BELLANGERE. Sister, I do not know what has to be done, but I will wait with you.

AGLOVALE. I, too, will wait, my daughter. My soul has long been ill at ease. You will try; we have tried more than once.

YGRAINE. You have tried — you also?

AGLOVALE. They have all tried. But at the last moment their strength has failed them. You, too, you shall see. If she were to command me to go up to her this very evening, I would put my two hands together and say nothing; and my weary feet would climb the staircase, without lingering and without hastening, though I know full well that none come down again with eyes unclosed. There is no courage left in me against her; our hands are helpless, and can touch no one. Other hands than these are wanted, and all is useless. But you are hopeful, and I will assist you. Close the doors, my child. Awaken Tintagiles; bare your little arms and enfold him within them, and take him on your knees — we have no other defense.

ACT III

SCENE. *The same room. Ygraine and Aglovale.*

YGRAINE. I have been to look at the doors. There are three of them. We will watch the large one. The two others are low and heavy. They are never opened. The keys were lost long ago, and the iron bars are sunk into the walls. Help me close this door; it is heavier than the gate of a city. It is massive; the lightning itself could not pierce through it. Are you prepared for all that may happen?

AGLOVALE (*seating himself on the threshold*). I will go seat myself on the steps; my sword across my knees. I do not think this is the first time I have waited and watched here, my child; and there are moments when one does not understand all that one remembers. I have done all this before, I do not know when; but I have never dared draw my sword. Now, it lies there before me, though my arms no longer have strength; but I intend to try. It is perhaps time that men should defend themselves, even though they do not understand.

[*Bellangere, carrying Tintagiles in her arms, comes out of the adjoining room.*

BELLANGERE. He was awake.

YGRAINE. He is pale; what ails him?

BELLANGERE. I do not know; he was very silent. He was crying.

YGRAINE. Tintagiles.

BELLANGERE. He is looking away from you.

YGRAINE. He does not seem to know me. Tintagiles, where are you? It is your sister who speaks to you. What are you looking at so fixedly? Turn around; come, I will play with you.

TINTAGILES. No, no.

YGRAINE. You do not want to play?

TINTAGILES. I cannot stand, sister Ygraine.

YGRAINE. You cannot stand? Come, come, what is the matter with you? Are you suffering any pain?

TINTAGILES. Yes.

YGRAINE. Tell me where it is, Tintagiles, and I will cure you.

TINTAGILES. I cannot tell you, sister Ygraine — everywhere.

YGRAINE. Come to me, Tintagiles. You know that my

arms are softer, and I will put them around you, and you will feel better at once. Give him to me, Bellangere. He shall sit on my knee, and the pain will go. There, you see? Your big sisters are here. They are close to you, we will defend you, and no evil can come near.

TINTAGILES. It has come, sister Ygraine. Why is there no light, sister Ygraine?

YGRAINE. There is a light, my child. Do you not see the lamp that hangs from the rafters?

TINTAGILES. Yes, yes; it is not large. Are there no others?

YGRAINE. Why should there be others? We can see what we have to see.

TINTAGILES. Ah!

YGRAINE. Oh! your eyes are deep.

TINTAGILES. So are yours, sister Ygraine.

YGRAINE. I did not notice it this morning. I have just seen in your eyes. We do not quite know what the soul thinks it sees.

TINTAGILES. I have not seen the soul, sister Ygraine. But why is Aglovale on the threshold?

YGRAINE. He is resting a little. He wanted to kiss you before going to bed; he was waiting for you to wake.

TINTAGILES. What has he on his knees?

YGRAINE. On his knees? I see nothing on his knees.

TINTAGILES. Yes, yes; there is something.

AGLOVALE. It is nothing, my child. I was looking at my old sword; and I scarcely recognize it. It has served me many years, but for a long time past I have lost confidence in it, and I think it is going to break. Here, just by the hilt, there is a little stain. I had noticed that the steel was growing paler, and I asked myself: — I do not remember what I asked myself. My soul is very heavy to-day. What is one to do? Men must needs live and await the unforeseen. And after that they must still act as if they hoped. There are sad evenings when our useless lives taste bitter in our mouths, and we would like to close our eyes. It is late, and I am tired.

TINTAGILES. He has wounds, sister Ygraine.

YGRAINE. Where?

TINTAGILES. On his forehead and on his hands.

AGLOVALE. Those are very old wounds, from which I suffer no longer, my child. The light must be falling on them this evening. You had not noticed them before?

TINTAGILES. He looks sad, sister Ygraine.

YGRAINE. No, no; he is not sad, but very weary.

TINTAGILES. You too are sad, sister Ygraine.

YGRAINE. Why no, why no; look at me, I am smiling.

TINTAGILES. And my other sister too.

YGRAINE. Oh, no, she too, is smiling.

TINTAGILES. No, that is not a smile; I know.

YGRAINE. Come, kiss me, and think of something else.
  [*She kisses him.*

TINTAGILES. Of what shall I think, sister Ygraine? — Why do you hurt me when you kiss me?

YGRAINE. Did I hurt you?

TINTAGILES. Yes. I do not know why I hear your heart beat, sister Ygraine.

YGRAINE. Did you hear it beat?

TINTAGILES. Oh! Oh! it beats as though it wanted to —

YGRAINE What?

TINTAGILES. I do not know, sister Ygraine.

YGRAINE. It is wrong to be frightened without reason, and to speak in riddles. Oh! your eyes are full of tears. Why are you unhappy? I hear your heart beating, now; people always hear them when they hold one another so close. It is then that the heart speaks and says things that the tongue does not know.

TINTAGILES. I heard nothing before.

YGRAINE. That was because — Oh! But your heart! What is the matter? It is bursting!

TINTAGILES (*crying*). Sister Ygraine! Sister Ygraine!

YGRAINE. What is it?

TINTAGILES. I have heard. They — they are coming!

YGRAINE. Who? Who are coming? What has happened?

TINTAGILES. The door! the door! They are there!

[*He falls backwards on to Ygraine's knees.*

YGRAINE. What is it? He has — he has fainted.

BELLANGERE. Take care — take care. He will fall.

AGLOVALE (*rising brusquely, his sword in his hand*). I, too, can hear — there are steps in the corridor.

YGRAINE. Oh!

[*A moment's silence; they all listen.*

AGLOVALE. Yes, I hear. There is a crowd of them.

YGRAINE. A crowd — a crowd — now?

AGLOVALE. I do not know; one hears and one does not hear. They do not move like other creatures, but they come. They are touching the door.

YGRAINE (*clasping Tintagiles in her arms*). Tintagiles! Tintagiles!

BELLANGERE (*embracing him*). Let 'me 'too! let me!— Tintagiles!

AGLOVALE. They are shaking the door — listen — do not breathe. They are whispering.

[*A key is heard turning harshly in the lock.*

YGRAINE. They have the key!

AGLOVALE. Yes, yes; I was sure of it. Wait. (*He plants himself, with sword outstretched, on the last step — to the two sisters*) Come! come both!

[*For a moment there is silence. The door opens slowly. Aglovale thrusts his sword wildly through the opening, driving the point between the beams. The sword breaks with a loud report under the silent pressure of the timber, and the pieces of steel roll down the steps with a resounding clang. Ygraine leaps up, carrying in her arms Tintagiles, who has fainted; and she, Bellangere and Aglovale, putting forth all their strength, try, but in vain, to close the door, which slowly opens wider and wider, although no one can be seen or heard. Only a cold and calm light penetrates into the room. At this moment Tintagiles, suddenly stretching out his limbs, regains consciousness, sends forth a long cry of deliverance, and embraces his sister — and at this very instant the door, which resists no longer, falls to brusquely under their pressure, which they have not had time to stop.*

YGRAINE.   Tintagiles!

[*They look with amazement at each other.*

AGLOVALE (*waiting at the door*).   I hear nothing now.

YGRAINE (*wild with joy*).   Tintagiles! Tintagiles! Look! Look! He is saved! Look at his eyes; you can see the blue. He is going to speak. They saw we were watching. They did not dare. Kiss us! Kiss us, I say! Kiss us! All! all! Down to the depths of our soul!

[*All four, their eyes full of tears, fall into each other's arms.*

ACT IV

SCENE.   *A corridor in front of the room in which last act took place.*

Three Servants of the Queen enter. They are all veiled, and their long black robes flow down to the ground.

FIRST SERVANT (*listening at the door*).   They are not watching.

SECOND SERVANT.   We need not have waited.

THIRD SERVANT.   She prefers that it should be done in silence.

FIRST SERVANT.   I knew that they must fall asleep.

SECOND SERVANT.   Quick! open the door.

THIRD SERVANT.   It is time.

FIRST SERVANT.   Wait there; I will enter alone. There is no need for three of us.

SECOND SERVANT.   You are right; he is very small.

THIRD SERVANT.   You must be careful with the elder sister.

SECOND SERVANT.   Remember, the Queen does not want them to know.

FIRST SERVANT.   Have no fear; people seldom hear my coming.

SECOND SERVANT.   Go in then; it is time. (*The First Servant opens the door cautiously and goes into the room*) It is close on midnight.

THIRD SERVANT.   Ah!

[*A moment's silence. The First Servant comes out of the room.*

SECOND SERVANT. Where is he?

FIRST SERVANT. He is asleep between his sisters. His arms are around their necks; and their arms enfold him. I cannot do it alone.

SECOND SERVANT. I will help you.

THIRD SERVANT. Yes; do you go together. I will keep watch here.

FIRST SERVANT. Be careful; they seem to know. They were all three struggling with a bad dream.

[*The two Servants go into the room.*

THIRD SERVANT. People always know; but they do not understand.

[*A moment's silence. The First and Second Servants come out of the room again.*

THIRD SERVANT. Well?

SECOND SERVANT. You must come too; we cannot separate them.

FIRST SERVANT. No sooner do we unclasp their arms than they fall back around the child.

SECOND SERVANT. And the child nestles closer and closer to them.

FIRST SERVANT. He is lying with his forehead on the elder sister's heart.

SECOND SERVANT. And his head rises and falls on her bosom.

FIRST SERVANT. We shall not be able to open his hands.

SECOND SERVANT. They are plunged deep down into his sister's hair.

FIRST SERVANT. He holds one golden curl between his little teeth.

SECOND SERVANT. We shall have to cut the elder sister's hair.

FIRST SERVANT. And the other sister's, too, you will see.

SECOND SERVANT. Have you your scissors?

THIRD SERVANT. Yes.

FIRST SERVANT. Come quickly; they have begun to move.

SECOND SERVANT. Their hearts and their eyelids are throbbing together.

FIRST SERVANT. Yes; I caught a glimpse of the elder girl's blue eyes.

SECOND SERVANT. She looked at us but did not see us.

FIRST SERVANT. If one touches one of them, the other two tremble.

SECOND SERVANT They are trying hard, but they cannot stir.

FIRST SERVANT. The elder sister wishes to scream, but she cannot.

SECOND SERVANT. Come quickly; they seem to know.

THIRD SERVANT. Where is the old man?

FIRST SERVANT. He is asleep — away from the others.

SECOND SERVANT. He sleeps, his forehead resting on the hilt of his sword.

FIRST SERVANT. He knows of nothing; and he has no dreams.

THIRD SERVANT. Come, come, we must hasten.

FIRST SERVANT. You will find it difficult to separate their limbs.

SECOND SERVANT. They are clutching at each other as though they were drowning.

THIRD SERVANT. Come, come.

[*They go in. The silence is broken only by sighs and low murmurs of suffering, held in thrall by sleep. Then the three Servants emerge very hurriedly from the gloomy room. One of them carries Tintagiles, who is fast asleep, in her arms. From his little hands, twitching in sleep, and his mouth, drawn in agony, a glittering stream of golden tresses, ravished from the heads of his sisters, flows down to the ground. The Servants hurry on. There is perfect silence; but no sooner have they reached the end of the corridor than Tintagiles awakes and sends forth a cry of supreme distress.*

TINTAGILES (*from the end of the corridor*). Aah!

[*There is again silence. Then from the adjoining room the two sisters are heard moving about restlessly.*

YGRAINE (*in the room*). Tintagiles! Where is he?

BELLANGERE. He is not here.

YGRAINE (*with growing anguish*). Tintagiles! A lamp, a lamp! Light it!

BELLANGERE. Yes — yes.

[*Ygraine is seen coming out of the room with a lighted lamp in her hand.*

YGRAINE. The door is wide open!

[*The voice of Tintagiles, almost inaudible, in the distance.*

TINTAGILES. Sister Ygraine!

YGRAINE. He calls! He calls! Tintagiles! Tintagiles!

[*She rushes into the corridor. Bellangere tries to follow, but falls fainting on the threshold.*

ACT V

SCENE. *Before a great iron door in a gloomy vault. Enter Ygraine, haggard and dishevelled, with a lamp in her hand.*

YGRAINE (*turning wildly to and fro*). They have not followed me here! Bellangere! Bellangere! Aglovale! Where are they? They said they loved him and they leave me alone! Tintagiles! Tintagiles! Oh, I remember; I have climbed steps without number, between great pitiless walls, and my heart bids me live no longer. These vaults seem to move. (*She supports herself against the pillars*) I am falling. Oh! Oh! My poor life! I can feel it — it is trembling on my lips — it wants to depart. I know not what I have done; I have seen nothing. I have heard nothing. Oh, this silence! All along the steps and all along the walls I found these golden curls, and I followed them. I picked them up. Oh! oh! They are very pretty! Little childie — little childie — what was I saying? I remember; I do not believe in it. When one sleeps — all that has no importance and is not possible. Of what am I thinking? I do not know. One awakes, and then — After all — come, after all — I must think this out. Some say one thing, some say the other; but the way of the soul is quite different. When the chain is removed, there is much more than one knows. I came here with my little lamp. It did not go out, in spite of the wind on the staircase. And then, what is one to think? There are so many things which are vague. There must be people who know them; but why do they not speak? (*She looks around her*) I have never seen all this before. It is difficult to get so far — and it is all forbidden. How cold it is; and so dark one is afraid to breathe. They say there is poison in these gloomy shadows. That door looks very terrible. (*She goes up to the door and touches it*) Oh! how cold it is. It is of iron — solid iron — and there is no lock. How can they open it? I see no hinges; I suppose it is sunk into the wall. This is as far as one can go. There are no more steps. (*Suddenly sending forth a terrible shriek*) Ah! more golden hair between the panels! Tintagiles! Tintagiles! I heard the door close just now — I remember! I remember! It must be! (*She beats frantically against the door with hands and feet*) Oh! Monster! Monster! It is here that I find you! Listen! I blaspheme! I blaspheme and spit on you!

[*Feeble knocks are heard from the other side of the door; then the voice of Tintagiles penetrates very feebly through the iron panels.*

TINTAGILES. Sister Ygraine, sister Ygraine!

YGRAINE. Tintagiles! What! What! Tintagiles, is it you?

TINTAGILES. Quick, open, open! She is here!

YGRAINE. Oh! Oh! Who? Tintagiles, my little Tintagiles, can you hear me? What is it? What has happened? Tintagiles! Have they hurt you? Where are you? Are you there?

TINTAGILES. Sister Ygraine, sister Ygraine! Open for me — or I shall die.

YGRAINE. I will try — wait, wait. I will open it, I will open it.

TINTAGILES. But you do not understand! Sister Ygraine! There is no time to lose! She tried to hold me back! I struck her, struck her; I ran. Quick, quick, she is coming!

YGRAINE. Yes, yes — where is she?

TINTAGILES. I can see nothing, but I hear — oh, I am afraid, sister Ygraine, I am afraid. Quick, quick! Quick, open! for the dear Lord's sake, sister Ygraine!

YGRAINE (*anxiously groping along the door*). I am sure to find it. Wait a little — a minute — a second.

TINTAGILES. I cannot, sister Ygraine. I can feel her breath on me now.

YGRAINE. It is nothing, Tintagiles, my little Tintagiles; do not be frightened — if I could only see.

TINTAGILES. Oh, but you can see — I can see your lamp from here. It is quite light where you are, sister Ygraine. Here I can see nothing.

YGRAINE. You see me, Tintagiles? How can you see? There is not a crack in the door.

TINTAGILES. Yes, yes, there is; but it is so small!

YGRAINE. On which side? Is it here — tell me, tell me — or is it over there?

TINTAGILES. It is here. Listen! Listen! I am knocking.

YGRAINE. Here?

TINTAGILES. Higher up. But it is so small; a needle could not go through!

YGRAINE. Do not be afraid, I am here.

TINTAGILES. Oh, I know, sister Ygraine! Pull! pull! You must pull! She is coming! If you could only open a little — a very little. I am so small!

YGRAINE. My nails are broken, Tintagiles. I have pulled, I have pushed, I have struck with all my might, with all my might! (*She strikes again, and tries to shake the massive door*) Two of my fingers are numbed. Do not cry. It is of iron.

TINTAGILES (*sobbing in despair*). You have nothing to open with, sister Ygraine? nothing at all, nothing at all? I could get through — I am so small, so very small — you know how small I am.

YGRAINE. I have only my lamp, Tintagiles. There! There! (*She aims repeated blows at the gate with her earthenware lamp, which goes out and breaks, the pieces falling to the ground*) Oh! it has all grown dark! Tintagiles, where are you? Oh! listen, listen! Can you not open from the inside?

TINTAGILES. No, no; there is nothing. I cannot feel anything at all. I cannot see the light through the crack any more.

YGRAINE. What is the matter, Tintagiles? I can scarcely hear you.

TINTAGILES. Little sister, sister Ygraine. It is too late now.

YGRAINE. What is it, Tintagiles? Where are you going?

TINTAGILES. She is here! Oh, I am so weak. Sister Ygraine, sister Ygraine. I feel her on me!

YGRAINE. Whom? whom?

TINTAGILES. I do not know — I cannot see. But it is too late now. She — she is taking me by the throat. Her hand is at my throat. Oh, oh, sister Ygraine, come to me!

YGRAINE. Yes, yes.

TINTAGILES. It is so dark.

YGRAINE. Struggle — fight — tear her to pieces! Do not be afraid. Wait a moment! I am here. Tintagiles! answer me! Help! ! ! Where are you? I will come to you, kiss me, through the door — here, here.

TINTAGILES (*very feebly*). Here — here — sister Ygraine.

YGRAINE. I am putting my kisses on this spot here, do you understand? Again, again!

TINTAGILES (*more and more feebly*). Mine too — here — sister Ygraine! Sister Ygraine! Oh!

[*The fall of a little body is heard behind the iron door.*

YGRAINE. Tintagiles! Tintagiles! What have you done? Give him back, give him back! For the love of God, give him back to me! I can hear nothing. What are you doing with him! You will not hurt him? He is only a little child; he cannot resist. Look! look! I mean no harm. I am on my knees. Give him back to us, I beg of you. Not for my sake only, you know it well. I will

do anything. I bear no ill-will, you see. I implore you
with clasped hands. I was wrong. I am quite resigned,
you see. I have lost all I had. You should punish me
some other way. There are so many things which would
hurt me more — if you want to hurt me. You shall see.
But this poor child has done no harm. What I said was
not true — but I did not know. I know that you are very
good. Surely the time for forgiveness has come! He is so
young and beautiful, and he is so small! You must see
that it cannot be! He puts his little arms around your
neck; his little mouth on your mouth; and God himself
could not say him nay. You will open the door, will you
not? I am asking so little. I want him for an instant,
just for an instant. I cannot remember. You will understand. I did not have time. He can get through the tiniest opening. It is not difficult. (*A long inexorable silence*)
Monster! Monster! Curse you! Curse you! I spit on
you!

[*She sinks down and continues to sob softly, her arms out-
spread against the gate, in the gloom.*

THE CONFLICT

CLARICE VALLETTE McCAULEY

CLARICE VALLETTE McCAULEY was born in Philadelphia, Pa., and is a graduate of the public schools of that city. After teaching for a few years in that city she went on the stage, getting her early training as a member of the Girard Avenue Stock Company and for three years played continuously in resident and travelling stock companies.

In 1912 she won a five hundred dollar prize for a short story called *The Prairie* and her first book, *The Garden of Dreams* was brought out by A. C. McClurg & Co. of Chicago. Lately the stage, particularly in its Little Theatre and community activities, has claimed a great deal of her attention. She has directed pageants and festivals in Columbus and Des Moines, writing some of these herself, and is at present in charge of a class in Play Production in the extension work of Columbia University.

Mrs. McCauley has been director of The Morningside Players for the last two seasons. This is a group of Columbia University students interested in putting on original plays written by the students in the classes in playwriting. She has written and produced a number of one-act plays, among them *The Threshold, The Conflict, The Queen's Hour* and *A Return.*

THE CONFLICT

A PLAY IN ONE ACT

By CLARICE VALLETTE McCAULEY

"The Conflict" was originally presented by the Vagabond Players, Baltimore, December 6th, 1920.

Original Cast

EMELIE	Mrs. J. A. Dushane Penniman
BESS	{ Rose Kohler
. . . .	{ Harriet Gibbs
BOB	John Stuart
MOTHER	Mrs. S. Johnson Poe

Presented by May Standish Rose.

THE CONFLICT

SCENE. *The kitchen of an old-fashioned farmhouse.*

TIME. *Late afternoon of an April day.*

In the back wall, well to the right, is a door leading into the garden. Left of center a broad window curtained in crisp white muslin. In the right wall — down stage — a door leading to the living rooms at the front of the house. Just opposite — in the left wall — a door which when opened reveals a narrow flight of stairs which turns and disappears — evidently the back stairway leading to the rear bedrooms.

In the upper left-hand corner a built-in kitchen range with copper preserving kettle above it. In the upper right a small sink with pump attachment — a little oak-framed mirror over it — a roller towel on the wall beside it. Farther down, on the right, a cupboard filled with old-fashioned china — a nest of yellow bowls — a pan of apples. A drop-leaf table down right of center is covered with a pretty blue and white cloth — a cane-seated rocker on the right of it — on the left a straight chair to match. Between outer door and window is a little table with a workbasket on it — a clock hangs on the wall above it. Near the window a chair — on the sill potted geraniums in bloom. The window is open and through it you get a glimpse of a white lilac bush in flower. The square of sunshine on the floor is gradually cut off diagonally — as though by a slanting roof — till near the end it disappears entirely.[1]

---

[1] The room should suggest by every detail of its cheery, wholesome orderliness a certain sympathetic plea for the mother. Otherwise, if the home were unattractive, there would at once be furnished a reason for the children's wish to leave it; but there is no fundamental reason — other than the primordial urge to try our wings, which gets us all, sometime; and which no mother can successfully deny without forever crippling her child. In contrast to the crisp, clear-cut details of the kitchen is the vague, hazy sunshininess of the garden outside the door.

As the curtain rises Emelie is discovered seated at left of the center table, writing a letter. (On this table stands a small black traveling bag, and scattered around it gloves, purse, a few letters.)

Emelie is a tall girl of about twenty-three, not exactly beautiful, but with a certain nobility of purpose in her face that lends her distinction, and the lines of her slender figure in its solemn black are full of allurement. Her face quivers as she writes, and she stops a moment to wipe her eyes. There is the cheery, impudent call of a robin in the garden, and Bess enters from the living room.

Bess is a girl of seventeen. She is not in mourning like her sister, but her white skirt and middy blouse are set off by a black tie, and a black ribbon on her hair. She has emptied a vase of withered flowers on to a newspaper, and carries them carefully before her.

EMELIE (*looking up and referring to the flowers*). Gone — are they?

BESS. Yes — lilacs droop so soon. I cut these for you to take with you on the train.

EMELIE (*absentmindedly, looking at her letter*). I'm sorry, Puss —

BESS. I'm not; I'm, oh, so glad — you stayed! (*She has stopped back of the chair to give her sister a hug*) You can't think how much even two days more means to us. You're surely going this time?

EMELIE. Yes.

BESS (*going up towards window*). Then I'd better cut you some more. The white ones by the window — they're in bloom now — and they last longer, I think. Do you like them just as well?

EMELIE (*writing*). Just as well, dear.

BESS (*raising the lid of the range and emptying newspaper*). My! It's good I looked at this fire. It's almost gone. (*Reaches into wood-box and puts wood on fire as she speaks*) And Mother *told* Bob to tend to it, but of course he's out — as usual — dear knows where. (*There's the sound of a*

*rapidly passing train, and the sky above the window is dark-
ened — as is the square of sunlight on the floor. Bess looks
at the clock)* There goes the express now. I suppose
you'll take the 5:05?

EMELIE. Yes.

BESS. Well — You'll want supper before you go.

EMELIE. No, Bess, don't bother. I'm not hungry — I
can get tea on the train.

BESS *(coming down)*. Sister, you haven't changed your
mind?

EMELIE. No.

BESS. You're really going to New York?

EMELIE. Yes.

BESS. Does Mother know? *(Emelie nods)* But she doesn't
believe you'll do it?

EMELIE. I suppose not.

BESS. And when Mother sets her mind against anything
we want to do — you know how it is — even Father
always gave in to her — in the end. Don't you feel
afraid — she'll persuade you not to go?

EMELIE. I hate to vex her, dear, but — well — neither of
you quite understand. My whole future, my very life
depends on this. *(Under her breath)* More than my life,
perhaps.

BESS *(who has caught the last phrase, looks at her searchingly)*
Sister — *(Coming down back of the table)* you know that
talk — we — had — last night? After we had gone to
bed?

EMELIE. Yes — I kept you awake till all hours.

BESS. It was I kept you. Well — you know what you
said — about how, sometimes, when you wanted something that wasn't good for you and didn't feel very strong
— how it was awfully foolish to hang around in sight of it,
and how it was much, much wiser to *run away* from
temptation?

EMELIE. Yes.

BESS (*coming around and kneeling softly beside her*). Are you — running away — from temptation?

EMELIE. Little sister, dear little sister, what are you saying?

BESS (*with the frank persistence of a child*). Are you?

EMELIE (*frames the earnest face in her hands, and as she stoops to kiss her, whispers*). Sh — yes.

BESS. Oh, I was sure of it! Then that's why you're not going back to Boston. I knew it — I knew it — It's those letters!

[*Reaches towards them.*

EMELIE (*checking her*). Darling! You don't know what you're talking about. Those letters are from a very, very dear friend —

BESS (*convictingly*). In Boston!

EMELIE. Well, yes —

BESS. And they always make you cry — such funny tears!

EMELIE. They spoke of Father — of our loss, dear. If they made me cry it was because they were so full of tenderness — of sympathy —

BESS. You think so much of him, sister?

EMELIE. So much, dear. He's the best, the truest friend I ever had.

BESS (*puzzled*). Then why?

EMELIE. Don't, darling. I've no right — I don't dare — Oh, I can't explain —

BESS (*jealously*). Well — just the same — I'm glad you're going to New York instead. I wish I were. Is that really an honest-to-goodness contract — that long one?

[*Indicating envelope.*

EMELIE (*laughing and abandoning hope of writing for the time*). Not exactly. It's an offer, though — from one of the biggest magazines in New York — suggesting subjects for four of my kiddie pictures. If they like them — and they *shall* like them — they'll produce them in colors. And then — it's up to the public. If the public like them — if it laughs — and applauds — and clamors for more — why, then I can ask, oh, just anything I want for my work — in reason, of course — and they'll give it to me. That's the way of the world.

BESS. Isn't it splendid? And that's when you'll send for me?

EMELIE. Yes, dear — if Mother will let you —

BESS (*despairingly*). Oh, Mother —

EMELIE. Don't cross bridges, Honey. You know I must first be very sure that I can take care of you — before I talk to Mother.

BESS. You don't think I'll be too old, by then?

EMELIE. For music? You goosie, of course not! If you don't strain those sweet little vocal cords of yours, you'll be just right to begin. Pussy, run along now and cut the lilacs, won't you? — while I finish my letter. And send Bobs if you see him about. I want him to mail this for me.

BESS (*going*). I shouldn't wonder if that's where he's gone — to the postoffice. Shall I raise the shade?

EMELIE. Yes, dear; and leave the door open — the air's so good to-day.

BESS (*taking a large scissors from a hook near the door, wistfully*). I wish I was going to New York.

[*Goes out, leaving door open.*

Through the open door the sun falls in a tessellated square — as though through a trellis — across the threshold. Emelie resumes her letter-writing. Bess is seen through the window at the lilac bush. There is no sound for a moment but the twittering of birds and a little dry sob from the girl at the table. Then a boy's clear whistle is heard, to which Bess replies, and presently a boy's shadow falls across the threshold, and an instant later he is apparently joined by Bess, who has gone to meet him. By this time Emelie has sealed her letter and is addressing it.

EMELIE (*calling*). Bobbie!

BOB (*from outside*). All right, Sis! I'm coming. (*Entering*) Bess *said* you wanted me.

[*Bobbie is a boy of twelve or thirteen — perfectly clean but barefooted, and in the boyish dishabille of a fellow that lives*

*close to the ground.   There is no subtlety about Bobbie —
he's just plain Boy.*

EMELIE.   Yes, I — goodness, Bobs! Bare feet, so early in
spring! Won't you catch cold?

BOB.   Cold! Forget it! D'ye think I'm a girl? Say,
Em! You're sure some letter writer. Gettin' 'em and
sendin' 'em every mail — must keep you busy. Don't
you want a secr'tary?

EMELIE.   If I did, I wouldn't hire you — you fourth-grader,
you!

BOB (*good-naturedly*).   Gee, what a wallop! Don't I make
a pretty good fist at corresponding, though? Oh, well!
Who wants to write, anyway? I got no use for a pen;
but gimme a hammer an' saw an' some nails, an' I'll make
you own up that I can't be beat turnin' out chick'n-coops.
Ain't that right?

EMELIE (*laughing*).   It surely is; but good gracious, Bobs,
haven't you any ambition? Don't you ever think what
you want to be when you're a man?

BOB.   Sure I do! I'm goin' to stay right here and have the
best little chick'n-farm in the county. Nothin' but
Wy'ndottes an' Barr'd Rocks in mine! Well — mebbe
some Leghorns f'r the eggs.

EMELIE (*smilingly*).   Oh, well! In that case, it's all right, I
suppose. It's a good thing one of us wants to stick to the
old place. If it were only Jim, now — By the way,
Bobs, where *is* Jim? I haven't seen him all day.

BOB.   Off with the gang, I guess.

EMELIE.   Oh, dear! That isn't right. He ought to cut that
out! — that's how he got into all that trouble.

BOB.   *You* got it doped out wrong. Cutting it out's what
got him in Dutch!

EMELIE.   Bob! What do you mean? I don't understand.

BOB (*loftily*).   No, and nobody takes the trouble to understand a fellow around here.

EMELIE.   Robert! I don't think that's quite fair — not to
me!

BOB. Oh, well, it makes me sore. Jim's all right — even if he does get pretty bossy sometimes. And Jim never got a square deal in this mixup — never, from nobody. Seems to me any one could understand that you can't go out with fellers one day an' cut 'em out the next — just like that! (*He makes a little perpendicular chopping-off gesture with one hand*) But you know how Mother is! When she says cut it out — it means cut it out — *just like that!* Not to-morror', or th' next day — or lettin' 'em down easy — but *now!* Well, the night she said "No more of it!" the gang was meetin' at Dutch Heinie's for a game o' cards —

EMELIE. Oh, Bobbie!

BOB. Oh, well — they'd been meetin' all winter — nothin' to it! But somebody must've got wind of it — an' the whole crowd gets pinched! — an' of course, just 'cause Jim had cut it out so sudden and shame-faced like, they thought *he* was the squealer — and mebbe they didn't have trouble planted for *him* from that on. Say, he didn't any more break into Martin's show-case than I did.

EMELIE. Of course he didn't! My own brother! Don't I know that, Bobs?

BOB. Well, if you'd heard Mother questioning him — you'd 'a' thought he was a liar as well as a thief.

EMELIE. Sh — Bobbie! That's the unfortunate part of it. That's what he got for going with bad company.

BOB. Well — he sure had enough of 'em. When he got out didn't he just beg Mother to let him get away from here? He knows they're no good — but in a little place like this what's a fellow goin' to do? He wanted to go to Fall River; Uncle Zack'd 'a' got him a job there. But Mother said he was too young to be *breaking home ties.*

EMELIE. Oh, Bobbie — you don't understand, dear. Mother didn't want him away *then*, with Father sick.

BOB (*sullenly*). No, and she won't let him go *now*, with Father —

[*He stops, gulps, and turns away suddenly, brushing his eyes with his coat-sleeve.*

EMELIE (*going to him*). There, there, Bobbie — I know! It does seem as if everything was set against his getting a chance. But we will have to think hard — and stand together — and just be patient a little longer.

BOB. Well, I'll tell you something! It wouldn't surprise me none if he'd run away and enlist some day.

EMELIE. He can't! He's too young.

BOB. What's the matter with lying?

EMELIE. Bobby!

BOB. Oh, well, Jiminy Crickuts! If I wanted to get out of a place as bad as Jim does out 'a this one, my brain 'u'd get so cracked I'd forget my name — let alone my birthday. Where's Mother? Out?

EMELIE. I think she's taking a nap, dear — she went up to lie down. You know she's all worn out with nursing —

BOB (*nodding and speaking quickly*). Does she *take* it all right — your going?

EMELIE. Bobs, dear! I don't like to hear you speak of Mother that way.

BOB. Aw, gee!

EMELIE. Well, I don't! It sounds so disrespectful. And you love her.

BOB. Course I do — you know it!

EMELIE. Sure I know it. Why, just think! You are *her baby!*

BOB (*slyly*). Say, I don't get no chance to forget that neither.

EMELIE (*shaking him*). Bobbie, you're incorrigible.

BOB (*purposely as ungrammatical as he knows how to be*). I ain't never goin' to get no chance to grow up! I'm like that guy — what's his name? *Peter Pan!* That's me! Well, where's this letter you wanted me to mail?
[*Going to table.*

EMELIE. You haven't been to the postoffice?

BOB. No. (*Half sheepishly*) Mrs. Lane's. She promised to have something for me. (*Picks up letter*) Bosting,

eh? Well — Jumpin' *Jee*-hosaphat! What do you want
to mail this here for? Why don't you take it along?

EMELIE. I'm not going that way.

BOB. You ain't going by the 5.15 to Boston?

EMELIE. No, dear youth — I take the 5.05 to New York.

BOB (*whistles*). Mother know?

[*Enter Bess with lilacs. She stays up at door.*

EMELIE. Yes, *she — knows.*

BOB. Well, I'm off. (*To Bess*) Shall we show her what
I got?

[*Exits. Emelie looks up questioningly.*

BESS (*explaining Bob's last speech*). Some plants, Emelie.

EMELIE. Oh, for Father! (*Taking the lilacs from Bess*)
Thank you, dear — they're beautiful — and like you.
They'll go along to take care of me, Sweetheart.

[*Reënter Bob with a broad, shallow basket filled with pansy
plants.*

BOB. Pansies! Ain't they beauts? Mrs. Lane gave 'em
to me. It looks so rough up there — no sod, nor nothin'
growin'. Bess an' I were goin' to set 'em out this afternoon, but they can wait till morning. I won't have
more'n time to get to the postoffice and back before your
train goes. Well — you don't have far to go — that's
one comfort. Comes in sort o' handy, this havin' a private
railroad station at your back door, eh? Well — I'm off.

EMELIE. Wait, Bobbie. I don't want you to come back
here.

BOB. What! Not to say good-by?

EMELIE. I can't say good-by to you children that way. I
don't want either of you here when — they're going to be
so hard — these last few moments with Mother. Bess
will take the pansies and wait for you — you know the
little siding where the train almost stops? I'll wave
good-by to you there; and after the train's gone, why
you two can go to the cemetery together, and all the way
to New York I'll be seeing you setting out the pansies on
Father's grave.

BOB. Don't, Em! Funny how a feller misses him — though he hardly ever *said* much — Aw' Gee! (*Disgusted with himself for showing emotion*) Take care of yourself, Em. Write soon!

[*Rushes blindly off.*

The two girls stand a moment in each other's arms, then they break away with a guilty look at the clock.

BESS. Do you think she's sleeping?

EMELIE. No.

BESS. Then why —

EMELIE. Oh, it makes it so hard for me! It's her way, you know — Will you go up and tell her, dear, that I'm almost ready to go — and that there isn't much more time?

BESS (*crossing towards the door to the back stairway*). Yes. What did you do with your suitcase, Sister?

EMELIE. I sent it over early this afternoon. And Bess — I don't want to go up to the room again — you might just bring my hat and coat, dear — I have everything else.

[*Bess runs up the back stairway, leaving the door swing open behind her.*

Emelie gathers up her writing materials, dropping the letters into the little satchel. One of these she stops to reread; in the midst of it, with a little sob, and a gesture of renunciation, she tears up the letter and drops the pieces into the fire. Coming back she stops and picks a pansy which she slips into the book on the table before she drops that into the satchel, too.

Bess comes down the stairs carrying Emelie's hat and coat.

BESS. She'll be down in a minute. (*Then, in reply to the question in Emelie's face*) She was up — looking out of the window.

EMELIE. What did she say?

BESS. Only that she thought you'd given up going.

EMELIE (*sighs*). Good-by, dear.

BESS. You won't forget you're going to send for me?

EMELIE. I won't forget.

BESS (*taking up basket*). Bobs and I'll be at the siding.

EMELIE. And I'll be sure to lean out of the window and throw you kisses as far as I can see you.

BESS (*tremulously*). Good-by.

[*She goes out waving her hand and is seen passing the window.*

EMELIE. Good-by, little sister — and God keep you, darling — as you are.

(*She turns and sees Mother, who during the last speech has come down the stairway. She has taken down the kitchen apron that is hanging on nail inside of door, and is putting it on. There is a moment's embarrassed pause, then Emelie speaks*) Mother — I hated to disturb you; but I was beginning to be afraid you might not waken till the last minute.

MOTHER (*placidly*). I wasn't asleep. I thought you'd reconsidered going.

EMELIE. Mother — you make it *so hard* for me —

MOTHER. I mean to make it hard — very hard. (*She goes to the dresser and takes from it a large pan of apples, a knife and a bowl. Then she draws the cane-seated rocker to the left of the table and proceeds to peel the apples in long, thin, unbroken curls — possible only for the woman with a steady hand and no troublesome nerves*). For that matter, I've never said that staying right here was going to be the *easy* thing for you to do; but you can't get out of the fact that it's your duty, Emelie. (*The rocker stops a moment, as though its occupant expected a reply; then, as there is none, it continues its placid rhythmic swing, as the Mother resumes her argument*) You can't always have things the way you want them — and I don't think it would be good for you if you could. (*Emelie, who has come down behind the table, makes a sudden sharp movement as though to speak, then closes her lips firmly. She picks up one of her gloves, examines it mechanically for a moment — and then goes up stage to the work basket, and stands there finding needle and thread, etc., during next speeches. Meanwhile all the mother's attention appears to be centered on the careful coring and quartering of the apple in her hand. She leisurely selects another before continuing)* Now that you've got used to your freedom and your own way, it's asking a sacrifice of you — I realize that; but you'll have to make lots of them before you're as old as I am.

EMELIE *(with a sudden lift of her head, and in a tone crisp, clean-cut, that somehow shows the fight is on)* It's your idea of life, isn't it, Mother?

MOTHER. Making sacrifices?

EMELIE. Yes.

MOTHER. Well, it's a pretty big part of it — as you'll find out.

EMELIE. I'm a poor scholar.

MOTHER. When you don't like the lesson?

EMELIE. Yes. For nearly twenty years I've tried to learn it, but — I can't do it.

MOTHER. How you exaggerate, Emelie!

[There is nothing impetuous in the speech of these women — there is power — repose — reserve — at bottom both are very much alike.

EMELIE. Oh, no, I don't! Stop and think. I was three years old when Robert was born. I was expected to grow out of babyhood right then and there. And when he died — there was James to do for — and give in to. Do you remember what a naughty child I used to be? Poor little tempestuous mite — always being punished — hardly ever understanding what for —

MOTHER. Well, you *did* have a bad temper.

EMELIE. And, of course, *that had* to be sacrificed! *(At the little exclamation of surprise from her mother she continues hastily)* Oh, I know that must sound absurd to you, because you don't — perhaps you can't see it as I do; but all the *little things* you didn't like about me — had to be lopped off, even if I was as surely maimed thereby as though you had cut off my arms and legs. Dear Mother! I know you meant everything for the best — always! You were determined I should be unselfish — well-

disciplined — and self-controlled — cut out and fashioned
by a pattern on your nail; weren't you?

[*She has come down right of table during this speech, and on
the last two words, to soften the unfilial tone of it, reaches out
and just touches her mother's hand.*

MOTHER (*not hurt at all by the criticism — and equally un-
touched by the caress*).   Do you think you're any the worse
for it?

EMELIE.   Who knows?

MOTHER.   I don't think I understand you, Emelie.   Just
what do you mean to complain of?

EMELIE.   I don't mean to complain of anything, dear.   You
loved us all devotedly — no one could have been a better
mother — if only — (*she hesitates, then finishes whimsically*)
If only you could have individualized us a bit, dear, instead
of lumping us all together as just "*your children.*"

MOTHER (*her hands idle for a moment, she revolves what seemed
to her an absurd arraignment; then, surrendering to the
apparent need for justification*).   I suppose you will admit,
Emelie, that you were a very jealous child?

EMELIE.   Oh, undoubtedly!   Frightfully so!   Did you
think you had cured me, Mother?

MOTHER.   I tried —

EMELIE.   On the contrary, you fed the flame — don't you
see?   You *exercised* the unlovely thing till it grew strong.
I learnt jealousy as a fine art at the mature age of seven.
It frightens me to think how I used to feel — how I could
feel now if any — (*she catches herself up and finishes rather
lamely — as she goes back to the sewing table*) any one gave
me cause.

MOTHER (*looking back after her a moment — then down at
her work*).   Emelie!   You've never told us — me — much
about your friends.

EMELIE.   No?   (*She lingers a bit unnecessarily over the smooth-
ing out of the gloves, but finally places them beside her hat
and coat and comes slowly down to her mother's side*)   What
is it you would like to know, Mother?

MOTHER. Something about the way you're living now — the people who have helped you in your work. That girl you roomed with first — for instance; what's become of her?

EMELIE. I don't know. I never see her any more.

MOTHER. Why not?

EMELIE. Mother! Let's not go into that. It's a long story — and it would have no bearing on the subject we are discussing.

MOTHER (*mildly*). I thought that was settled.

EMELIE (*her eyes flashing ominously, but her voice quiet*). Did you? You thought that all my life to come was to be narrowed within the limits of your "NO"; that I'd give up my plan to go to New York, forego all the splendid opportunities this year is holding out to me, just because you believe my duty is here. And after all, is that your real reason, Mother? Isn't it rather that you're afraid — that you distrust your child — and your teaching? If not, why is it that you seem to resent each problem that I dare to solve for myself, each step I take unaided, each fresh proof that I'm no longer a child at your apron-strings?

MOTHER. Emelie!

EMELIE. Yes, Mother, I beg your pardon. I know I'm going to hate myself presently for talking to you like this — but can't you see that I've got to fight you? All my life with you has been a fight — a fight to keep true to myself — a constant conflict of wills — ideals and principles that clash and clash — it's terrible — terrible! Can't you see —

[*She stops to get hold of herself.*

MOTHER. Can't I see what, Emelie?

EMELIE (*more gently*). Can't you see that you cannot hope to *always* have the ordering of your children's lives? We grow up; it is the way of children, Mother. We have adult responsibilities — problems of our own which we have a right to face ourselves; and to each one of our battles we bring all that we have inherited from our parents — and all the teaching we've got at their hands — but something of our own besides. And, Mother — (*she kneels beside her*) that something is the God within us! Forever to do violence to that something is to kill the individual. Can't you — can't you try to understand before it's too late? Jim — Bess — Bobs, even, will have his future some day to decide for himself.

MOTHER. That's just why you're needed at home; you're the eldest. You always were more like a boy than a girl — Jim'll listen to you.

EMELIE. It took me a long time, Mother, to realize how exacting your love was. Do you remember how you opposed the idea of my studying in Boston? Why, if I had not gotten that first scholarship at the art school, I'd never have had my chance at all — and *then* I had to go with the bitter thought of your displeasure at my heart like a stone all summer long.

MOTHER (*rather proudly*). You had it in you! You'd have gotten there just the same — no matter where you studied — *if a little later*, perhaps.

EMELIE. Yes, but that's *such* a tragedy! The joy of battle and achievement belongs to youth! *I want it now! Not when I'm forty.* And you know that if I hadn't made good — right from the very start — I should have had to come home. Not because my people couldn't afford it — that I would have understood — but just because Fate — in your own person — said "No!" Talk about signs from heaven! I fairly worshiped those first checks. Why, fifty dollars was a fortune that meant room-rent for a month — yes, and food, too. It took so little to live in a hall bedroom with the aid of a twenty-five-cent gas-stove and the delicatessen around the corner.

MOTHER (*dryly*). No wonder you've ruined your digestion.

EMELIE. Digestion depends upon the frame of mind, Mother. Mine was better in the hall bedroom than it has been here in my father's house, bottling up my sorrow and fighting your displeasure.

[*The girl's lips quiver pitifully. The Mother rises, and, on her way back to the sink with the apples, she stops with a half-clumsy caress and says gently*

MOTHER. You're a good girl, Emelie, lots of ways. You mustn't think I'm always finding fault with you. It's strange how you've taken your father's death harder than any of the other children — though you were away from home so much — and never his favorite.

EMELIE. I guess there's no grief quite so bitter as the loss of some one we have loved imperfectly. Oh, it's all so irrevocable — and it's such a pity. Father — working, slaving all his life for us — unrecompensed, unappreciated.

MOTHER. Why, Emelie! I think we all did our duty by Father.

EMELIE. Duty? Oh, yes. Duty — weighed — measured; so much politeness, so much service, so much tolerance of individual likings — with a sort of affection, too, of course. We all loved Father — Oh, as a father, all very much according to the letter of the law — but did any of us ever try to understand him — as an individual, like ourselves? And now it's too late! Oh, Mother dear, I do wish *we* could understand each other a little better before I go.

MOTHER (*in the act of crossing to the range with the saucepan of apples*). But I thought you'd come to see it my way — about going.

EMELIE (*with a little wail of hopeless desperation in her voice*). Yes, yes, I know you did! And the pity of it is that you'll keep on thinking so till the whistle blows. We talk round and round in a circle — and my train will be here in fifteen minutes. Couldn't you just give in once — kiss me good-by and wish me success? It takes lots of strength to travel the hard lonely road in a strange city.

MOTHER (*she is through with her work. NOW they will have it out. She turns her back definitely upon the range, and for the first time speaks directly to the girl. All through the preceding scene she has made you feel that Emelie and her problem must take second place to this dish of apple-sauce — the duty of the moment).* That's another thing I don't understand. You might as well be frank with me, Emelie. I've never liked secrecy — and you're mighty close about your affairs. You were perfectly content with Boston when you came here a month ago. What's changed you — why this sudden notion for going to New York, instead?

EMELIE (*half-heartedly*). We'll all need more money now that Father's gone — and Jim's not making much yet. I think I can earn more in New York.

MOTHER. And spend more, too. A year ago you were delighted with your place.

EMELIE. That was a year ago. Now, the drawing of insipid faces and faultless figures in absurd gowns seems intolerable — because I've grown and my work has grown. Fashion-work was just a means to keep me in food and lodging while I studied.

MOTHER. Suppose you don't get anything to do — what then?

EMELIE. I'm pretty sure to fall into something. If I fail, there's always the fashion-work to fall back on. But I have offers — good ones.

MOTHER. Who from?

EMELIE. Friends who have faith in me.

MOTHER. That's another thing I don't like. You never *talk* about your friends. 'Tain't natural — unless you're ashamed of them.

EMELIE. Mother!

MOTHER. I don't care — it doesn't look right. You've had letters and sent some every day — even the day of the funeral — but I notice how careful you were not to let them lie around none.

EMELIE (*looks nervously around the room — her eyes light on the clock*). Mother, we're wasting time. You've known all along that I couldn't stay on here indefinitely.

MOTHER. I can't see why not. *Why is one place any better*

than another to make pictures in? The boys are away all day. You needn't be afraid I'd expect much housework of you.

EMELIE (*looks at her mother in silence for a moment. There grows in her face a determination to force the issue, yet she reads the unspoken trouble at her mother's heart and her sense of justice counsels her to be very patient under the probe*). Mother, suppose we quit fencing like this — get down to facts. Just why are you so determined to keep me here?

MOTHER. I *don't* trust you, Emelie, and that's the truth. You are changed somehow. You're older and more world-wise — and nervous — and there's something going on that you don't tell me. You never were one to talk much, but you don't give me your confidence at all, now.

EMELIE. And you think you can force it? Have I ever given you any real cause for not trusting me?

MOTHER (*reluctantly*). Not as I know of.

EMELIE. Am I necessarily guilty of something unless I continually prove myself innocent?

MOTHER. I don't like it. You're not frank with me.

EMELIE. I'm all right, Mother. Oh, why should I worry *you* with my problems? I can't do it — though I love you, dear. (*She flings her arms impulsively around her mother's neck; but the whole unyielding figure is so prohibitive, so keenly censorious, that the next moment her hands fall limply to her side*) Well — what is it you want to know, Mother?

MOTHER (*grasping at the permission, without noticing what she pays for it*). This man you've been getting letters from — who is he?

EMELIE. A gentleman I met through my work, Mother. He's been very good to me — in a business way —

MOTHER. Yes, but it don't look like *just business* to be writing letters back and forth every day —

EMELIE. Then it would be safe to conclude that there was more than *just business* between us.

MOTHER. What's his name?

EMELIE (*flinching*). Is that necessary?

MOTHER. Are you ashamed of him?

EMELIE. No.

MOTHER (*after a dissatisfied pause*). What's he do?

EMELIE. He's — he's on a magazine, Mother — what they call "Managing Editor."

MOTHER. That how you came to meet him?

EMELIE. Yes. I illustrated some articles for him.

MOTHER (*not looking at her*). Known him long — do you see much of him?

EMELIE. About a year. Yes, I see quite a great deal of him.

[*The girl's steady eyes have never wavered from her mother's face. There is a cold, bitter little smile about her lips. She could quicker understand a storm of passionate, anxious scolding than this inquisitorial skirmishing that keeps getting closer and closer to the vital question, but that dreads to ask it.*

MOTHER. I suppose he takes you out — sometimes?

EMELIE. Frequently.

MOTHER. You go — alone — with him?

EMELIE. Usually.

MOTHER. Of course — he's single?

EMELIE. No.

MOTHER. What!

EMELIE (*stiffening against the table — her nervous hands fingering the edge of the cloth, her coat, her gloves*). He's married. I don't think I am hurting his wife. She does not care.

MOTHER (*indignantly*). How do *you* know?

EMELIE. They have not lived together for years; she's abroad most of the time.

MOTHER (*speaking the word as though it were sacrilege*). Divorced?

EMELIE. No — there's a child — a girl, just reaching womanhood. For her sake — well, they've never just happened to —

MOTHER. And you run around with him like this — *you?*
I want to know — he says he loves you?

EMELIE (*laughing shortly*). Yes.

MOTHER. And you?

EMELIE. I love him — yes.

[*The last speeches have been spoken almost flippantly. Her
attitude, during the earlier part of the scene, has been that of a
child whistling in the dark. Now that her secret has been
dragged boldly, nakedly into the daylight her attitude becomes
one of impregnable, hurt defiance. In her anxiety the
mother is blind.*

MOTHER. I can't grasp it! I've felt there was something
like this in the wind all along — yet I couldn't believe it
of you, Emelie. Mind you, I'm not saying you've done
anything really bad —

EMELIE. Thank you.

[*There is a flash of gratitude in her face but it fades into
bitterness as her mother quite unconsciously spoils it.*

MOTHER. *You've had too good training for that* — but I didn't
think you'd cheapen yourself so. How can you believe
this man —

EMELIE. Because belief is the very life of love — something
you've never learnt, Mother. You kill love by doubting
it.

MOTHER. Can't very well believe in a married man who
makes love —

EMELIE. Mother! Might I suggest that you do not know
either the man or the circumstances?

MOTHER (*very emphatically*). There aren't any circumstances
that can make wrong right.

EMELIE. Oh! (*Pause*) Very well. Then, since you've
judged me, what do you propose to do?

MOTHER. I am trying to think. You want to go to New
York. Why?

EMELIE. I told you —

MOTHER. You didn't! You told me a lot of nonsense.
You never gave me the real reason.

EMELIE. Which is —

MOTHER. This man! He lives in New York — or he's going to live there. Ain't that why you want to go?
[The girl looks at her mother incredulously — her whole attitude one of helpless aloofness. It is as though she looked across an ever-widening gulf at the dead.

EMELIE *(with a gesture of hopelessness).* Well —

MOTHER. Do you think I can't put two and two together? Those big envelopes you got from New York yesterday and again to-day — and you walking about like one in a dream! He's on a magazine you say — and look at *you* — so sure of getting work in a strange city. Well, why don't you speak? Isn't it so?

EMELIE. What's the use of speaking? You can't expect to extract truth with a probe — and get it out undamaged. You have chosen to put your own construction on appearances — go on! I'm anxious to see what you're going to make of it. *Just what you will do to my life.*
[The train is heard whistling in the distance.

MOTHER. You shall not go to New York to-night.

EMELIE. No? Well, that looks exceedingly probable. I should have to run now to catch the train. Yet I could make it! Quick, Mother! I know all that's worrying you. But of what good was your training if you can't trust me? I've made my choice — I want to abide by it. Just say that I may.

MOTHER. You see! Why are you so set on going by this very train if it isn't an appointment? If you are so determined on leaving home to-night it will have to be for Boston. You're playing on the brink of a precipice — — and you don't know it!

EMELIE. Take care, Mother, that you don't push me over —

MOTHER. Oh, yes — I know you're stubborn — but after all, you're my child! Maybe when you've had a night to think —
[The unwonted stimulus of opposition has aroused the mother quite out of her quiet calm. All the majesty of outraged

*motherhood is in her bearing as she sweeps to the outer door
and locks it. After the first little cry of "Mother, don't do
that!" the girl makes no protest. Listlessly she goes to the
sink; as in a dream she washes her hands and dries them
on the roller-towel, and at the little mirror studies her face
curiously while she fastens on her hat. While she is doing
this the smoke of the New York train darkens the window.
The girl parts the curtains and stands watching. You hear
the grinding of brakes, the hissing of escaping air, the momentary portentous silence, the clang of the bell, the exhaust —
and then the throbbing of the departing south-bound train.
The girl slips into her coat and picks up her bag as the mother
moves stolidly over to the door and throws it open. Once more
a shaft of sunlight — a long, pale one this time — falls across
the threshold, and the birds break out into a joyous twittering.
The girl joins her mother in the doorway, and for a moment
they stand there in silence, so incongruously out of it all —
all that the spring would tell them if they could but hear.*

EMELIE. Well, Mother — good-by.

MOTHER. I suppose you'll have to go, now. You wouldn't
care to stay till morning?

EMELIE. Hardly.

MOTHER (*flustered by the girl's steady eyes, takes refuge in a
commonplace*). I'd 'a' thought you'd have more pride,
Emelie. I had when I was your age. You'll write?

EMELIE. I don't know — it depends.

MOTHER. On what?

EMELIE. I can't see the outcome of this, Mother. But
whatever happens I want you to feel that I'll not hold you
responsible for *my* decisions.

MOTHER. Emelie!

EMELIE. Funny! You believe in predestination — don't
you, Mother? I never did — before. I never could see
Fate as a cat playing with a mouse — I never believed
that God played with us in wanton sport, but what's the
difference if He lets His creatures do it for Him?

MOTHER. You mustn't talk like that — I don't understand.

EMELIE. I hope you never will.

MOTHER (*drawing her quickly to her in alarm*). Emelie!

EMELIE. Oh, don't! *Please* don't! (*In a sudden burst of anger she tears herself brusquely out of her mother's arms*) You've faith in no one but yourself! Well, you can sleep to-night very sure of how beautifully you've managed every one's life. (*Train whistles*) Let me go! I don't want to miss my train.

[*Emelie goes quickly out of the door and down the walk without a backward look.*

MOTHER (*making a movement after her*). Emelie! What a way for a girl to speak to her mother! (*Muttering to herself*) Well, she needn't feel so bitter about it. I'm sure I did it all for her own good. But that's the way with children. (*Coming down*) They never understand — till it's too late. She's forgot her flowers. Well, it's too late for them, too. I wonder what she meant by —

[*Bess is heard calling from right "Emelie! Oh, Emelie! Where are you?" She runs excitedly in at the door down right, and takes in her mother's appearance with an evident start of dismay. Train is heard stopping.*

BESS. Why, Mother! Where's Emelie? Didn't she go? We waited for her at the siding. I'm sure she wasn't on the train, for it stopped an awful long time there. We ran all the way back. I came cross-lots and through the front because Bob got a —

BOB (*who has run around the house is seen passing window and runs in at kitchen door*). Didn't she go?

[*Train is heard going rapidly in distance.*

MOTHER (*after a pause*). Yes — she went.

BESS. To New York?

MOTHER. No — to Boston.

BESS. Oh! I wonder what made her change her mind.

BOB. Shucks! And I found this telegram for her at the postoffice, too! That chump of a green kid of Sweeny's put it in our mail box.

MOTHER. A telegram?

BOB. Yes; do you suppose it's anything important?

MOTHER. Give it to me. I'll see. (*She opens it — reads — looks stunned. Still clutching the envelope, in a dazed sort of way she drops the telegram, and crosses unsteadily towards the door, left*) Emelie! My girl! Oh, why didn't you tell me? Why didn't you tell me? (*She goes heavily, brokenly up the stairs, muttering*) I — I didn't understand her — she said — Oh, my God — my God! What have I done?

BOB. Why, whatever's the matter with Mother? What's in the thing, anyway? (*Picks up telegram*) That's funny — I don't see anything in this —

BESS (*faintly*). What's — it say, Bobs?

BOB. Why, all it says is — "You can't mean to go out of my life like this. Think how I need you. I shall be waiting at South Station for you to-night, with what anxiety you can imagine. Don't fail me. Devotedly, Craig." Who's Craig? Do you know? Well, anyway, it's from Boston. I don't see anything the matter with that. She'll meet him O K since she got that train. (*Goes to stairway*) Oh, Mother! It's all right! That telegram was from Boston, you know. (*Waits a moment; then starts up the stairs*) Say, Mother! What's the matter? Ain't you goin' to have any supper?

BESS (*staring down at the forgotten flowers, and speaking a lou frightened voice*). She — didn't take — my lilacs.

CURTAIN

THE LAMP AND THE BELL

EDNA ST. VINCENT MILLAY

EDNA ST. VINCENT MILLAY was born February 22, 1892, at Rockland, Maine. After a childhood spent almost entirely in New England, she attended Vassar College, graduating in 1917. Since that time she has lived in New York City.

Miss Millay's chief fame is as a poet. Her play "Aria da Capo," produced by the Provincetown Players, is probably one of the finest short plays written by an American. The "Lamp and the Bell" (included in this volume) and the one-act pieces "The Princess Marries the Page" and "Two Slatterns and a King" constitute her contributions to the theatre.

THE LAMP AND THE BELL

A DRAMA IN FIVE ACTS

By EDNA ST. VINCENT MILLAY

Written on the occasion of the Fiftieth Anniversary of the Founding of the Vassar College Alumnae Association.

Dedicated to "1917"

Original Cast

LORENZO, King of Fiori . .	.Julia Lovejoy Cuniberti '11
MARIO, King of Lagoverde .	.Valeria Knapp '20
GUIDO, Duke of Versilia, illegitimate nephew to Lorenzo	.Louisa Brook Jones '07

GIOVANNI		. . .	.Katherine Jones '20
LUIGI	Gentlemen		.Muriel Izard '17
ANSELMO	at the court		.Lucia Cole Waram '01
RAFFAELE	of Lorenzo .		.Eleanor Kissam '20

FIDELIO, Jester at the court of
   Lorenzo . . . . . . .Geneva Harrison '20

GIUSEPPE, Agent for the Duke's
   estates . . . . . . .Eleanor Fatman Morgen-
                     thau '13

CESCO	Townsmen .	.Gertrude Taylor Watkins '07
HORATIO	of Fiori . .	.Lucille Stimson Harvey '09

BEPPO, a little boy, son to
   GIULIANA . . . . . .Marcelle Furman New-
                     burg '19

RIGO, little boy, son to Leonora .Ruth Delepenha '17

CLERK . . . . .Lucy Madeira Wing '96

MESSENGER . . . . . . .Esther Saville Davis '06

OCTAVIA, Lorenzo's second Wife .Montgomery Cooper '09

BEATRICE, "Rose-Red,"
   Daughter to Lorenzo by a
   former marriage . . . .Clifford Sellars '21

BIANCA, "Snow-White,"
   Daughter to Octavia by a
   former marriage . . . .Lois Duffie '20

LAURA		.Frances Stout Kellman '17
CARLOTTA		.Kathleen Millay Young ex-'21
FRANCESCA		.Dorothy Comstock '19
VIOLA	Ladies at	.Lillian White '18
LILINA	the court of	.Caroline Goodrich '16
LELA	Lorenzo	.Sylvia Brockway '20
ARIANNA		.Margaret Hughes '18
CLAUDIA		.Janet Lane '18
CLARA		.Jeanette Baker '18
LUCIA		.Ellen Hasbrouck '15

GRAZIA, Nurse to Beatrice and
    Bianca . . . . . . .Eleanor Ray Broeniman '99

GIULIETTA, Servant to Bianca .Virginia Archibold '17

"LITTLE SNOW-WHITE" . . .Gretchen Tonks

"LITTLE ROSE-RED" . . . .Joy Macracken '36

LEONORA		.Catherine Barr '20
GIULIANA		.Mabel Hastings Humpstone '94
CLARA	Women	.Olive Remington '19
GIOVANITTA	of Fiori	.Caroline Curtis Johnson '83
ANNA		.Frances Haldeman Sidwell '84
EUGENIA		.Helen Hoy Greeley '99

ELEANORA ⎱ little girls, daughters
LUISA   ⎰ to Leonora

GILDA, a little girl, sister to
    Beppo . . . . . . .Ruth Benedict '20

ADELINA, another little girl . .Maiserie MacCracken '31

NURSE . . . . .Edith Ward

PIERROT	
HARLEQUIN	
PANTALOON	Strolling
POLICHINELLO	players
COLOMBINE	

Courtiers, Ladies-in-waiting, Soldiers, Pages, Musicians,
Towns-people, Children

THE LAMP AND THE BELL

PROLOGUE

[Anselmo and Luigi]

ANSELMO. What think you, — lies there any truth in the tale
The King will wed again?

LUIGI. Why not, Anselmo?
A king is no less lonely than a collier
When his wife dies. And his young daughter there,
For all her being a princess, is no less
A motherless child, and cries herself to sleep
Night after night, as noisily as any,
You may be sure.

ANSELMO. A motherless child loves not,
They say, the second mother. Though the King
May find him comfort in another face, —
As it is well he should — the child, I fancy,
Is not so lonely as she is distraught
With grief for the dead Queen, and will not lightly
Be parted from her tears.

LUIGI. If tales be true,
The woman hath a daughter, near the age
Of his, will be a playmate for the Princess.

CURTAIN

ACT I

SCENE 1

A garden of the palace at Fiori; four years later.
Discovered seated Laura, Francesca and Fidelio, Laura embroidering, Fidelio strumming his flute, Francesca lost in thought.

LAURA. You — Fool! If there be two chords to your lute,
Give us the other for a time!

FRANCESCA. And yet, Laura,
　I somewhat fancied that soft sound he made.
　'Twas all on the same tone, — but 'twas a sweet tone.
LAURA. 'Tis like you. As for myself, let music change
　From time to time, or have done altogether
　Sing us the song, Fidelio, that you made
　Last night, — a song of flowers, and fair skies,
　And nightingales, and love.
FIDELIO. I know the song.
　It is a song of winter.
LAURA. How is that?
FIDELIO. Because it is a song of summer set
　To a sad tune.
FRANCESCA (sadly). Ah, well, — so that it be not
　A song of autumn, I can bear to hear it.
LAURA. In any case, music. I am in a mood for music.
　I am in a mood where if something be not done
　To startle me, I shall confess my sins.
　[Enter Carlotta.
CARLOTTA. Ha! I will have that woman yet by the hair!
LAURA. What woman, pray, Carlotta?
CARLOTTA. Ho! What woman!
　Who but that scullery-wench, that onion-monger,
　That slatternly, pale bakeress, that foul witch,
　That coroneted Fishwife of Fiori,
　Her Majesty, the Queen!
FRANCESCA. Hush — hush — Carlotta!
　You could be put to death for less than that!
CARLOTTA. Not I, my duck. When I am put to death
　'Twill be for more! Oh, I will have her yet
　By the hair! (For the first time noticing Fidelio)
　　　　　Fidelio, if you breathe one word
　Of this, I will scratch the Princess into ribbons,
　Whom you love better than your wit.
FIDELIO. I' faith,
　I did but hear you say you are a fishwife,
　And all the world knows that.

LAURA. Fear not, Carlotta,
He is as dumb as a prophet. Every second word
He utters, eats the one before it. Speak,
But softly.

CARLOTTA. Nay, 'tis nothing. — Nay, by my head,
It is a townful! 'Tis the way she has
Of saying "That should be done like this, and this
Like that"! The woman stirs me to that point
I feel like a carrot in a stew, — I boil so
I bump the kettle on all sides!

LAURA. My dear,
Were you as plump as I you would not dare
Become so angry. It would make your stays creak.

CARLOTTA. Well, I am done. Fidelio, play me a dirge
To put me in good spirits. Merry music
Is sure to make me sad.

(Fidelio plays. Pause).

'Tis curious
A woman like her should have a child like that —
So gentle and so pretty-mannered. Faith, —

FIDELIO. Hush! Hush! Here come the prettiest pair of
birds
That ever sat together on a bough so close
You could not see the sky between. How now,
Snow-White and Rose-Red! Are you reconciled
One to another?

[Enter Beatrice and Bianca, with their arms about each other.

BIANCA. Reconciled, Fidelio?
We had not quarreled!

[Laughter from Fidelio and the ladies.

BEATRICE. Do not listen to him,
Bianca, 'tis but the jingling of his bells.
Fidelio, Do you make a better jest than that
At once, or have the clappers cut from them.

FIDELIO. Alas, alas, — all the good jests are made.
I made them yesterday.

CARLOTTA. If that be true,
You would best become a wise man for a time,
My friend, — there are plenty of wise words not yet
said!

FIDELIO. I shall say them all to-morrow.

LAURA. If you do,
You will be stoned to death.

FIDELIO. Not I. No one
Will hear me. — Well, I am off. — I know an old man
Who does not know the road runs past his house;
And yet his bees make honey.

[*Exit Fidelio.*

CARLOTTA (*looking after him*). 'Tis the one wise fool
We have among us.

[*Enter Grazia.*

GRAZIA. Oh, here you are, my ducklings!
Always together, like a beggar and a flea!
I looked for you at dinner-time; I forget now
What for; but then 'twas a matter of more weight
Than laying siege to a city, — la, how time
Does carry one on! An hour is like an ocean,
The way it separates you from yourself! —
(*To Bianca and Beatrice*) What do you find to talk about
all day?

BEATRICE. We do not talk all day.

CARLOTTA. Nay, 'tis you, Grazia,
That talk all day.

BEATRICE. We ride, and play at tennis.

BIANCA. 'Tis you that ride, Beatrice. I but on a heaving
hill, and strive my best to stick there.

GRAZIA. I' faith, I have seen you going forth,—you sidewise
aslant your pretty palfrey; and Her Highness, as God's
my judge, astride the devil himself.

BEATRICE. What, Cupid? — La, he's gentle as a kitten!
Though he's a little young, 'tis true, not settled yet
In his mind.

LAURA.   As to his mind, 'twere a small matter,
Were he a bit more settled in his legs!

GRAZIA.   What did I come here for? — I must go back
To where I started, and think of it again!
[*Exit Grazia.*

CARLOTTA (*calling after her*).   Are you sure that you remember where you started?
— — The woman hath a head like a sieve.

LAURA.   And yet,
You may be sure 'tis nothing more than the thimble
Of the matter she's forgotten.   I never knew her
Mislay the thread or the needle of a thing.

BIANCA.   We must study now, Beatrice, we indeed must.
We have not opened a book since yesterday.

LAURA.   La, as for me, I have not opened a book
Since yesteryear, — I'd liefer open a vein!

CARLOTTA.   Lessons, — troth, I remember well those lessons.
As for what I learned, — troth, that's a different matter.

FRANCESCA.   'Tis curious; the things that one remembers
Are foolish things.   One does not know at all
Why one remembers them.   There was a blackbird
With a broken foot somebody found and tamed
And named Euripides! — I can see it now.

CARLOTTA.   Some of the silly rhymes we used to write
In the margins of our books, I still remember!

LAURA.   And eating sweets behind the covers of them!

FRANCESCA.   And faces — faces — faces — and a little game
We used to play, all marching in a row
And singing! — I wish I were a child again.

BEATRICE.   You are not old, Francesca.   You are very young.
And very beautiful!

FRANCESCA.   I have been beautiful
Too many years to be so very young.

CARLOTTA.   How now, Francesca!   Would you have it said
You are enamoured of some beardless youth,
That so you see the wrinkles suddenly?
Have done!   Have done!

BIANCA.　　　　　　　　　Where shall we study, Bice?

BEATRICE.　Indoors.　I cannot study out of doors.

[*Exeunt Beatrice and Bianca.*

LAURA.　I vow I never knew a pair of lovers
More constant than those two.

CARLOTTA.　　　　　　　　A pair of lovers?
Marry, I find your figure lacking force!
Since when were lovers true?

FRANCESCA.　　　　　　　　Oh, peace, Carlotta!
You bear too sharp a weapon against the world, —
A split tongue full of poison, in a head
That darts at every heel! — I'm going in.

[*Exit Francesca.*

LAURA.　You should not say such things when she is with us,
Carlotta.

CARLOTTA.　Is the woman in love?

LAURA.　　　　　　　　　　In love!
She is so far gone she does not know which way
To sail, — all shores are equally out of sight.

[*Exeunt Laura and Carlotta.*
Music off stage.　Enter Fidelio, singing.

FIDELIO.　"What was I doing when the moon stood above?
What did I do?　What did I do?
I lied to a lady that had given me her love, —
I swore to be true!　I swore to be true!"

(*He picks up from the grass a white scarf which Beatrice was
wearing, and which slipped from her shoulders unnoticed as
she went out*)

My mistress!

(*He thrusts the scarf under his cloak and continues his song,
just as Guido enters from another direction*)

"And what was I doing when the sun stood above?　What
did I do?　What did I do? —"

GUIDO.　　　　　　　　By my sacred word, Fidelio,
I do not like your song.

FIDELIO.   Faith, and small wonder! —
   It is a song that sets the evil eye
   To staring in upon itself.

GUIDO (*stopping in his walk*).   What mean you
   By that, my throaty friend?

FIDELIO.   I mean to say
   That, taking it all in all and by and large,
   You have no ear for music.

GUIDO.   I have no ear
   For yours, but it is possible Apollo
   Had a better tenor.   I never heard him sing.

FIDELIO.   Nay, and how could you? — He died when you
      were born!

GUIDO.   He died, that is, in giving birth to me?

FIDELIO.   Aye, if you like, — you bear as much resemblance
   To him as to your mother's husband, surely.

GUIDO.   Take care, Fidelio!

FIDELIO (*lightly*).   So!   Then it angers you
   Apollo should be deemed your sire!   I told you (*sadly*)
   You have no ear for music!

GUIDO.   You are a sly fool,
   My merry friend.   What hide you under the cloak?

FIDELIO.   Why, 'tis a little patch of snow the sun
   Would lay too hot a hand on.

GUIDO.   By my life, —
   And what are you that you can keep the sun
   From shining where it will?

FIDELIO.   Why, by your life, —
   And a foul oath it is! — why, by your life,
   I am a cloud, — that is an easy riddle.

SCENE 2

*A garden with a fountain, at Fiori.   Beatrice and Bianca
sitting side by side on a low step.   Evening.*

BEATRICE.   How beautiful it is to sit like this,
   Snow-White. — to think so much, and to say little.

BIANCA.　Ay, it is beautiful.　I shall remember
All my life long these evenings that we spent
Sitting just here, thinking together.　(*Pause*)　Rose-Red,
It is four years to-day since first we met.
Did you know that?

BEATRICE.　　　　　Nay, is it?

BIANCA.　　　　　　　Four years to-day.
I liked you from the moment that I saw you,
Beatrice!

BEATRICE.　I you, Bianca.　From the very moment!
I thought you were the prettiest little girl
That I had ever seen.

BIANCA.　　　　　I was afraid
Of you, a little, at first, — you were a Princess,
You see.　But you explained that being a Princess
Was much the same as anything else.　'Twas nice,
You said, when people were nice, and when they were not
　nice
'Twas hateful, just the same as everything else.
And then I saw your dolls, and they had noses
All scratched, and wigs all matted, just like mine,
Which reassured me even more! — I still, though,
Think of you as a Princess;　the way you do things
Is much more wonderful than the way I do them! —
The way you speak to the servants, even the way
You pick up something that you drop.

BEATRICE.　　　　　　You goose!
'Tis not because I'm a princess you feel that way —
I've always thought the same thing about you! —
The way you draw your gloves on is to me
More marvelous than the way the sun comes up!

(*They both burst out laughing*)

Oh, lud, — how droll we are!

BIANCA.　　　　　Oh, I shall die
Of laughing!　Think you any one else, Rose-Red,
Was ever half so silly?

BEATRICE. I dare wager
There be a thousand, in this realm alone,
Some even sillier!

BIANCA. Here comes Fidelio!

[*Enter Fidelio.*

BEATRICE. Fidelio, sing to us, — there is no nightingale
Abroad to-night, save you. And the night cries
For music!

BIANCA. Sing, Fidelio!

FIDELIO. I have no thorn
To lean my breast on. I've been happy all day,
And happiness ever made a crow of me.

BEATRICE. Sing, none the less, — unless you have a cold,
Which is a singer's only rock of refuge.
You have no cold, or you would not be happy.
So sing.

FIDELIO (*singing*). "Oh, little rose-tree, bloom!
Summer is nearly over.
    The dahlias bleed and the phlox is seed,
        Nothing's left of the clover,
    And the path of the poppy no one knows, —
    I would blossom if I were a rose!

    Summer for all your guile
        Will brown in a week to autumn,
    And launched leaves throw a shadow below
        Over the brook's clear bottom,
    And the chariest bud the year can boast
    Be brought to bloom by the chastening frost!
    Oh, little rose-tree, bloom!"

[*As he finishes the song Fidelio goes out, softly strumming
the last chords. Bianca and Beatrice sit quite still for a
moment.*

BIANCA. Do you know what I am thinking, Bice?

BEATRICE. You're wondering where we'll be ten years from
    now,
Or something of that nature.

BIANCA.   Ay, I was wondering
   Which would be married first, and go away,
   And would we still be friends.

BEATRICE.   Oh, do you doubt it,
   Snow-White?

BIANCA.   Nay, nay, — I doubt it not, my dear, —
   But I was wondering.   I am suddenly sad,
   I know not why.   I do not wish to leave you
   Ever.

BEATRICE.   I know.   I cannot bear to think
   Of parting.   We have been happy these four years
   Together, have we not?

BIANCA.   Oh, Beatrice!
   [*She weeps.*

BEATRICE.   Nay, do not weep! — Come, you must go to bed.
   You are tired to-night.   We rode too far to-day.
   (*She draws Bianca's head down to her shoulder*)
   Oh, you are tired, tired, you are very tired.
   You must be rocked to sleep, and tucked in bed,
   And have your eyelids kissed to make you dream
   Of fairies!   Come, dear, come.

BIANCA.   Oh, I do love you,
   Rose-Red!   You are so sweet!   Oh, I do love you
   So much! — so much!   I never loved any one
   The way that I love you!   There is nobody
   In all the world so wonderful as you!
   [*She throws her arms about Beatrice and clings to her.*

SCENE 3

*A room in the palace at Fiori.   Lorenzo and Beatrice playing
chess.   Twilight.*

LORENZO.   You'll not be able to get out of that,
   I think, my girl, with both your castles gone.

BEATRICE.   Be not so sure! — I have a horse still, father,
   And in a strong position: if I move him here,
   You lose your bishop; and if you take my bishop,
   You lose your queen.

LORENZO. True, but with my two rooks
Set here, where I can push them back and forth,
My king is safe till worms come in and eat him.

BEATRICE. What say you then to this? — Will you take this pawn,
Or will you not?

LORENZO (*studying the board*). Od's bones! — where did that come from?

[*Enter Octavia.*

OCTAVIA. La, would you lose your eyesight, both of you? —
Fumbling about those chessmen in the dark?
You, Beatrice, at least, should have more wit!

LORENZO. "At least" — hm! — Did you hear her say, "at least,"
Bice, my daughter?

BEATRICE. Ay. But it is true
The twilight comes before one knows it.

LORENZO. Ay.
'Tis true, but unimportant. Nevertheless,
I am a tractable old fellow. — Look you,
I will but stay to map the lay of the pieces
Upon this bit of letter. 'Tis from a king
Who could not tell the bishop from the board, —
And yet went blind at forty. — A little chess
By twilight, mark you, and all might have been well.

[*Enter Bianca.*

BIANCA. Oh, — I've been looking everywhere for you?

OCTAVIA (*drily*). For me?

BIANCA. Nay, mother, — for Beatrice. Bice,
The rose is out at last upon that bush
That never blossomed before, — and it is white
As linen, just as I said 'twould be!

BEATRICE. Why, the bud
Was redder than a radish!

BIANCA. Ay, I know.
But the blossom's white, pure white. Come out and see!
(*Politely*) Would you like to see it, mother?

OCTAVIA. Nay, not now, child.
Some other time.

BEATRICE. Father, we'll end the game
To-morrow; and do you not be scheming at it
All night!

LORENZO. Nay, I will not unfold the chart.

BEATRICE. But you remember well enough without;
Promise me not to think of it.

LORENZO. I' faith,
You are a desperate woman. Ay, I promise.

[*Exeunt Bianca and Beatrice. Octavia seats herself. Pause.*

OCTAVIA. I tell you, as I've told you often before,
Lorenzo, 'tis not good for two young girls
To be so much together!

LORENZO. As you say,
Octavia. For myself, I must confess
It seems a natural thing, enough, that youth
Should seek out youth. And if they are better
pleased
Talking together than listening to us,
I find it not unnatural. What have we
To say to children? — They are as different
From older folk as fairies are from them.

OCTAVIA. "Talking together," Lorenzo! What have they
To talk about, save things they might much better
Leave undiscussed? — you know what I mean, — lovers,
And marriage, and all that — if that be all!
One never knows — it is impossible
To hear what they are saying; they either speak
In whispers, or burst out in fits of laughter
At some incredible nonsense. There is nothing
So silly as young girls at just that age. —
At just Bianca's age, that is to say.
As for the other, — as for Beatrice,
She's older than Bianca, and I'll not have her
Putting ideas into my daughter's head!

LORENZO. Fear not, my love. Your daughter's head will doubtless,
  In its good time, put up its pretty hair,
  Chatter, fall dumb, go moping in the rain,
  Be turned by flattery, be bowed with weeping,
  Grow gray, and shake with palsy over a staff, —
  All this, my love, as empty of ideas
  As even the fondest mother's heart could wish.

OCTAVIA. You mock me, sir?

LORENZO.   I am but musing aloud,
  As is my fashion. — And indeed, my dear,
  What is the harm in lovers-and-all-that
  That virtuous maidens may not pass the time
  With pretty tales about them? — After all,
  Were it not for the years of looking forward to it
  And looking back upon it, love would be
  Only the commonest bird-song in the hedge, —
  And men would have more time to think, — and less
  To think about.

OCTAVIA.   That may be. But young girls
  Should not be left alone too much together.
  They grow too much attached. They grow to feel
  They cannot breathe apart. It is unhealthy.

LORENZO. It may be true. But as for me, whom youth
  Abandoned long ago, I look on youth
  As something fresh and sweet, like a young green tree,
  Though the wind bend it double. — 'Tis you, 'tis I,
  'Tis middle age the fungus settles on.

OCTAVIA. Your head is full of images. You have
  No answers. I shall do as I spoke of doing,
  And separate them for a little while,
  Six months, maybe a year. I shall send Bianca
  Away within a fortnight. That will cure them.
  I know. I know. Such friendships do not last.

CURTAIN

ACT II

SCENE 1 — *Four months later*

A garden, near the palace at Fiori. The young Duke Guido is discovered standing with one foot resting on a garden bench, looking off, lost in thought. Enter Giovanni.

GIOVANNI.   That is a merry face you wear, my Guido!
Now that the young King Mario visits the court
And walks all morning in the woods with the Princess,
Or gives her fencing lessons, — upon my word,
You are as gay as a gallows!

GUIDO.   She is never
Alone with him.   Laura — Carlotta — some one
Is always there.

GIOVANNI.   Ah — ah — but even so,
No matter who is there, I tell you, lovers
Are always alone!

GUIDO.   Why do you say these things,
Giovanni?

GIOVANNI.   Because I love you, you lean wolf,
And love to watch you snuff the air.   My friend,
There was a time I thought it all ambition
With you, a secret itching to be king —
And not so secret, either — an open plot
To marry a girl who will be Queen some morning.
But now at times I wonder.   You have a look
As of a man that's nightly gnawed by rats,
The very visage of a man in love.
Is it not so?

GUIDO.   I do not know, Giovanni.
I know I have a passion in my stomach
So bitter I can taste it on my tongue.
She hates me.   And her hatred draws me to her
As the moon draws the tide.

GIOVANNI.   You are like a cat —
There never was a woman yet that feared you
And shunned you, but you leapt upon her shoulder!

Well, I'll be off. The prettiest girl in Fiori, —
Unless it be Her Highness, waits for me
By a fountain. All day long she sells blue plums,
And in the evening what she has left of them
She gives to me! You should love simply, Guido,
As I do.

[*Exit Giovanni.*

Guido sits on the bench and drops his head in his hand.
Enter Francesca.

FRANCESCA (*softly*). Guido! Guido!

GUIDO.   Who calls me?

FRANCESCA. Guido!

GUIDO. Francesca! Why do you follow me here? — You know
I do not wish to see you!

FRANCESCA.   Do not be angry.
'Tis half a week since you have spoken to me,
And more than a week since you have so much as laid
Your hand upon my arm! And do you think,
Loving you as I do, I can do without you,
Forever, Guido, and make no sign at all?
I know you said you did not wish to see me
Ever again, — but it was only a quarrel —
And we have quarreled before!

GUIDO.   It was not a quarrel.
I am tired of you, Francesca. You are too soft.
You weep too much.

FRANCESCA.   I do not weep the less
For having known you.

GUIDO.   So; — it will save you tears, then,
To know me less.

FRANCESCA.   Oh, Guido, how your face
Is changed, — I cannot think those are the eyes
That looked into my eyes a month ago!
What's come between us?

GUIDO.   Nothing has come between us.
It is the simple snapping of a string
Too often played upon.

FRANCESCA.   Ah! — but I know
Who snapped it! It will do you little good
To look at her, — she'll never look at you!

GUIDO.   Be silent a moment! — Unless you would be silent
Longer!

FRANCESCA.   Indeed! I shall speak out my mind!
You go beyond yourself! There is proportion
Even in a nature like my own, that's twisted
From too much clinging to a crooked tree!
And this is sure: if you no longer love me,
You shall no longer strike me!

MARIO (*off stage*).   Beatrice!
Wait for me! Wait!

BEATRICE (*off stage*).   Not I! Who does not run
As fast as I run, shall be left behind me!

GUIDO.   They are coming here! I do not wish to see
them!

FRANCESCA.   Oh, Guido!
[*She follows him off. Exeunt Guido and Francesca.*
Enter Beatrice, running, followed by Mario.

MARIO.   Beatrice, you run like a boy!
You whistle like a boy! And upon my word,
You are the only girl I ever played
At jousting with, that did not hold her sword
As if it were a needle! Which of us,
Think you, when we are married, will be King?

BEATRICE.   When we are married! Sir, I'll have you know
There's an ogre to be tamed, a gem to be pried
From out a dragon's forehead, and three riddles
To be solved, each tighter than the last, before
A Princess may be wed!

MARIO   Even by a King?

BEATRICE.   For Kings the rules are sterner! — One more
riddle,
And a mirror that will show her always young.

MARIO.   And if I do these things, then, will you have me,
Rose-Red?

BEATRICE.   Maybe.   And if you do not do them,
Maybe.   Come — I will race you to the bridge!

MARIO (*catching her hand*).   Nay, not so fast! — Have you
no wish to be
Beside me, ever, that you are forever running
Ahead?

BEATRICE.   Indeed, if you would have the truth
It has come into my mind more times than once
It would be sweet to be beside you often.

MARIO.   Rose-Red!

BEATRICE.   Come — I will race you to the bridge!

[*Exeunt Beatrice and Mario.*

SCENE 2

*Courtyard of the palace at Fiori.   Entire court assembled.
A band of strolling players, with a little stage on wheels, are
doing a Harlequinade pantomime to amuse the young King
Mario, the guest of honor.   Beatrice sits beside him.   In this
scene the two people who are oblivious to the pantomime are
Guido and Octavia.   Guido is apparently brooding over something.   From time to time he looks at Beatrice and Mario.
Once, having gazed for some moments at the pair, he looks at
Octavia and sees that she, too, is looking at them, which seems
to satisfy him.   The Queen does not take her eyes from the two
during the entire scene.   Beatrice and Mario do not conduct
themselves precisely as lovers, but they are very gay and happy
to be in each other's company, apparently.   Lorenzo watches
the show with a benign, almost childish interest.   Pantomime
begins.*

GIOVANNI.   You, Pierrot, are you not a little thick
For such a sorrowful fellow?

PIERROT.   Nay, indeed!
Sorrow may come to all.   And 'tis amazing
How much a man may live through and keep fat.

[*Pantomime continues.*

CARLOTTA. Ho! Now he stumbles! Look you, Pantaloon,
If you were not so learned i' the head
You might know better where to put your feet!

LAURA (*to Carlotta*). 'Tis curious how it addles a man's
bones
To think too much.

CARLOTTA.   Nay, truth. Wise men were ever
Awkward i' the legs.

[*Pantomime continues.*

RAFFAELE.   Have at him, Polichinello.

GIOVANNI. Lay on! Lay on!

ANSELMO.   Leave not a nail of him!

GIOVANNI. Dog! Would you have him write a book about
you?

LUIGI. Spit him i' the liver! It is his only organ!

BEATRICE (*to Mario*). Nay, it is cruel. I cannot look at it.

MARIO. It is but play.

BEATRICE.   Ay, but 'tis cruel play.
To be so mocked at! — Come, take heart, good Doctor!
'Tis a noisy fellow, but light withal! — Blow at him!

GIOVANNI (*to Guido*). She has the softest heart that ever
I saw
In a hard woman. It may be, seeing she has pity
For one rogue, she has pity for another!
Mark you, my Guido, there is hope yet!

GUIDO.   Nay,
There's not. I have opened up my mind to her,
And she will none of me.

GIOVANNI (*jestingly*).   That was the last thing
You should have done! — Speak, — did she give for answer
She loves the King?

GUIDO.   Not she. She gave for answer
She does not love the Duke.

[*Pantomime continues.*

ANSELMO (*to Colombine*).   Ah, pretty lady!

CARLOTTA. La, she is fickle! How she turns from one face
To another face, — and smiles into them all!

FRANCESCA.   Oh, ay, but 'tis the Pierrot that she loves.

[*Pantomime continues and comes to a close.   All applaud.*

LUIGI.   Well done!

ANSELMO.   Bravo!

GIOVANNI.   A monstrous lively play!

BEATRICE.   Oh, is it over? — I would it were not over!

MARIO.   And yet it pleased you not!

BEATRICE.   When it pleased me not,
I looked at you.

MARIO.   And when I pleased you not — ?

BEATRICE.   I looked at Harlequin.   However, I saw him
But fleetingly.   Pray, was he dark or fair?

LUIGI.   Laura!

LAURA.   Who calls?   La, it is only Luigi!

LUIGI.   Laura, there'll be a moon to-night.

LAURA.   I' faith,
There was a moon last night.

[*She sighs.*

LUIGI.   At ten o'clock,
Were I by a certain gate, would you be there?
What say you?

LAURA.   Ay, — if weariness overtook me,
And I could not get further!

CARLOTTA.   La, 'tis sun-down!

[*In the meantime the crowd has been breaking up and dis-
persing.   The curtain falls on the disappearing spectators
and on Pierrot and his troupe packing up their wagon to go
to the next town.*

SCENE 3

*Fiori.   A garden with a fountain.   Evening.   Enter Octavia
and ladies.*

OCTAVIA.   It would amuse me if I had a lily
To carry in my hand.   You there, Carlotta!
You have a long arm, — plunge it in the pool
And fish me forth a lily!

CLAUDIA.   Majesty,
They close at night.

OCTAVIA.   Well — we will open them.

CARLOTTA (*going to pool and scanning it*).   Go to — I am not
a frog!

OCTAVIA.   What did you say?

ARIANNA.   She says she sees a frog, Your Majesty.

FRANCESCA (*aside to Carlotta*).   You are mad!   Can you not
keep your tongue in your head?

CARLOTTA.   Ay, I can keep it in my cheek. — There's one.
God grant it have an eel at the end of it, —
I'll give the dame good measure.

[*While the ladies are at the pool enter Guido.*

GUIDO.   Greeting, madam!

OCTAVIA.   Who greets me? — Ah, it is the Duke.   Good
even, Guido.   You seek an audience with me?

GUIDO.   Nay — nay — but if you send away your women, —
We shall be more alone.

OCTAVIA (*after considering him a moment*).   You may leave
me now,
Laura, Francesca — all of you — and you would best go in
At an early hour, instead of walking the gardens
All night; I would have you with your wits
About you in the morning.

CARLOTTA (*aside*).   Oh, indeed?
You would best go in yourself, lest the dew rust you,
You sauce-pan!

[*Exeunt ladies.*

OCTAVIA.   Now, my good sir, — you may speak.

GUIDO (*as if by way of conversation*).   It is a long time, is it
not, your daughter —
Is absent from the court?

OCTAVIA.   Why say you that?

GUIDO.   Why but to pass the time, till she returns?

OCTAVIA.   Nay, Guido.   That is well enough for some,
But not for me.   I know the slant of your fancy;
'Tis not in that direction.

GUIDO.   Yet me thinks
 The sooner she is back again at court
 The happier for us both.
OCTAVIA.   "Us both?"   What "both"?
GUIDO.   You Madam, and myself.
OCTAVIA.   And why for me?
GUIDO (*carefully*).   Why, are you not her mother?
OCTAVIA.   Hah!   (*Pause*)   Guido,
 What festers in your mind?   Do you speak out now,
 If you await some aid from me.
GUIDO.   Madam,
 I have but this to say: if I were a woman
 With a marriageable daughter, and a King rode by,
 I'd have her at the window.
OCTAVIA.   So.   I thought so.
 (*With an entire change of manner*)
 Guido, what think you, — does she love the King, —
 I mean Lorenzo's daughter?
GUIDO.   Ay, she loves him.
OCTAVIA.   And loves he her?
GUIDO.   Oh, ay.   He loves the moon,
 The wind in the cypress trees, his mother's portrait
 At seventeen, himself, his future children —
 He loves her well enough.   But had she blue eyes
 And yellow hair, and were afraid of snakes,
 He yet might love her more.
OCTAVIA.   You think so, Guido?
 I am content to learn you of that mind.
 There had occurred to me — some time ago,
 In fact — a similar fancy.   And already
 My daughter is well on her way home.
 [*Exeunt Guido and Octavia.*
 Music.   Enter Beatrice and Fidelio.   Fidelio strums his lute
 softly throughout the next conversation, up to the words "and
 cease to mock me."
BEATRICE.   Fidelio,
 Were you ever in love?

FIDELIO. I was never out of it.

BEATRICE. But truly?

FIDELIO. Well, I was only out of it
What time it takes a man to right himself
And once again lose balance. Ah, indeed,
'Tis good to be in love. I have often noticed,
The moment I fall out of love, that moment
I catch a cold.

BEATRICE. Are you in love, then, now?

FIDELIO. Ay, to be sure.

BEATRICE. Oh! Oh! With whom, Fidelio?
Tell me with whom!

FIDELIO. Why, marry, with yourself, —
That are the nearest to me, — and by the same troth,
The farthest away.

BEATRICE. Go to, Fidelio!
I am in earnest, and you trifle with me
As if I were a child.

FIDELIO. Are you not a child, then?

BEATRICE. Not any more.

FIDELIO. How so?

BEATRICE. I am in love.

FIDELIO. Oh — oh — oh, misery, misery, misery, misery!

BEATRICE. Why do you say that?

FIDELIO. Say what?

BEATRICE. "Misery, misery."

FIDELIO. It is a song.

BEATRICE. A song?

FIDELIO. Ay, 'tis a love-song.
Oh, misery, misery, misery, misery, oh!

BEATRICE. Nay, sweet Fidelio, be not so unkind!
I tell you, for the first time in my life
I am in love! Do you be mannerly now,
And cease to mock me.

FIDELIO. What would you have me do?

BEATRICE. I would have you shake your head, and pat my
  shoulder,
And smile and say, "Godspeed."

FIDELIO (*doing so very tenderly*). Godspeed.

BEATRICE (*bursting into tears*). I' faith I do not know if I am
  happy or sad.
But I am greatly moved. I would Bianca
Were here. I never lacked her near so much
As to-night I do, although I lack her always.
She is a long time gone. — If I tell you something,
Will you promise not to tell?

FIDELIO. Nay, I'll not promise,
But I'll not tell?

BEATRICE. Fidelio, I do love so
The King from Lagoverde! I do so love him!

FIDELIO. Godspeed, Godspeed.

BEATRICE. Ay, it is passing strange;
Last week I was a child, but now I am not.
And I begin my womanhood with weeping;
I know not why. — La, what a fool I am!
'Tis over. Sing Fidelio.

FIDELIO. Would you a gay song,
My Princess?

BEATRICE. Ay. — And yet — nay, not so gay.
A simple song, such as a country-boy
Might sing his country-sweetheart. — Is it the moon
Hath struck me, do you think? I swear by the moon
I am most melancholy soft, and most
Outrageous sentimental! Sing, dear fool.

FIDELIO (*singing*).
  "Butterflies are white and blue
  In this field we wander through.
  Suffer me to take your hand.
  Death comes in a day or two.
  All the things we ever knew
  Will be ashes in that hour.

Mark the transient butterfly,
How he hangs upon the flower.
Suffer me to take your hand.
Suffer me to cherish you
Till the dawn is in the sky.
Whether I be false or true,
Death comes in a day or two."

CURTAIN

ACT III

SCENE 1. *The following summer*

A field or meadow near Fiori. As the curtain rises voices are heard off-stage singing a bridal song.

SONG: Strew we flowers on their pathway!
 Bride and bridegroom, go you sweetly.
 There are roses on your pathway.
 Bride and bridegroom, go you sweetly.
 Sweetly live together.

Enter Viola, Lilina, Lela, Arianna and Claudia, laden with garlands, flowering boughs and baskets of flowers. They meet Anselmo coming from another direction, also bearing flowers

VIOLA. How beautiful, Anselmo! Where did you find them?
ANSELMO. Close by the brook.

LILINA. You gathered all there were?
ANSELMO. Not by one hundredth part.

LELA. Nay, is it true?
We must have more of them!

ARIANNA. And are they fragrant
As well?

ANSELMO. Ay, by my heart, they are so sweet
I near to fainted climbing the bank with them.

[*The ladies cluster about Anselmo and smell the flowers.*

LILINA. Oh!
VIOLA. Ah!

CLAUDIA.   How drowsily sweet!

LELA.   Oh, sweet!

ARIANNA.   What fragrance!
[*Enter Laura and Giovanni, followed by Carlotta and Raffaele.*

LAURA. La, by my lung! I am as out of breath
As a babe new-born! Whew! Let me catch the air!
[*She drops her flowers and seats herself beside them.*

CARLOTTA (*to the younger ladies and Anselmo, by way of greeting*). How hot the sun is getting!

ANSELMO.   'Tis nigh noon,
I think.

GIOVANNI. 'Tis noon.

CLAUDIA.   We must be starting back.

LAURA. Not till I get my breath.

RAFFAELE.   Come, — I will fan you.
[*He fans her with a branch.*

LAURA. 'Tis good — 'tis very good — oh, peace — oh,
slumber —
Oh, all good things! You are a proper youth.
You are a zephyr. I would have you fan me
Till you fall dead.

CARLOTTA.   I tell you when it comes
To gathering flowers, much is to be said
For spreading sheets on the grass, — it gives you less
The backache.

LAURA.   Nobly uttered, my sweet bird.

GIOVANNI. Yet brides must have bouquets.

CARLOTTA.   And sit at home,
Nursing complexions, whilst I gather them.

LILINA (*running to Carlotta, along with Lela and Viola, and throwing her arms about her*).
Nay, out upon you now, Carlotta! Cease now
To grumble so, — 'tis such a pretty day!

VIOLA. And weddings mean a ball!
                              And one may dance all night
At weddings!

LILINA.   Till one needs must dance to bed,
Because one cannot walk there!

GIOVANNI.   And one eats
Such excellent food!

ANSELMO.   And drinks such excellent wine!

CLAUDIA. And seldom will you see a bride and bridegroom
More beautiful and gracious, or whom garlands
Do more become.

GIOVANNI.   'Tis so, — upon my sword! —
Which I neglected to bring with me — 'tis so,
Upon Anselmo's sword!

CARLOTTA.   Nay, look you, Laura!
You must not fall asleep! (*To Raffaele*) Have done, you
    devil!
Is it a poppy that you have there? (*To Laura*) Look you,
We must be starting back!

[*Laura rouses, then falls back again.*

LAURA.   Ay, that we must.

ARIANNA. Where are the others?

ANSELMO.   Scattered all about.
I will call to them. Hola! You fauns and dryads!
Where are you?

VOICES.   Here! Here! Is it time to go?

ANSELMO. Come this way! We are starting back!

VOICES.   We are coming!
We'll come in a moment! We cannot bear to leave
This place!

GIOVANNI (*as they enter*). A thousand greetings, lovely
    Clara!
Lucia, a thousand greetings! How now, Luigi!
I know you, man, despite this soft disguise!
You are no flower-girl!

LUIGI.   I am a draught-horse,
That's what I am, for four unyielding women!
Were I a flower-girl, I'd sell the lot
For a bit of bread and meat — I am so hungry
I could eat a butterfly!

CARLOTTA.   What ho, Francesca!
I have not seen you since the sun came up!

FRANCESCA.   This is not I, — I shall not be myself
Till it goes down!

LELA.   Oh, la, what lovely lilies!

FRANCESCA.   Be tender with them — I risked my life to get
them!

LILINA.   Where were they?

FRANCESCA.   Troth, I do not know.   I think
They were in a dragon's mouth.

LAURA (*suddenly waking*).   Well, are we going?

[*All laugh.*

LUIGI.   No one is going that cannot go afoot.
I have enough to carry!

LAURA.   Nay, take me too!
I am a little thing.   What does it matter —
One flower more?

LUIGI.   You are a thousand flowers,
Sweet Laura, — you are a meadow full of them —
I'll bring a wagon for you.

CARLOTTA.   Come.   Come home.

[*In the meantime the stage has been filling with girls and men
bearing flowers, a multitude of people, in groups and couples,
humming the song very softly.   As Carlotta speaks several
more people take up the song, then finally the whole crowd.
They move off slowly, singing.*

SONG.   "Strew we flowers on their pathway," etc.

SCENE 2

*Bianca's boudoir in the palace at Fiori.   Bianca, with a
mirror in her hand, having her hair done by a maid.   Several
maids about, holding perfume flasks, brushes, and veils, articles
of apparel of one sort or another.   Beatrice standing beside her,
watching.*

BIANCA.   Look at me, Rose-Red.   Am I pretty enough,
Think you, to marry a King?

BEATRICE. You are too pretty.
There is no justice in it. Marry a cobbler
And make a king of him. It is unequal, —
Here is one beggarly boy king in his own right,
And king by right of you.

BIANCA. Mario is not
A beggarly boy! Nay, tell me truly, Bice,
What do you think of him?

BEATRICE. La, by my soul!
Have I not told you what I think of him
A thousand times? He is graceful enough, I tell you,
And hath a well-shaped head.

BIANCA. Nay, is that all?

BEATRICE. Nay, hands and feet he hath, like any other.

BIANCA. Oh, out upon you for a surly baggage!
Why will you tease me so? You do not like him,
I think.

BEATRICE. Snow-White! Forgive me! La, indeed,
I was but jesting! By my sacred word,
These brides are serious folk.

BIANCA. I could not bear
To wed a man that was displeasing to you.
Loving him as I do, I could not choose
But wed him, if he wished it, but 'twould hurt me
To think he did not please you.

BEATRICE. Let me, then,
Set your sweet heart at rest. You could not find
In Christendom a man would please me more.

BIANCA. Then I am happy.

BEATRICE. Ay, be happy, child.

BIANCA. Why do you call me child?

BEATRICE. Faith, 'tis the season
O' the year when I am older than you. Besides,
A bride is always younger than a spinster.

BIANCA. A spinster! Do you come here to me, Rose-Red,
Whilst I pinch you smartly! You, Arianna, push me
Her Highness over here, that I may pinch her!

(To Loretta) Nay, is it finished? Aye, 'tis very well.
Though not so well, Loretta, as many a day
When I was doing nothing! — Nay, my girl,
'Tis well enough. He will take me as I am
Or leave me as I was. You may come back
In half an hour, if you are grieved about it,
And do it again. But go now, — all of you.
I wish to be alone. *(To Beatrice)* Not you.
(Exeunt all but Beatrice and Bianca)
                Oh, Rose-Red,
I trust 'twill not be long before I see you
As happy as you see me now!

BEATRICE.   Indeed,
I could not well be happier than I am.
You do not know, maybe, how much I love you.

BIANCA. Ah, but I do, — I have a measure for it!

BEATRICE. Ay, for to-day you have. But not for long.
They say a bride forgets her friends, — she cleaves so
To her new lord. It cannot but be true.
You will be gone from me. There will be much
To drive me from your mind.

BIANCA.   Shall I forget, then,
When I am old, I ever was a child?
I tell you I shall never think of you
Throughout my life, without such tenderness
As breaks the heart, — and I shall think of you
Whenever I am most happy, whenever I am
Most sad, whenever I see a beautiful thing.
You are a burning lamp to me, a flame
The wind cannot blow out, and I shall hold you
High in my hand against whatever darkness.

BEATRICE. You are to me a silver bell in a tower.
And when it rings I know I am near home.

SCENE 3

A room in the palace. Mario alone. Enter Beatrice.

BEATRICE. Mario! I have a message for you! — Nay,
You need not hang your head and shun me, Mario,
Because you loved me once a little and now
Love somebody else much more. The going of love
Is no less honest than the coming of it.
It is a human thing.

MARIO.   Oh, Beatrice!
What can I say to you?

BEATRICE.   Nay, but indeed,
Say nothing. All is said. I need no words
To tell me you have been troubled in your heart,
Thinking of me.

MARIO.   What can I say to you!

BEATRICE. I tell you, my dear friend, you must forget
This thing that makes you sad. I have forgotten,
In seeing her so happy, that ever I wished
For happiness myself. Indeed, indeed,
I am much happier in her happiness
Than if it were my own; 'tis doubly dear,
I feel it in myself, yet all the time
I know it to be hers, and am twice glad.

MARIO. I could be on my knees to you a lifetime,
Nor pay you half the homage is your due.

BEATRICE. Pay me no homage, Mario, — but if it be
I have your friendship, I shall treasure it.

MARIO. That you will have always.

BEATRICE.   Then you will promise me
Never to let her know. I never told her
How it was with us, or that I cherished you
More than another. It was on my tongue to tell her
The moment she returned, but she had seen you
Already on the bridge as she went by,
And had leaned out to look at you, it seems,
And you were looking at her, — and the first words

She said, after she kissed me, were, "Oh, sister,
I have looked at last by daylight on the man
I see in my dreams!"

MARIO (*tenderly*). Did she say that?

BEATRICE (*drily*). Ay, that
Was what she said. — By which I knew, you see,
My dream was over, — it could not but be you.
So that I said no word, but my quick blood
Went suddenly quiet in my veins, and I felt
Years older than Bianca. I drew her head
Down to my shoulder, that she might not see my face,
And she spoke on, and on. You must not tell her,
Even when you both are old, and there is nothing
To do but to remember. She would be withered
With pity for me. She holds me very dear.

MARIO. I promise it, Rose-Red. And oh, believe me,
I said no word to you last year that is not
As true to-day! I hold you still the noblest
Of women, and the bravest. I have not changed.
Only last year I did not know I could love
As I love now. Her gentleness has crept so
Into my heart, it never will be out.
That she should turn to me and cling to me
And let me shelter her, is the great wonder
Of the world. You stand alone. You need no shelter,
Rose-Red.

BEATRICE. It may be so.

MARIO. Will you forgive me?

BEATRICE. I had not thought of that. If it will please
you,
Ay, surely. — And now, the reason for my coming:
I have a message for you, of such vast import
She could not trust it to a liv'ried page,
Or even a courier. She bids me tell you
She loves you still, although you have been parted
Since four o'clock.

MARIO (*happily*). Did she say that?

BEATRICE. Ay, Mario.
I must return to her. It is not long now
Till she will leave me.
MARIO. She will never leave you,
She tells me, in her heart.
BEATRICE (*happily*). Did she say that?
MARIO. Ay, that she did, and I was jealous of you
One moment, till I called myself a fool.
BEATRICE. Nay, Mario, she does not take from you
To give to me; and I am most content
She told you that. I will go now. Farewell,
Mario!
MARIO. Nay, we shall meet again, Beatrice!

SCENE 4

*The ballroom of the palace at Fiori, raised place in back, sur-
mounted by two big chairs, for Lorenzo and Octavia to sit while
the dance goes on. Dais on one side, well down stage, in full
sight of the audience, for Mario and Bianca. As the curtain
rises, the stage is empty except for Fidelio, who sits forlornly
on the bottom steps of the raised place in the back of the stage, his
lute across his knees, his head bowed upon it. Sound of laughter
and conversation, possibly rattling of dishes, off stage, evidently
a feast going on.*

LAURA (*off stage*). Be still, or I will heave a plate at you!
LUIGI (*off stage*). Nay, gentle Laura, heave not the wedding-
crockery
At the wedding guest! Behold me on my knees
To tell the world I love you like a fool!
LAURA. Get up, you oaf! Or here's a platter of gravy
Will add the motley to your folly!
LUIGI. Hold her,
Some piteous fop, that liketh not to see
Fine linen smeared with goose! Oh, gracious Laura,
I never have seen a child sucking an orange
But I wished an orange, too. This wedding irks me

Because 'tis not mine own.   Shall we be married
Tuesday or Wednesday?

LAURA.   Are you in earnest, Luigi?

LUIGI.   Ay, that I am, if never I was before.

LAURA.   La, I am lost!   I am a married woman!
Water! — Nay, wine will do!   On Wednesday, then.
I'll have it as far off as possible.

[*Enter from banquet-room Guido, Giovanni and Raffaele.*

GIOVANNI.   Well met, Fidelio!   Give us a song!

FIDELIO.   Not I!

GUIDO.   Why, what is this?   You, that are dripping with song
Week days, are dry of music for a wedding?

FIDELIO.   I have a headache.   Go and sit in a tree,
And make your own songs.

RAFFAELE.   Nay, Fidelio.
String the sweet strings, man!

GIOVANNI.   Strike the pretty strings!

GUIDO.   Give us the silver strings!

FIDELIO   Nay then, I will that!
(*He tears the strings off the lute and throws them in Guido's
face*)
Here be the strings, my merry gentlemen!
Do you amuse yourself with tying knots in them
And hanging one another! — I have a headache.

[*He runs off, sobbing.*

RAFFAELE.   What ails him, think you?

GIOVANNI.   Troth, I have no notion.

[*Enter Nurse.*

GUIDO.   What ho, good Grazia!   I hear the king my uncle
Is ill again!

GRAZIA.   Where heard you that, you raven?

GUIDO.   Marry, I forget.   Is't true?

GRAZIA.   It is as false
As that you have forgotten where you heard it.
Were you the heir to his power, which I bless God
You're not! — he'd live to hide the throne from you
Full many a long day yet! — Nay, pretty Guido,

Your cousin is not yet Queen, — and when she is — Faith,
She weareth a wide petticoat, — there'll be
Scant room for you beside her.

[Exit Nurse across stage.

GUIDO (*To his companions*).   None the less
I do believe the king is ill.

RAFFAELE.   Who told you?

GUIDO. His wife. She is much exercised about him.

GIOVANNI. 'Tis like enough. This woman would rather lie
Than have her breakfast served to her in bed.

[Exeunt Guido, Giovanni and Raffaele.

*Music. Enter Musicians and take place on stage. Enter
four pages and take places on either side the door from the
banquet hall and on either side the throne in the back. Enter
Lorenzo and Octavia, Lorenzo apparently quite well, and seat
themselves on throne in back. Enter courtiers and ladies,
Carlotta with Anselmo, Laura with Luigi, etc., and stand
in little groups about the stage, laughing and talking together. Enter Beatrice alone, her train held by two pages in
black. Enter twelve little Cupids, running, and do a short
dance in the center of the room, then rush to the empty dais
which is awaiting Mario and Bianca, and cluster about it.
Enter Bianca and Mario, she in white and silver, with a deep
sky-blue velvet train six yards long, held up by six silver
pages (or Cupids); he in black and gold, with a purple velvet
train of the same length held by six gold pages (or Cupids).
His arm is about her waist, she is leaning back her head
against him and looking up into his face. They come in
slowly, talking softly together, as utterly oblivious of the court,
the pages, the music, everything, as if they were a shepherd and
a shepherdess walking through a meadow. They walk slowly
across the stage and seat themselves on the dais. The music
changes, strikes up a gay pavane; the ladies and courtiers
dance. Guido, Giovanni and Raffaele reënter just as the
music starts and go up to the ladies; Guido goes to Beatrice,
and she dances with him. In the midst of the dance Lorenzo
slips a little sidewise in his chair, his head drops forward on*

*his chest; he does not move again.   Nobody notices for some
time.   The dance continues, all who are not dancing watching
the dancers, save Octavia, who watches with great pride and
affection Bianca and Mario, who in turn are looking at one
another.   Octavia turns finally to speak to Lorenzo, stares at
him, touches him, then screams.   Music stops in confusion on
a discord, dance breaks up wildly, everybody rushes to throne.*

Scene 5

*The same room later that evening, entirely empty, disordered.
Musicians' benches overturned, a couple of instruments left
about, garlands trampled on the floor, a wing of one of the
Cupids clinging to the dais of Bianca and Mario.   Enter
Beatrice, weeping, goes to her father's throne and creeps
up into it, with her face towards the back of it and clings there,
sobbing quietly.   Enter Bianca and Mario.*

BIANCA (*softly*).   Ay.   She is here.   I thought she would be
    here.
There are so many people by his bed
Even now, she cannot be alone with him.

MARIO.   Is there no hope?

BIANCA.   Nay, there is none.   'Tis over.
He was a kind old man.

MARIO.   Come, let us go,
And leave her to herself.

BIANCA.   Nay, Mario.
I must not leave her.   She will sit like that
All night, unless I bid her come away,
And put her into bed.

MARIO.   Will you come to me
After she sleeps?

BIANCA.   Ay.   If she sleeps.

MARIO.   And if not?

BIANCA.   I could not leave her.

MARIO.   Bianca, do you love me?

BIANCA.   Ay, Mario!

MARIO.   Ah, but not as I love you!

BIANCA.   You do not think that, Mario; you know
How much I love you.   But I could not be happy
Thinking of her awake in the darkness, weeping,
And all alone.

MARIO.   Oh, my sweet love!

BIANCA.   It may be
She will sleep.

MARIO.   I shall be waiting for you.

[*They embrace.*

[*Exit Mario.   Bianca goes to Beatrice and sits at the foot
of the throne, putting her head against Beatrice's feet.*

BIANCA.   Sister.

[*After a moment Beatrice slowly reaches down her hand, and
Bianca takes it.*

CURTAIN

ACT IV

SCENE 1 — *Five years later*

*A marketplace in Fiori, vegetables, fruits and flowers exposed
for sale in little stalls and wagons, crowd of townspeople moving
about, talking, laughing, buying.   Group of children playing
a game in a ring.   Supper time.*

CHILDREN.   One, two, three,
The dough is in the oven!
One, two, three,
The bread is on the board!
One, two, three,
The dough is in the oven!
One, two, three,
The bread is on the board!
One, two, three,
All follow me!

EUGENIA.   Good-even, Giovanitta.   Those are beautiful
Onions you have there.

GIOVANITTA. Ay, it has been a good year
For onions.

EUGENIA. I am taking seven.

GIOVANITTA. Each year,
You buy another onion!

EUGENIA. Faith, each year
I have another mouth to thrust it in!
Beautiful carrots, too, you have.

GIOVANITTA. Ay, carrots
Are well enough. One cannot complain. 'Tis a good year
For carrots.

CLARA. 'Tis a good year for many things.
Prices are low, — but not too low for profit.

GIULIANA. And there are fewer taxes than there once were
On things one cannot live without.

ANNA. 'Tis a good Queen
We have, it must be granted.

GIOVANITTA. Ay, and a wise one.

GILDA. And pretty, too.

GIULIANA. Ho, ho! When did you see her?

GILDA. This morning, mother. I was at the edge of the wood
With Beppo, when they rode by to the hunt,
Talking together, and laughing.

BEPPO (*calling from across the stage*). And the horses
With feet like this!

[*Arching his hands and feet to represent a horse stepping
delicately.*

GILDA. And glittering in the sunshine
In a thousand places, mother! I wanted to tell you
When we returned, but you had gone to the brook
With the linen. They were so near us we could hear them
Talking.

BEPPO (*coming up*). And hear the horses breathe!

ANNA. What said they?

GILDA. Well, one of them said — what was the name?

BEPPO. Anselmo.

GILDA. Oh, ay. She said, "Anselmo, am I getting thinner
Do you think? If I be not thinner than I was at starting,
I shall descend at once! I like not this;
It chatters my teeth."

BEPPO. And then she said —

GILDA. What said she?

Oh, ay, — about the boat.

BEPPO. She said, "Next time
I shall go fishing instead of hunting. A boat
Hath a more mannerly gait!"

GILDA. There was one horse, mother,
That was all white! There was not one hair upon him
That was not white!

GIULIANA. And who was riding that horse?

BEPPO. A man. And riding well.

GILDA. He was dressed in green,
And had a yellow beard. And there was a lady
With hair the color of Adelina's, bright
Like fire. She was dressed in blue, and was most
beautiful.

BEPPO. And she was mounted on a dappled mare.

GILDA. But, oh, it was the Queen that was more lovely —
Than any of the rest!

GIOVANITTA. How did you know, now,
It was the Queen?

GILDA. Nay, but you could not help
But know! She was not laughing like the rest, —
Just smiling; and I should not have been afraid
To toss a flower to her from the wood,
If I had a flower.

BEPPO. You knew her, though,
Because she was in scarlet. All the world knows
She wears a scarlet mantle!

GILDA. Nay, if that were all,
It might have been the Pope!

BEPPO. I would it had been.
I never saw the Pope.

GILDA. You never saw
The Queen until this morning! — Mother, she rides
Clothed like a man, almost!

BEPPO. With sword at side!

GILDA. And, oh, the sword had a jeweled — what is the
name of it?

BEPPO. Scabbard, of course!

GILDA. A jeweled scabbard, mother!
I wish I were a queen.

BEPPO. Ho, you would make
A proper queen, with that droll nose of yours!

GILDA. I know a boy who likes my nose!

BEPPO. Ho, ho!
He must be a hunchback!

GIULIANA. You must not tease her, Beppo.

GILDA. I wish I were queen. If I were a queen,
You would not dare to say my nose is droll.

BEPPO. It would be, all the same.

GIOVANITTA. You should be content
With what you have, not wish to rise beyond it.
It is a sin to covet.

GIULIANA. Being a queen,
My bird, is not all riding to the hunt
Of a sunny morning.

ANNA. Nay, 'tis riding back
At times, of a rainy night, to such a burden
Of cares as simple folk have little mind of.

GILDA. I'd rather have a queen's cares than my own.

BEPPO. Ho, ho! Your cares! What cares have you?

GILDA. I have
A brother that will be teasing me all times!
'Tis cares enough for one, I tell you.

ADELINA (*across the stage*). Beppo!
Come help me fetch the milk!

GILDA. Oh, Mister Beppo,
Your sweetheart calls you! Run and fetch the milk!

LEONORA (*from a house, coming out*). Come in to supper, children!

RIGO. Oh, not just yet!

ELENORA. Father's not home yet!

LEONORA. You need not wait for him.

LOUISA. May we come out again?

LEONORA (*joining other women*). Ay, for a time. Till it gets dark.

RIGO (*to Louisa*). 'Tis dark now, almost.

LOUISA. Hush! She does not know it.

GIULIANA. 'Tis dark now.

LEONORA. Ay, I know.
I let them play a little after dark
Sometimes, when the weather's fine. I would not have them
Afraid of shadows. They think I do not know
Darkness from light.

ELENORA. There's father now!

RIGO. I see him!

[*Elenora, Louisa and Rigo run off the stage and along the path.*

LEONORA. He is late home to-day. I cannot think
What may have held him. 'Twill be deep night already
In the woods.

CESCO (*off stage, harshly*). Down! Down! Do you run back to your mother!
See you not I am in haste? — Hang not upon me!

EUGENIA. La! He is in a temper!

LEONORA. I never knew him
So out of patience with them.

GIULIANA. He is hungry, maybe.

LEONORA. He is often hungry, but I never knew him
So out of patience.

(*The children come running back. To Elenora*)

Why do you weep, my heart?

LUIGI. Father is some one else to-night.

ELENORA (*weeping*). He pushed me!

[*Enter Cesco, with game on his shoulder.*

SEVERAL WOMEN. Good-even, Cesco.

CESCO (*to Leonora*). Look you, Leonora,
Have we a bed fit for a queen to lie in?

LEONORA. Nay, faith! Not we!

GILDA. She can have my bed, mother.

GIULIANA. Ay, true. There is a bed in my house, Cesco.

GIOVANITTA. What will the queen do here?

GIULIANA. I would indeed
She had let us know that she was coming!

CESCO. The Queen
Knew not herself. Nor is she coming of herself.
They are bringing her, — on a litter of crossed boughs.

GILDA. She is not *dead?*

CESCO. Nay. Wounded i' the arm
A little, and in a swoon. But the young King
Of Lagoverde is no more!

WOMEN. How so?

CESCO. I tell you my two eyes have looked this day
On a sad and useless thing! — A fine lad, young,
And strong, and beautiful as a lad may be,
And king of a fair country, thrust from horse
By a foul blow, and sprawled upon the ground, —
Legs wide asunder, fist full of brown mud,
Hair in his eyes, — most pitiful unkingly!
Bring me a mug of wine, good wife!

[*Leonora goes out.*

GIOVANITTA. You, Gilda!
There is a queen you would not be to-night,
I'll warrant you, — the Queen of Lagoverde,
With her two fatherless babes!

EUGENIA. Nay, now, good Cesco,
What is this matter?

CESCO. You'll know it quick enough.
They will be bringing the queen here ere I have breath

To tell you.   They are coming by the road.
I took the mountain path, and ran.

GIULIANA.   I must hasten
To put fresh sheets on. (*To Gilda*) Look you,— listen well
If he should talk, and tell me afterwards.
[*Exit.*

EUGENIA.   Here comes Horatio!   The boats are in.
[*Some children rush down to the water-side.*
A good day, husband?

HORATIO.   Ay, a heavy day.
What think you of that? — A big one, eh? — Came in
With a school of little fish, — too greedy that time!
What happens here? — The air is full of breathing!
[*The men come up from the boats with children clinging to
them. Beppo and Adelina return from another direction
with the milk.*

LEONORA (*somewhat proudly*).   Cesco will tell you.

CESCO.   In a word 'tis this: To-day the Queen of Fiori,
Returning from the hunt, is set upon
By brigands; whereat the King of Lagoverde,
Being hunting in that quarter and hearing cries,
Comes up to give his aid; in rendering which
He gives his life as well, and at this moment,
On other men's legs, goes heavily home to supper.
The Queen of Fiori, wounded, and in a swoon
Only less deep than death itself, comes this way.

CROWD.   Ay, here they come!
[*Enter Anselmo.*

ANSELMO.
                              Make way, make way, good people—
Fall back a little — leave a clear space — give air!
(*Enter Laura and Francesca, Luigi, several gentlemen, and
several attendants, four of them bearing a litter on which lies
Beatrice, in a scarlet cloak, her hair flowing. Luigi is with
Laura, who clings to him. If possible to arrange, several of
the party may lead on their horses and lead them off across the
stage. The litter is set down stage in full sight of the audience.*

*Beppo comes down stage near it, as does also, from another
direction, Gilda. Giuliana returns)*
Who has a bed that we may lay her on?
She cannot leave this place to-night.

GIULIANA.   This way, sir.

[*The attendants pick up the litter and go off, the crowd following.*

GILDA (*stealing back*).   Hist, Beppo!

BEPPO.   Ay?

GILDA.   Heard you not something fall,
When they picked her up again?

BEPPO.   Ay, that I did.

GILDA.   What was it, think you?   (*They search*)   Nay, 'twas
nearer here.

BEPPO.   I have it. — 'Tis her sword!

GILDA.   The Queen's?   Ay, — truly.
How beautiful!

BEPPO (*slowly and with awe drawing it from its scabbard*).
Look, — there is blood on it!

SCENE 2

*A room in the palace at Lagoverde.   Bianca and her two
little daughters discovered at the rise of the curtain, she in a big
chair, they at her feet.*

BIANCA.   And so the fairy laid a spell on her:
Henceforth she should be ugly as a toad.
But the good fairy, seeing this was done,
And having in no wise power to alter this,
Made all toads beautiful.

LITTLE ROSE-RED.   They are not beautiful
Now, mother!

LITTLE SNOW-WHITE.   That was in another country! —
What country, mother?

[*Bianca, lost in thought, does not answer.*

LITTLE ROSE-RED.   Where is father, mother? —
I have not seen him in so many days!

BIANCA. Father is gone away.

LITTLE ROSE-RED. Will he come back?

BIANCA. Nay. He will not come back. But we shall go
Where he is.

LITTLE SNOW-WHITE. Soon?

BIANCA. God grant it may be soon!
Now — shall we play a game?
[*Enter Octavia.*

OCTAVIA. Bianca.

BIANCA. Ay.

OCTAVIA. It is a folly to remain indoors
Like this. You should be out in the sunshine.

BIANCA. Nay.
I have no business with the sunshine.

OCTAVIA. Ah,
My daughter, say not so! — The children, then, —
They have much need of it, and they have need
Of you, at the same time. Take them without.

BIANCA. I do not wish to be in the sunshine.

LITTLE SNOW-WHITE. Mother,
Come out of doors!

OCTAVIA. You see, now!

BIANCA. Do you run out, dears,
And play at ball. Mother will join you later.

LITTLE ROSE-RED. Where *is* my ball?

BIANCA. Nay, do you not remember?
We put it in the ear of the stone griffin,
Because he hears too much.

LITTLE ROSE-RED. Ay, so we did!

LITTLE SNOW-WHITE. Come on, Rose-Red!
[*Exeunt children.*

OCTAVIA. It is a curious thing
This friend of yours you rate so monstrous high
Has not come nigh you in your sore affliction!

BIANCA. I beg you not to speak of that again,
Mother. 'Tis the third time to-day you have said that,
Or hinted at it. And I answer always,

"There is some reason for it," as I should answer
Though you cried daily till the day of doom,
"It is a curious thing!" There is some reason,
There is some good reason why she does not come.

OCTAVIA. Oh, ay, I doubt it not! But there are reasons
And reasons!

BIANCA. And what am I to learn from that?

OCTAVIA. 'Tis scarce by reason of too much love for you
She leaves you friendless in your greatest need.

BIANCA. I cannot say. 'Tis one thing or another.
You have no words can turn me to believe
She has forgotten me, or loves me less.
'Tis a big thing, to leave me thus alone, —
And there is some big reason.

OCTAVIA. Ay. Oh, ay.
'Tis possible she grieves for Mario's death
No less than you.

BIANCA (*simply*). Ay, it is possible.
I mind she told me on my marriage-day
She was as happy as I.

OCTAVIA. 'Tis a curious thing,
When he was here she came to see you often,
But now that he is gone comes not at all.

BIANCA (*simply*). Ay, it is curious.
(*Catching Octavia's expression*)
Nay, what evil thing
Is in your mind, gives you that evil smile?

OCTAVIA. Only a little thought.

BIANCA. A little thought,
I'll warrant you! — You'd have me to believe
She loved my husband?

OCTAVIA. Ay, I know she loved him.

BIANCA. It is a lie!

OCTAVIA. How dare you say I lie!

BIANCA. Oh, do not be so proud! Let us speak truth
At length, a little! We are so garnished up
With courtesies, so over-sauced and seasoned,

We cannot taste each other!   Why do you tell me
A thing like that? — You have no love for me!

OCTAVIA (*weeping*). I love you too much — you are the only thing
I do love!

BIANCA.   Nay, it is not love of me
For my own self.   Else would you do the thing
Would make me happiest.   You know how I have loved her,
Since we were children.   You could not be to me
What she was;   one forgets too many things.
You could not know my thought.   I loved you dearly,
But you were hard to love;   one never knew
Whether you would be hot or cold to touch.
Whilst she and I, — oh, we were two young trees
So nearly of a height we had the same world
Ever within our vision! — Yet all these years,
Even from the time we first went to Fiori,
You have been bearing me your little tales, —
"She had done this and that, she was thus and so —,"
Seeking to stir and poison the clear water
Of my deep love for her!   And now this thing.
Which is not true.   But if it had been true,
It would not be so out of all reason cruel
As that you should have told me of it now.
Nay, do not weep.   All day 'tis one of us
Making the other weep.   We are two strange,
Unhappy women.   Come, let us be at peace.
(*Pause.   Bianca rises suddenly*)
Mother, farewell a little while.   I go now
To her, seeing that she does not come to me.
But not to question her, not to demand,
"How comes it: this?   What can you say to that?"
Only to sit beside her, as in the old days,
And let her lay her quiet on my heart.

Scene 3

The garden at Fiori, same as in Act I, Scene 1. Discovered seated on a stone bench in the sunshine, Beatrice, clad in a loose gown, looking very ill. Fidelio sings off stage.

FIDELIO (*singing*).

> "Let the little birds sing,
> Let the little lambs play.
> Spring is here, and so 'tis spring, —
> But not in the old way.
>
> I recall a place
> Where a plum-tree grew, —
> There you lifted up your face
> And blossoms covered you.
>
> If the little birds sing,
> And the little lambs play,
> Spring is here, and so 'tis spring, —
> But not in the old way."

BEATRICE.   It is a pretty song.   There be some things
That even the tortured heart's profoundest anguish
Cannot bring down from their high place.   Music
Is one of them.

[*Enter Grazia, carrying a bowl.*

GRAZIA.   Now, will you drink this broth,
Or will you not?   I swear upon my shroud —
And 'tis a solemn oath — I never nursed
So vaporous a patient! — Come, my bird!

BEATRICE (*taking the bowl, then setting it down*).   Nay, Nurse,
I cannot.

GRAZIA.   Oh, alackaday!
What shall I do with you?   Come now, and drink me
The pretty broth, my dear!

BEATRICE.   I will drink it later.
'Tis too hot.

GRAZIA. Ay, and in a moment 'twill be
Too cold! And you'll not drink it! I could cry.

[*Exit Grazia. Enter Fidelio.*

BEATRICE. Fidelio, as you love me, do you drink this,
And quickly, man!

FIDELIO (*with grief*). Oh, my dear mistress!

BEATRICE. Drink!

FIDELIO (*sadly drinking*). I best would leave a little else
she'll know
'Twas never you.

BEATRICE. Ay, so you would. I' faith,
It is a knave's trick, but I cannot touch it.
Go now, Fidelio, ere she come again.

[*Exit Fidelio. Enter Bianca.*

BIANCA (*softly*). Rose-Red.

[*Beatrice looks up and listens, thinking it a dream.*

BIANCA Rose-Red, dear sister!

BEATRICE (*bowing her head and weeping*). Oh, my heart!

BIANCA (*coming towards her*). Why do you weep?

BEATRICE (*looking up startled and seeing her, jumping to her
feet*). Oh, no! Oh, God above!
Go back! Go back!

BIANCA (*amazed, quietly*). Beatrice, are you mad?
'Tis I, Bianca.

BEATRICE (*more quietly*). Ay, I know 'tis you.
And you must go away.

BIANCA (*breaking down*). You are mad, my dear!

BEATRICE. I would I were. For madmen have their
moments
Of light into the brain. — Hear me, Bianca,
You must return at once to Lagoverde,
And come to me no more, and think of me
No more.

BIANCA. Ay. I will go. But ere I go
Tell me you do not love me. 'Tis apparent
You do not. I but wish to hear the words.

BEATRICE. Nay, that I will not say. It would be well,
To say it, and let it be. But I'll not say it,
It is not true.

BIANCA. You love me still?

BEATRICE. I love you
More than all else on earth. But I have wronged you
So hugely that I cannot think of it
And stand here talking with you —I am ill —(*She staggers*)
You must pardon me — I have been very ill —

BIANCA. Then it is true?

BEATRICE (*with a cry as of relief*). Ay, it is true! Who told you?

BIANCA. My mother told me. I said it was not true.
But if 'tis true — I pity you, Rose-Red.
I pity him. I pity us all together.

BEATRICE (*feverishly*). Ah, I can see it now! — the quiet road
In the deep wood's gathering darkness, the reins loose
On the horses' necks, that nodded, nodded, and we
Speaking from time to time, and glad to think
Of home, — and suddenly out of nowhere, — fury,
And faces, and long swords, and a great noise!
And even as I reached to draw my sword,
The arm that held the scabbard set on fire,
As if the sleeve were burning! — and my horse
Backing into the trees, my hair caught, twisted,
Torn out by the roots! Then from the road behind
A second fury! And I turned, confused,
Outraged with pain, and thrust, — and it was Mario!

BIANCA (*wildly*). What are you saying? What are you say-
ing? What is this
You are telling me? That it was you? Your hand — ?
Oh, God have mercy upon me! Let me go!

BEATRICE (*pitifully reaching out her arms towards her*).
Snow-White! Snow-White! — farewell!

BIANCA (*without turning*). Oh, God have mercy!
[*Exit Bianca*
Beatrice falls unconscious to the floor.
CURTAIN

ACT V

Scene 1

A room in the palace at Fiori.   Anselmo and Luigi.

LUIGI.   Nay, is that true, Anselmo?

ANSELMO.   Aye, 'tis true.
But no one saw save me.   I drew her sword
Out of his heart and thrust it in its scabbard,
Where she lay senseless.

LUIGI.   Oh, unhappy Queen!

ANSELMO.   Ay, she does not forget.   Has it not struck you
She rides no more?   Her black horse stands in stable,
Eating his head off.   It is two years now
Since she has visited Lagoverde; and the Queen
Of Lagoverde comes not nigh this place.

LUIGI.   There's not the reason that there was to come
Before Octavia's death.

ANSELMO.   Nay, 'tis not that.

LUIGI.   Think you that Beatrice told her?

ANSELMO.   Ay,
I doubt it not.

LUIGI.   'Tis hard.   They were close friends.

ANSELMO.   And since that day her hand upon the sceptre
Trembles, — and Guido sees.   She goes too much
Among the people, nursing them.   She loves them;
Their griefs are hers, their hearts are hers, as well.
But Guido has a following in this court
That hangs upon his word, and he has taught them
Her gentleness is weakness, and her love
Faint-hearted womanish whims, till they are eager
To pull her down, and see a man in place of her.

LUIGI.   Her throne is like a raft upon a sea,
That shifts, and rights itself, and may go down
At any moment.

ANSELMO.   The more especially
For all these drowning beggars that cling to it,
Chattering for help.   She will not strike them off.

LUIGI.   Unhappy Queen.   And there's a storm approaching,
If ever I smelled wind.

ANSELMO.   I fear it, Luigi.

[*Exeunt Anselmo and Luigi.   Enter Guido and Francesca.*

FRANCESCA.   How do I know you love her still? — I know,
The way you fall a-tapping with your fingers,
Or plucking at your eyebrows, if her name
Be spoken, or she move across the court.
How do I know? — Oh, Guido, have I learned you
So little, then, in all these bitter years?
I know you very well.

GUIDO.   You know too much
I'll have an end of this, I tell you!

FRANCESCA.   Ay.
You've told me that before. — An end of what?
What is this thing you'll put this mighty end to?
'Fore God I would I knew.   Could I but name it,
I might have power to end it then, myself!

GUIDO.   I'll have an end of these soft words at twilight,
And these bad mornings full of bile!   I'll have an end
Of all this spying on me!

FRANCESCA (*gently*).   'Tis not so.
I do not spy upon you.   But I see you
Bigger than other men, and your least gesture —
A giant moving rocks. — Oh, Guido, tell me
You do not love her!   Even though I know
You lie, I will believe you, — for I must!

GUIDO (*pause*).   Nay, I am done with you.   I will tell you
    nothing.
Out of my way! — I have that on my mind
Would crush your silly skull like the shell of an egg!
Od's body, will you keep your ugly claws
From scratching at my sleeve?

[*He thrusts her roughly aside and rushes out.*

FRANCESCA (*creeping away, sobbing*).   Oh, God — oh, God —
I would whatever it is, that it were over.

[*Exit.   Enter Fidelio, and crosses the stage, singing.*

FIDELIO (*singing*).
>   "Rain comes down
>   And hushes the town.
>   *And where is the voice that I heard crying?*
>   Snow settles
>   Over the nettles.
>   *Where is the voice that I heard crying?*
>   Sand at last
>   On the drifting mast.
>   *And where is the voice that I heard crying?*
>   Earth now
>   On the busy brow.
>   *And where is the voice that I heard crying?*"

[*Exit Fidelio.*

Scene 2

The court-room in the palace at Fiori, crowded with restless and expectant people. The crowd is arranged on both sides of the stage, in such a way that a broad avenue is left in the middle, leading from the footlights to the back of the stage and gradually narrowing to a point at Beatrice's throne. On the extreme right and left of the stage, along the back of the crowd, stands the guard, a large body of armed soldiers, at attention, in double row. On either side the throne stands an armed soldier. As the curtain rises the court is all standing and looking off stage in a certain direction. Enter the Queen, Beatrice, from that direction, walks in, looking straight ahead, goes to the throne and seats herself. The court sits. The clerk begins to read.

CLERK.   The first case to be heard is that of Lisa,
    A widow with two small children, who resides
    Near the Duke's wood, and has been caught in the act
    Of cutting trees there, and hauling them home to burn.
BEATRICE.   Stand, Lisa. You are a widow, I am told,
    With two small children.
LISA.   Ay, your Majesty,
    Two little boys.

BEATRICE.   I know another widow, Lisa,
   With two small children, — but hers are little girls.
   Have you been cutting trees on the Duke's land?
LISA.   No, Majesty.   I could not cut a tree.
   I have no axe.
BEATRICE.   And are you strong enough
   To break a tree with your hands?
LISA.   No, Majesty.
BEATRICE.   I see.   What do you do, then?   There must be
   Some reason for this plaint.
LISA.   I gather wood
   That's dead, — dried boughs, and underbrush that's been
   A long time on the ground, and drag it home.
BEATRICE.   Have you a woodpile?
LISA.   Nay.   I gather enough
   Each day for the day's need.   I have no time
   To gather more.
BEATRICE.   And does the dry wood burn
   As well as other wood?
LISA.   Oh, better!
BEATRICE.   I see.
   You would as lief, then, have this wood you gather,
   This dead wood, as a green tree freshly cut?
LISA.   Ay, I would liefer have it, Majesty.
   I need a fire quickly.   I have no time
   To wait for wood to season.
BEATRICE.   You may sit down,
   Lisa.   Is the Duke's agent here?
AGENT.   Ay, here.
BEATRICE.   What is it the Duke's custom to have done
   With this dead wood on his estate?
AGENT.   He burns it,
   Your Majesty.
BEATRICE.   You mean to say, I think,
   He pays a price to have it gathered and burned.
AGENT.   Ay, Majesty.
BEATRICE.   Where is it burned?

AGENT. In a clearing.

BEATRICE. And what is cooked upon it?

AGENT. Nothing is cooked.
The Duke is not a gypsy.

[*With irritation.*
Pause. Slight titter in court-room, instantly hushed into profound silence.

BEATRICE (*evenly*). If he were,
He would be shrewder, and not be paying money
For what this woman is glad to do for naught.
Nothing is cooked, and nobody is warmed, —
A most unthrifty fire! Do you bid the Duke,
Until he show me sounder cause for plaint,
Permit this woman to gather unmolested
Dead wood in his forest, and bear it home. — Lisa,
Take care you break no half-green boughs. The next case?

CLERK. Is that of Mario, a miller, accused
Of stealing grain. A baker, by name Pietro,
Brings this complaint against him.

MESSENGER (*rushing in and up to throne*). Majesty,
Bianca of Lagoverde lies a-dying,
And calls for you!

BEATRICE (*rising*). She calls for me?

MESSENGER. Ay, Majesty.

[*Beatrice stands very still a moment, then turns to the towns-people.*

BEATRICE (*earnestly and rapidly*). You people, do you go
now and live kindly
Till I return. I may not stay to judge you;
Wherefore I set you free. For I would rather
A knave should go at large than that a just man
Be punished. If there be a knave among you,
Let him live thoughtfully till I return.

(*She steps down from the throne, and is immediately seized by the arm on either side by the two guards who have been standing beside the throne*)

Why, what is this, Enrico?

(*Looking up at the soldier on her right*)

Nay, it is not
Enrico! (*Looking to other side*) Nor is it Pablo! How is this?

(*From each side of the stage one row of the double row of
soldiers detaches itself, marches down around the front of the
stage and up towards the throne, making an armed alley for
the Queen to walk down, and entirely surrounding the crowd*)

Nay, all new faces. So! Upon my word,
This is a marvelous sight. — Do you stand back
And keep your fingers from me! — I see you there,
Angelo! Do not turn your head aside!
And you, Filippo! — Is the sick hand better
I bound the bandage on? — Is't well enough
To draw a sword against me? — Nay, I am sick.
I, that have loved you as your mothers love you —
And you do this to me! Lead me away.

[*The two guards lead out the Queen. Nobody else moves.
The townspeople cower and stare. The two little pages that
bore her train as she entered remain back of the throne, not
knowing what to do. As she goes by them, her train dragging
on the ground, the two ragged little boys of Lisa, the wood-
gatherer, run out from the group of citizens, pick up the ends
of her train, and go out, holding it up, one of them with his
arm over his eyes.*

Scene 3

*A dungeon. Beatrice alone, sitting on a bench, her head
bowed in her hands. Enter Guido.*

BEATRICE. Guido, is't you!

GUIDO.   Ay, it is I, my Queen.
You sent for me, an I mistake not?

BEATRICE.   Ay.
Guido, you will not keep me when I tell you
Snow-White is dying and calls my name!

GUIDO.   I knew that.

BEATRICE. You knew that, and you hold me here. Oh, Heaven!
What are you?

GUIDO. I am a man. You should have thought
Of that before. I could have been your friend
If it had pleased you. Failing that, I am
Your enemy. I am too aware of you,
And have been ever, to hold me in at less.

BEATRICE. Guido. I beg of you upon my knees
To let me go!

GUIDO. And why should I do that?

BEATRICE. For pity's sake!

GUIDO. I do not know the word.

BEATRICE. Then for the sake of my sworn hand and seal
Upon a paper yielding fair to you
This sovereignty you prize. It is to me
Little enough to-night. I give it gladly.

GUIDO. You have no power to give what I have taken
Already, and hold upon my hand, Rose-Red.

BEATRICE. Oh, do not speak that name! Oh, Guido, Guido,
I cannot suffer further! Let me go!
If only for a moment, let me go!
I will return, — I will but take her hand,
And come away! I swear it! Let me go!

GUIDO. On one condition only.

BEATRICE. Ay! 'Tis granted,
Ere it is spoken!

GUIDO. That upon returning
You come to me, and give yourself to me,
To lie in my arms lovingly. (*She is stricken speechless*)
You hear?
To lie in my arms lovingly.

BEATRICE. Oh, God!

GUIDO. It is my only word.

BEATRICE. Oh, God! Oh, God!

GUIDO. 'Tis granted?

BEATRICE. Nay, — I cannot! I will die
Instead. Oh, God, to think that she will lie there
And call for me, and I will never come!

GUIDO. Good night.

[*He goes to door.*

BEATRICE (*in a quiet voice*). Guido!
It shall be as you say.

GUIDO (*rushing to her*). Ah, Beatrice!

BEATRICE Nay, touch me not yet.
I will return. (*She laughs like a child*) Why, 'tis a simple
matter!
I wonder now that even for a moment
I held myself so dear! When for her sake
All things are little things! — This foolish body,
This body is not I! There is no I,
Saving the need I have to go to her!

Scene 4

A room at Lagoverde. Bianca lying in bed, ill to death.
The children clinging to the bed, their nurse trying to draw them
away. Giuletta, a maid, in the background. Possibly other
attendants about.

LITTLE ROSE-RED. Finish the story, mother!

NURSE. Come away, now!

LITTLE SNOW-WHITE. Finish the story!

BIANCA. Do you go away with nurse
A little while. You will bring them back to me
Later?

NURSE (*weeping*). Ay, madam.

[*She goes out with the children.*

BIANCA. Later — not much later,
I think. — Hear you no sound of horses yet,
Giulietta, galloping this way?

GIULIETTA. Nay, not yet.

BIANCA (*to herself*). I will not go until she comes. I will not.
Still, — if I should — Giulietta!

GIULIETTA (*coming quickly to the bed*). Ay, my mistress!

BIANCA. She will come, I tell you!

GIULIETTA.   Ay, I doubt it not.

BIANCA. Ay, she will come. But if she should come late,
And I no longer be here to receive her,
Show her all courtesy, I conjure you.
She will be weary, and mightily distraught.
Make her take wine, — and bring the children to her.
And tell her, they are hers now. She is their mother.
(Giulietta starts to go back to the window)
And say to her — wait! — I have a message for her.
Say to her this, Giulietta: The foot stumbles,
The hand hath its own awkward way; the tongue
Moves foolishly in the mouth; but in the heart
The truth lies, — and all's well 'twixt her and me.
Can you remember that?

GIULIETTA.   Ay, madam, I think so.
If not the words, at least the gist of it.

BIANCA. Forget it all, my good child, but forget not:
All's well 'twixt her and me.

GIULIETTA.   Nay, that I have.

BIANCA. I will sleep now a little. Do you leave me.
But go not far.   *(She lies still for a moment, then starts up)*
I hear the sound of hoof-beats!

GIULIETTA. Nay, madam.

BIANCA.   Ay, I tell you! I can hear them!
My face upon the pillow brings my ear
Nearer the ground! She is coming! Open the door!
[*She kneels up in bed and holds out her arms towards the door,
maintaining this position till Beatrice comes. Giulietta,
weeping, opens the door, and stands in it, shaking her head
sadly.*

GIULIETTA (*suddenly lifting her head and listening*). Nay, it
is so! I hear it now myself!
Ay, there's a horse upon the bridge!

BIANCA.   She's coming!
Stand back! Stand out of the doorway!
[*Pause.*

SERVANT (*entering*).   Majesty,
   The Queen is here.
   Ay, ay! Stand out of the doorway.
   [*Pause.*

GIULIETTA. She is here! She is in the court! She has
      leapt from horse!
   Madam, Oh God be praised! This way!

BIANCA.   Sister!
   [*Beatrice enters in her riding clothes, leaps to the bed, Bianca
   throws her arms about her neck, and dies.*

BEATRICE (*after a moment, looking down at her*). Snow-White!
   Oh, no! Snow-White! (*She screams*) Ah-h! Help me!
   She is dying!
   [*Attendants and nurses rush in, also the children.*

LITTLE SNOW-WHITE.   Mother, wake up!

LITTLE ROSE-RED.   Come out of doors!

BEATRICE. Take them away. Snow-White!
   [*Leaning over the bed.*

NURSE. Nay, it is over,
   Madam.

BEATRICE.   Leave me. Leave me alone with her.
   [*Exeunt all but Beatrice. She kneels beside the bed.*

SCENE 5

A room at Lagoverde. The next day. Beatrice alone.

BEATRICE.   In sooth, I do not feel the earth so firm
Under my feet as yesterday it was.
All that I loved have gone to a far land,
And left me here alone, save for two children
And twenty thousand enemies, and the thing
Of horror that's in store for me.   Almost
I feel my feet uprooted from the earth,
There's such a tugging at me to be gone.
Save for your children (*looking off stage towards Bianca's
room*), 'twould be simple enough

To lay me down beside you in your bed,
And call on Death, who is not yet out of hearing,
To take me, too.

[*Enter Fidelio.*

FIDELIO.   Mistress, I have news for you.
Guido is dead!
BEATRICE.   Is dead?
FIDELIO.   Ay, he is dead.
Dead of a dagger i' the back, — and dead enough
For twenty.   Scarce were you gone an hour's time
We came upon him cold.   And in a pool
Nearby, the Lady Francesca floating drowned,
Who last was seen a-listening like a ghost
At the door of the dungeon.   'Tis a marvelous thing!
But that's not all!
BEATRICE.   Why, what more can there be?
FIDELIO.   Mistress, in the night the people of Fiori
Rose like a wind and swept the Duke's men down
Like leaves!   Come home!   Come home!   We will have
     supper
On a flat web, behind a mulberry bush,
Of milk and tarts and honey and white bread —
All in one day!
BEATRICE.   There is but half of me
To hear your tidings.   I would clap my hands together
But one of them is stricken from my side.

[*Enter Giulietta.*

GIULIETTA.   Madam.
BEATRICE.   Ay, Giulietta.
GIULIETTA.   Madam, last night,
Before you came, she bade me tell you something,
And not forget.   'Tis this: That the foot stumbles,
The hand doth awkward things, and the foolish tongue
Says what it would not say, — but in the heart
Truth lies, — and all is well 'twixt her and you.

(*She starts to go out, and turns back at the door*)

She bade me above all things to forget not
The last: that all is well 'twixt her and you.
[*Exit.*

BEATRICE (*slowly and with great content*).
She is not gone from me. Oh, there be places
Farther away than Death! She is returned
From her long silence, and rings out above me
Like a silver bell! — Let us go back, Fidelio,
And gather up the fallen stones, and build us
Another tower.

CURTAIN

REHEARSAL

CHRISTOPHER MORLEY

CHRISTOPHER MORLEY was born at Haverford, Pennsylvania, May 5, 1890. He studied at Haverford College and was Rhodes Scholar 1910–1913. Upon his return to America he became associated with the editorial staffs of Doubleday, Page and Company, and the Curtis publications. He is now conductor of The Bowling Green, a column in the *New York Evening Post*.

Though better known as an essayist Mr. Morley has written three plays: "Three's a Crowd", "Thursday Evening", and "Rehearsal".

REHEARSAL

A COMEDY IN ONE ACT

By CHRISTOPHER MORLEY

Characters

FREDA . . . . .The Director

CHRISTINE
BARBARA
GERTRUDE } . . . . .The Players
SONIA

MARJORIE . . . . .The Stage Carpenter
and Property Man

REHEARSAL

SCENE. *Rehearsal of a play to be given by a college dramatic club.*

This is, as far as the setting is concerned, the easiest play to produce that you ever heard of. It requires only a bare stage, several plain chairs and a small table. Whatever is the natural and unadorned condition of your stage, leave it so. Nor are any special costumes necessary: the characters may attire themselves as suits their fancy and condition in life. The scene represents a rehearsal of an amateur play — I mean, a play performed by amateurs. As a matter of fact, the play they are at work on is supposed to be one of those Irish peasantry things. I have imagined the characters as being college girls, in whom is apparent that pleasing mixture of hilarity and importance characteristic of the sex in youth. However, it being to the author's interest that this play should be performed as frequently as possible, I will remark that by the change of a word or so here and there it is equally valid for girls' schools, or clubs of high-spirited ladies.

The house lights having been turned off, and the footlights on, as usual, the audience, eager to be entertained, attentively waits the rise of the curtain. But before the curtain goes up, the gutter is again darkened; so that for a moment the audience thinks some mistake has been made. This impression is perhaps confirmed when the curtain immediately rises upon the naked stage, which is adequately lit from above, but seems rather gloomy without the usual shine of the footlights.

Enter Freda, the director and manager, a brisk young person who enjoys her responsibility and takes it seriously. She carries a typescript, which she lays on the table at the front of the stage, — the sacred little table which still holds an empty jug and a glass to remind one that not long ago some British celebrity spent a happy evening lecturing there. Freda moves the table to one side, and rapidly begins to arrange the chairs (which are standing in a row at the back) in a calculated pattern. She puts four of them close together toward the back of the stage; and two, a little distance apart, one behind the other, toward the right side; two, similarly, toward the left. Two or three chairs she places with thoughtful precision in other places within the area thus marked out.

Enter Christine, Barbara, and Sonia, all carrying scripts.

FREDA. Hullo, Where's Gertrude?

CHRISTINE. She'll be here, I guess.

FREDA. She'd better be, or I'll get some one else to do her part. She doesn't seem to realize we've got to *play* this thing a week from to-night.

BARBARA. Horrid thought!

FREDA. Well, while we await the prima donna, let's get to work. Now you know your lines, we can develop some business.

SONIA. I wish you'd picked out some other play; this is so dreadfully gloomy. It'll put the audience into a morbid melancholy.

CHRISTINE. Yes, and there's some pretty strong stuff in it, too. My father and mother are going to be here, and really, I think one ought to be careful about saying some of these things before parents —

FREDA. You ought to be glad it's gloomy. People don't respect you if you play comedy. This kind of thing is much more artistic. Besides, don't blame me. The Professor of English Literature chose it; I didn't.

CHRISTINE. I know — but just looking at things from the parents' standpoint, English Literature is awfully outspoken sometimes.

SONIA. I'm glad my people live so far away there's no chance of their coming to the show.

BARBARA. Think of me, I have to play the stricken old father, brooding over his shame. You try being a stricken old father —

FREDA. Come now, we're wasting time.

[*Enter Marjorie, carrying a hammer, a paint pot and brush, electric bulbs, a roll of canvas and a dingy old suit of masculine garments.*

MARJORIE. Look here, what the deuce am I going to do for 'moonlight through cottage window'? I can't get an arc light anywhere. D'you suppose ordinary frosted bulbs will do?

FREDA. Don't bother *me*. That's your affair. Lord knows I've got enough to manage.

MARJORIE. Well, will these do for the stricken old father? [*Holds out horrible old trousers and coat.*

FREDA. Hurrah! Just the thing. (*Takes trousers and holds them against Barbara, who views them with much distaste*) A perfect fit!

BARBARA. Have I got to wear those things?

MARJORIE. I got them from the janitor.

FREDA. Better put them on right away, and get used to them.

[*Barbara shudders.*

MARJORIE. Yes, atmosphere, local color —

BARBARA. From the local colored man. No thanks.

[*She deposits trousers gingerly at one side of stage. Enter Gertrude, carrying script.*

GERTRUDE. Sorry to be late.

[*Marjorie goes rear of stage, and occupies herself quietly with paint and canvas while the rehearsal proceeds.*

FREDA. All right, now we can go ahead. I've put these chairs to show essentials of scenery. These (*indicating chairs at the back*) are the hearth. This (*to two chairs at one side*) is a door; this (*to two chairs on other side*) is another door. This (*to another chair, toward the rear*) is the window where the moonlight comes in. And here (*to another chair*) is the wheel-chair where the stricken old parent sits disconsolate.

CHRISTINE. There are going to be some stricken parents in the audience, too.

FREDA (*ignoring her*). Now get the scene well in mind. (*Reads from her script*) "A poor cottage in the Irish bogs. At the back, a faint glimmer of a scanty fire of peat on the hearth, with a pile of kelp drying beside it."

MARJORIE. Where am I going to get any kelp? What is kelp, anyway?

FREDA. Seaweed.

MARJORIE. I wonder if spinach would be all right?

FREDA (*continues to read*). "Through rear window, a clear beam of moonlight. In a wheel-chair by a lamp sits Shawn O'Connell, a stricken old man, reading the Bible. The setting indicates an atmosphere of extreme wretchedness and misery. From the shadows near the hearth, where Norah has flung herself prostrate in despair, comes an occasional low keening."

(*Christine and Sonia look humorously at Gertrude, who plays the part of Norah*)

Are you ready? Places!

(*Barbara sits down in one of the chairs; Gertrude, with a shame-faced air, lies down on the chairs assembled at the back. Christine and Sonia retire to one side of the stage, off the chair-marked area, and solemnly consult their scripts. Freda sits down at the little table, on the other side of the stage*)

Curtain!

(*There is a short pause, while Barbara gazes pensively at her hands, which she holds spread to represent a large book. Gertrude utters a low moan. It is not a success*)

You'll have to keen better than that. Throw a little agony into it.

GERTRUDE (*sits up*). Can't we have the footlights on? I can do much better then. It seems to make it more real.

FREDA. Good idea. Chris, switch 'em on.

(*Christine exit. The footlights go on, and Christine returns*) We've got to get into the spirit of this thing. Try to imagine the audience out there. (*She waves toward the auditorium*) Imagine the place crowded with intelligent

faces — proud parents, interested friends, hopeful young
men —

BARBARA. I'm damned if I want to wear trousers before a
mixed audience —

FREDA. Don't be so mid-Woodrovian. Look here, I told
you to bring something to use as a Bible. What did you
make me director for if you're not going to obey orders?
Wait a minute, I'll find something.

[*She rushes off.*

GERTRUDE. Tell me if this sounds any better.

[*She utters several throbbing tremulous wails.*

CHRISTINE. Somehow it doesn't seem to carry conviction.

SONIA. You must try to imagine terrible things. Imagine
you've flunked Physics.

GERTRUDE. The trouble is, it's so hard to find any place to
practice keening. I tried it in my room late at night, and
the watchman sent for a doctor.

MARJORIE. I wish Freda wouldn't insist on that moonlight.

GERTRUDE. I simply can't keen in cold blood. It'll be all
right when the audience is here.

SONIA. You're too self-conscious. You'll never be a great
actress.

GERTRUDE. You'd be self-conscious too if you had to play
this part before parents and younger brothers.

CHRISTINE. Younger brothers are the devil. They're as
bad as Doctor Freud.

SONIA. Write and tell them there's smallpox in town.

[*Reënter Freda, carrying large telephone directory.*

FREDA (*to Barbara*). Here you are — the Telephone Book.
It's the only thing I could find. Come now, Places!

BARBARA (*produces a clay pipe*). I thought that if I used
this pipe, it would help me to get the illusion.

[*Puts it in her mouth and sits down with the directory.*

FREDA. Curtain!

[*Barbara sits in the "wheel-chair", turning over the leaves of
the directory, and awkwardly holding the pipe in her mouth.
Gertrude is lying, face down, with her head buried in her arms,*

> *on the chairs at the back. She utters a dire dreadful moaning occasionally.*

BARBARA. Has Herself come yet?

GERTRUDE (*sobbing*). Not yet. Nor never will, I'm thinking.

BARBARA (*grav ly, with the tremulous voice of old age, but having great trouble to keep the pipe in her mouth while she speaks*). Fifty year and five it is that I'm living in this place, and never before now did shame come down upon the home of the O'Connell.

(*Gertrude utters only a low wail*)

Be leaving off your keening, my girl, I'll be having no stomach to my supper. Is that broth cooked?

GERTRUDE (*gets up languidly and pretends to look at the hearth*). No, father.

BARBARA. Come away out of the darkness now, and let me be seeing you.

(*Gertrude comes forward, slowly and shamefully, and crouches at Barbara's feet. Barbara tries to light her pipe*)

See how all the names are written here in the Book — names of the O'Connell, all numbered in the Good Book. (*Christine and Sonia cannot restrain a giggle*) Thirteen childer and never a word of shame agin one of them. Francey, Padraic, Finn, Bridget, Cathleen, Dennis. Think of Dennis, now, who killed three Englishmen in one Sunday. This has been a proud house, surely.

GERTRUDE. I'm thinking that the broth will soon be ready, father.

BARBARA. God be praised, I'm after keeping my appetite in spite of all this sorrow. (*Points to page in the book*) Thirteen childer, six dead of the bog fever, three drowned in the fishing, two in jail for the republic, one gone to America — all numbered in the Book.

CHRISTINE (*to Sonia*). Call Columbus 8200.

FREDA (*angrily*). Shhhh!

BARBARA (*in her own voice*). I've forgotten my lines. It isn't fair of the author to give any one a speech as long as this one.

GERTRUDE. It doesn't matter. The audience never listens to the first five minutes. They're busy climbing over each other's feet.

FREDA (*rapping on table*). How do you expect to get this thing across if you make a joke out of it?

BARBARA. I simply can't talk with this pipe in my mouth. It's funny — I've often seen men do it.

FREDA (*reading from her script*). "I am an old man — "

BARBARA. Oh, yes. (*Resumes her part*) I am an old man, and shamed in my own house. I am after looking for the third chapter of Isaiah. Does Isaiah come *after* Jeremiah or before it? I never can remember.

GERTRUDE. Yourself had thirteen childer, father, and if only one goes to hell, it's no bad proportion at all —

BARBARA. Whisht, whisht, Norah — is it the Bad Place Yourself is speaking of? Don't be naming that place to an old stricken man that maybe will have had sins of his own to be shriven. It's perished with hunger I am.

GERTRUDE (*rises, goes to chairs at the back and stoops over the imaginary fire*). Which is it that is troubling you more, father; the shame or the supper?

BARBARA (*absently turning over pages of the directory*). The third chapter of Isaiah. There's something about mantles and wimples and crisping pins.

GERTRUDE. Crisping pins, is it? Devil a crisping pin did I ever see in this house.

BARBARA (*reads*). "Because the daughters of Zion walk with stretched forth necks and wanton eyes, walking and mincing as they go, and making a tinkling with their feet. . . . the Lord will take away the bravery of their tinkling ornaments . . . the chains and the bracelets and the mufflers, the bonnets and the ornaments of the legs . . . the rings and nose jewels, the changeable suits of apparel, and the mantles and the wimples and the crisping pins. . . . And it shall come to pass, that instead of sweet smell there shall be stink; and instead of well-set hair baldness; and instead of a stomacher — " — Sure, Norah, isn't that broth ready?

GERTRUDE. Here it is, father.

[*Comes forward, carrying an imaginary bowl, which she sets down on an imaginary table beside Barbara, and pretends to set out imaginary dishes, spoons, etc.*

FREDA (*interrupting*). That's rotten! Barbara, you've got to be more tragic. Read that with more feeling.

BARBARA. I don't like reading the Old Testament. It's — well, it's so vulgar —

FREDA (*going to her*). Let me show you how that ought to go. Remember you're a broken old man. (*Takes the directory and sits down in Barbara's chair; assumes a quavering and senile solemnity, and pretends to read from the book, improvising the speech from memory*) Because the daughters of Zion walk with stretched forth legs and wanton stomachers the Lord will take away John J. Wimple plumber and steamfitter and instead of crisping pins there shall be Henry Wiesenfeldt Audubon 6543. (*Rises*) There, do you see? More pathos!

MARJORIE. Just a minute! I hadn't heard about all these mufflers and wimples and crisping pins — they aren't actual props, are they?

GERTRUDE. No, no, you poor fish. They're only mentioned.

MARJORIE. Well, how was I to know? Freda never gave me a copy of the script to look over. If anything goes wrong, it won't be my fault.

FREDA. Attention, please! Now go on with it from there.

[*Barbara resumes her place in the chair.*

BARBARA. Where were we? These interruptions get my goat.

FREDA. "Here it is, father."

GERTRUDE. Here it is, father. (*Again brings imaginary soup from the rear, and serves it as before. Barbara pretends to spoon it up with gusto*) Leave off feeding till I fix your napkin. Herself might be coming in, and you wouldn't want to be all speckled with the soup —

BARBARA. There's darker stains than spilling a little broth on your breastbone. Yourself might be thinking of the daughters of Zion.

GERTRUDE. Perhaps the daughters of Zion were not brought up all alone in the bogs, with no company but the moonlight and an old man dripping his soup. It's more of soup you are thinking than of salvation. Surely it's bitter.

BARBARA (*after a pause*). It *is* bitter. You've maybe dropped some of the kelp in it. (*A pause*) I'll be telling you the truth, I'm destroyed altogether with thirst. If you'd be slipping over to the shebeen to bring me a dram —

GERTRUDE (*goes to the chair that represents a window, and pretends to look out*). Here comes Herself now, God help us, and a foreigner with her. Be easy and go on with your supper. I'll be passing into the loft. (*She starts to the chair-doorway, right, and then impulsively returns to Barbara. Piteously*) Oh, Daddy, you'll not be thinking too hard of your Norah?

BARBARA (*still eating*). It's grand fine soup.

(Gertrude goes through chair-doorway, right, and stands near Freda. Christine and Sonia come to chair-doorway, left, and Sonia taps on the stage with her foot, to represent knocking at the door)

Who's that, God help us? (*Christine and Sonia enter*) Ah, it's yourself, Mrs. O'Toole, and a foreigner with you.

CHRISTINE. Yes. An English lady, God help her.

BARBARA. Come in and be set.

CHRISTINE. Surely it's quare and cold to-night, Shawn, and the bogs in the moonshine as white as soap.

BARBARA. Yes, I've finished my soup, thank you kindly.

CHRISTINE. A sorrowful night to be lying drowned in the bogs, I'm thinking. I mind the time when Katie O'Shaughnessy perished herself in the marsh. She floated face under, God help her, and they said it was because she was ashamed to look her Maker in the face. Indeed I don't wonder, with nothing on her but a shift.

BARBARA. The men folk float face upwards, Mrs. O'Toole.

CHRISTINE. To be sure you ought to know the rights of it, what with three sons floating in at the high tide. (*To Sonia*) We waked them all together, and Father Daly ran short on candles.

SONIA. Mr. O'Connell, I'm afraid I have dreadful news for you —

BARBARA. Indeed, Ma'am, bad news is an old friend in this house of shame. (*Plaintively*) If I had a drop of spirits it would be a consolation.

FREDA (*interrupting*). Fine! That's fine! (*The actors relax, and stand at ease*) I don't think your Irish brogue is very good, but you're beginning to get the spirit of the thing.

CHRISTINE. Yes, if we can do it like this I think the audience ought to be sufficiently depressed.

FREDA. We won't need to go over the part where the young Englishman's body is brought in, and Norah commits suicide. By the way, Marjorie, what are you going to do for the young Englishman's body?

MARJORIE. Oh, I'm going to play that myself. My only chance of glory.

FREDA. All right, then — we'll take it again from the beginning down to where Sonia and Christine come in.

SONIA. I don't think that's fair. You never give me a chance to rehearse the only decent bit I have.

BARBARA. Oh, rot, Sonia! Your stuff is a cinch. You don't even have to talk Irish.

GERTRUDE. Yes, for Heaven's sake let's do that first part again while we've got it hot. If I don't get used to watching Barbara I shall burst into yells of laughter —

BARBARA. Considering I have the rottenest part in the whole show, I think I do fairly well.

SONIA. Some people are certainly hard to please. Your part is the only one with a chance for any real acting. Pretty fat, I call it.

CHRISTINE. I agree with Sonia. We ought to rehearse the last half as often as we can. That bit where I have to break the news to the old man needs some doing. That seems to me the real crux of the play, and I don't feel at all sure of it yet.

MARJORIE. I thought you were going to check up that list of props with me. Here I've been hanging around —

FREDA. Ye gods, you girls think of no one but yourselves. Can't you forget your own parts for a moment and think of the good of the show?

SONIA. I don't care, you've skimped my part right along, and never give me a decent chance to rehearse. I know damn well you want me to flivver —

BARBARA. Sonia can have my part whenever she wants it. I'm fed up with the stricken old parent and his house of shame —

GERTRUDE (*looking at her wrist watch*). Well, what's the dope? I haven't got all day —

MARJORIE. You people make me tired. All wanting to grab off the footlight stuff. Suppose some of you lend *me* a hand in building the scenery.

FREDA (*angrily*). Who's directing this play, I'd like to know? You put it up to me, didn't you? *Somebody's* got to run things —

CHRISTINE. It was asinine to pick out a fool play like this. Why not something with some fun in it?

FREDA. Who ever heard of a one-act play with any fun in it? They don't write 'em. A one-act play *has* to be artistic —

SONIA. All I can say is, I hate to see an innocent audience suffer.

GERTRUDE. I know I'll *never* be able to live down this house of shame business with my young brothers. They'll be kidding me about it for the next five years.

SONIA. Come on now, all together — can't we do something else instead? Honestly, Freda, we'd rehearse all night for the next week if you'll choose something really decent —

FREDA. Don't be absurd. The announcements have gone out.

SONIA.   I bet the   thing will be a hideous failure —

FREDA.   Now let's be sensible.   I know exactly how you all feel.   Putting on a play is just like going to the dentist — the worst part is beforehand.   When the fatal evening comes, no one will suspect the agony we've been through. I bet the house will give us a big hand — even the younger brothers.

BARBARA.   Freda's right.   Come on, children, a little courage!

FREDA.   We'll do the second part of the play at the next rehearsal.   This time we'd better stick to what we've been doing, and get it set.   Places!

BARBARA.   Give the stricken old father time to light his pipe. [*As she fumbles with the pipe, the others take their positions — Freda at the little table; Marjorie at the rear; Christine and Sonia down-stage, left; Gertrude on the chairs toward the back; and Barbara then sits down with the telephone directory.*

FREDA.   Curtain!

[*And, as Barbara turns over the leaves of the book, and Gertrude utters her first "keen", the curtain falls.*

BEFORE BREAKFAST

EUGENE G. O'NEILL

EUGENE G. O'NEILL was born in New York City, October 16, 1888, the son of James O'Neill, the distinguished American actor. He has been seaman, laborer, newspaperman and dramatist. Mr. O'Neill was one of the original members of the Provincetown Players, the group of players and authors who have the honor of presenting most of his plays to the public.

Mr. O'Neill's published plays are as follows: "Thirst and Other One-act Plays", containing "Thirst"; "The Web", "Warnings", "Fog", and "Recklessness." Badger, Boston, 1914; "Before Breakfast", a Play in One Act. Shay, New York, 1916; "The Moon of the Caribbees and Six Other Plays of the Sea", containing: "Moon of the Caribbees", "Bound East for Cardiff", "The Long Voyage Home", "In the Zone", "Ile", "Where the Cross is Made", "The Rope." Boni and Liveright, New York, 1919; "Beyond the Horizon", a Play in Three Acts. Boni and Liveright, New York, 1920; "Gold", a Play in Four Acts. Boni and Liveright, New York, 1920; "The Emperor Jones" (8 scenes), "Diff'rent" (3 acts), "The Straw" (3 acts), Boni and Liveright, New York, 1921; "The Emperor Jones", a Play in Eight Scenes. Stewart Kidd, Cincinnati, 1921.

BEFORE BREAKFAST

A PLAY IN ONE ACT

By EUGENE G. O'NEILL

(1916)

"Before Breakfast" was originally produced by the Provincetown Players, in 1916.

Original Cast

MRS. ROWLAND	Mary Pyne
ALFRED, her Husband (not seen) . . .	Eugene G. O'Neill

BEFORE BREAKFAST

SCENE: *A small room serving both as kitchen and dining room in a flat on Christopher Street, New York City. In the rear, to the right, a door leading to the outer hallway. On the left of the doorway, a sink, and a two-burner gas stove. Over the stove, and extending to the left wall, a wooden closet for dishes, etc. On the left, two windows looking out on a fire escape where several potted plants are dying of neglect. Before the windows, a table covered with oilcloth. Two cane-bottomed chairs are placed by the table. Another stands against the wall to the right of door in rear. In the right wall, rear, a doorway leading into a bedroom. Farther forward, different articles of a man's and a woman's clothing are hung on pegs. A clothes line is strung from the left corner, rear, to the right wall, forward. A man's underclothes are thrown over the line.*

It is about eight-thirty in the morning of a fine, sunshiny day in the early fall.

Mrs. Rowland enters from the bedroom, yawning, her hands still busy putting the finishing touches on a slovenly toilet by sticking hairpins into her hair which is bunched up in a drab-colored mass on top of her round head. She is of medium height and inclined to a shapeless stoutness, accentuated by her formless blue dress, shabby and worn. Her face is characterless, with small regular features and eyes of a nondescript blue. There is a pinched expression about her eyes and nose and her weak, spiteful mouth. She is in her early twenties but looks much older.

She comes to the middle of the room and yawns, stretching her arms to their full length. Her drowsy eyes stare about the room with the irritated look of one to whom a long sleep has not been a long rest. She goes wearily to the clothes hanging on the right and takes an apron from a hook. She ties it about her waist, giving vent to an exasperated "damn" when the knot fails to obey her clumsy, fat fingers. Finally gets it tied and goes slowly to the gas stove and lights one burner. She fills the coffee pot at the sink and sets it over the flame. Then slumps down into a chair by the table and puts a hand over her forehead as if she were suffering from headache. Suddenly her face brightens as though she had remembered something, and she casts a quick glance at the dish closet; then looks sharply at the bedroom door and listens intently for a moment or so.

MRS. ROWLAND (*in a low voice*). Alfred! Alfred! (*There is no answer from the next room and she continues suspiciously in a louder tone*) You needn't pretend you're asleep. (*There is no reply to this from the bedroom, and, reassured, she gets up from her chair and tiptoes cautiously to the dish closet. She slowly opens one door, taking great care to make no noise, and slides out, from their hiding place behind the dishes, a bottle of Gordon gin and a glass. In doing so she disturbs the top dish, which rattles a little. At this sound she starts guiltily and looks with sulky defiance at the doorway to the next room*)

(*Her voice trembling*) Alfred!

(*After a pause, during which she listens for any sound, she takes the glass and pours out a large drink and gulps it down; then hastily returns the bottle and glass to their hiding place. She closes the closet door with the same care as she had opened it, and, heaving a great sigh of relief, sinks down into her chair again. The large dose of alcohol she has taken has an almost immediate effect. Her features become more animated, she seems to gather energy, and she looks at the bedroom door with a hard, vindictive smile on her lips. Her eyes glance quickly about the room and are fixed on a man's coat and vest which hang from a hook at right. She moves stealthily over to the open doorway and stands there, out of sight of any one inside, listening for any movement from within*)

(*Calling in a half-whisper*) Alfred!

(*Again there is no reply. With a swift movement she takes*

*the coat and vest from the hook and returns with them to her
chair. She sits down and takes the various articles out of
each pocket but quickly puts them back again. At last, in
the inside pocket of the vest, she finds a letter)*

(Looking at the handwriting — slowly to herself) Hmm! I
knew it.

*(She opens the letter and reads it. At first her expression is
one of hatred and rage, but as she goes on to the end it changes
to one of triumphant malignity. She remains in deep thought
for a moment, staring before her, the letter in her hands, a
cruel smile on her lips. Then she puts the letter back in the
pocket of the vest, and still careful not to awaken the sleeper,
hangs the clothes up again on the same hook, and goes to the
bedroom door and looks in)*

(In a loud, shrill voice) Alfred! *(Still louder)* Alfred!
(There is a muffled, yawning groan from the next room)
Don't you think it's about time you got up? Do you
want to stay in bed all day? *(Turning around and coming
back to her chair)* Not that I've got any doubts about
your being lazy enough to stay in bed forever. *(She sits
down and looks out of the window, irritably)* Goodness
knows what time it is. We haven't even got any way of
telling the time since you pawned your watch like a fool.
The last valuable thing we had, and you knew it. It's
been nothing but pawn, pawn, pawn, with you — anything to put off getting a job, anything to get out of going
to work like a man. *(She taps the floor with her foot nervously, biting her lips)*

(After a short pause) Alfred! Get up, do you hear me?
I want to make that bed before I go out. I'm sick of having this place in a continual muss on your account. *(With
a certain vindictive satisfaction)* Not that we'll be here
long unless you manage to get some money some place.
Heaven knows I do my part — and more — going out to
sew every day while you play the gentleman and loaf
around bar rooms with that good-for-nothing lot of artists
from the Square.

(*A short pause during which she plays nervously with a cup and saucer on the table*)

And where are you going to get money, I'd like to know? The rent's due this week and you know what the landlord is. He won't let us stay a minute over our time. You say you *can't* get a job. That's a lie and you know it. You never even look for one. All you do is moon around all day writing silly poetry and stories that no one will buy — and no wonder they won't. I notice I can always get a position, such as it is; and it's only that which keeps us from starving to death.

(*Gets up and goes over to the stove — looks into the coffee pot to see if the water is boiling; then comes back and sits down again*)

You'll have to get money to-day some place. I can't do it all, and I won't do it all. You've got to come to your senses. You've got to beg, borrow, or steal it somewheres. (*With a contemptuous laugh*) But where, I'd like to know? You're too proud to beg, and you've borrowed the limit, and you haven't the nerve to steal.

(*After a pause — getting up angrily*) Aren't you up yet, for heaven's sake? It's just like you to go to sleep again, or pretend to. (*She goes to the bedroom door and looks in*) Oh, you are up. Well, it's about time. You needn't look at me like that. Your airs don't fool me a bit any more. I know you too well — better than you think I do — you and your goings-on. (*Turning away from the door — meaningly*) I know a lot of things, my dear. Never mind what I know, now. I'll tell you before I go, you needn't worry. (*She comes to the middle of the room and stands there, frowning*)

(*Irritably*) Hmm! I suppose I might as well get breakfast ready — not that there's anything much to get. (*Questioningly*) Unless you have some money? (*She pauses for an answer from the next room which does not come*) Foolish question! (*She gives a short, hard laugh*) I ought to know you better than that by this time. When

you left here in such a huff last night I knew what would
happen. You can't be trusted for a second. A nice condition you came home in! The fight we had was only an
excuse for you to make a beast of yourself. What was
the use pawning your watch if all you wanted with the
money was to waste it in buying drink?

(*Goes over to the dish closet and takes out plates, cups, etc.,
while she is talking*)

Hurry up! It don't take long to get breakfast these days,
thanks to you. All we got this morning is bread and
butter and coffee; and you wouldn't even have that if it
wasn't for me sewing my fingers off. (*She slams the loaf
of bread on the table with a bang*)

The bread's stale. I hope you'll like it. *You* don't deserve any better, but I don't see why *I* should suffer.

(*Going over to the stove*) The coffee'll be ready in a
minute, and you needn't expect me to wait for you.

(*Suddenly with great anger*) What on earth are you doing
all this time? (*She goes over to the door and looks in*) Well,
you're *almost* dressed at any rate. I expected to find you
back in bed. That'd be just like you. How awful you
look this morning! For heaven's sake, shave! You're
disgusting! You look like a tramp. No wonder no one
will give you a job. I don't blame them — when you
don't even look half-way decent. (*She goes to the stove*)
There's plenty of hot water right here. You've got no
excuse. (*Gets a bowl and pours some of the water from the
coffee pot into it*) Here.

(*He reaches his hand into the room for it. It is a beautiful,
sensitive hand with slender, tapering fingers. It trembles
and some of the water spills on the floor*)

(*Tauntingly*) Look at your hand tremble! You'd better
give up drinking. You can't stand it. It's just your kind
that get the D. T.'s. *That would be* the last straw! (*Looking down at the floor*) Look at the mess you've made of
this floor — cigarette butts and ashes all over the place.
Why can't you put them on a plate? No, you wouldn't

be considerate enough to do that. You never think of me. You don't have to sweep the room and that's all you care about.

(*Takes the broom and commences to sweep viciously, raising a cloud of dust. From the inner room comes the sound of a razor being stropped*)

(*Sweeping*) Hurry up! It must be nearly time for me to go. If I'm late I'm liable to lose my position, and then I couldn't support you any longer. (*As an afterthought she adds sarcastically*) And then you'd have to go to work or something dreadful like that. (*Sweeping under the table*) What I want to know is whether you're going to look for a job to-day or not. You know your family won't help us any more. They've had enough of you, too. (*After a moment's silent sweeping*) I'm about sick of all this life. I've a good notion to go home, if I wasn't too proud to let them know what a failure you've been — you, the millionaire Rowland's only son, the Harvard graduate, the poet, the catch of the town — Huh! (*With bitterness*) There wouldn't be many of them now envy my catch if they knew the truth. What has our marriage been, I'd like to know? Even before your *millionaire* father died owing every one in the world money, you certainly never wasted any of your time on your wife. I suppose you thought I'd ought to be glad you were *honorable* enough to marry me — after getting me into trouble. You were ashamed of me with your fine friends because my father's only a grocer, that's what you were. At least he's honest, which is more than any one could say about yours. (*She is sweeping steadily toward the door. Leans on her broom for a moment*)

You hoped every one'd think you'd been forced to marry me, and pity you, didn't you? You didn't hesitate much about telling me you loved me, and making me believe your lies, before it happened, did you? You made me think you didn't want your father to buy me off as he tried to do. I know better now. I haven't lived with you all this time for nothing. (*Somberly*) It's lucky the poor thing was born dead, after all. What a father you'd have been!

(*Is silent, brooding moodily for a moment — then she continues with a sort of savage joy*)

But I'm not the only one who's got you to thank for being unhappy. There's one other, at least, and *she* can't hope to marry you now. (*She puts her head into the next room*) How about Helen? (*She starts back from the doorway, half frightened*)

Don't look at me that way! Yes, I read her letter. What about it? I got a right to. I'm your wife. And I know all there is to know, so don't lie. You needn't stare at me so. You can't bully me with your superior airs any longer. Only for me you'd be going without breakfast this very morning. (*She sets the brooms back in the corner — whiningly*) You never did have any gratitude for what I've done. (*She comes to the stove and puts the coffee into the pot*) The coffee's ready. I'm not going to wait for you. (*She sits down in her chair again*)

(*After a pause — puts her hand to her head — fretfully*) My head aches so this morning. It's a shame I've got to go to work in a stuffy room all day in my condition. And I wouldn't if you were half a man. By rights I ought to be lying on my back instead of you. You know how sick I've been this last year; and yet you object when I take a little something to keep up my spirits. You even didn't want me to take that tonic I got at the drug store. (*With a hard laugh*) I know you'd be glad to have me dead and out of your way; then you'd be free to run after all these silly girls that think you're such a wonderful, misunderstood person — this Helen and the others. (*There is a sharp exclamation of pain from the next room*)

(*With satisfaction*) There! I knew you'd cut yourself. It'll be a lesson to you. You know you oughtn't to be running around nights drinking with your nerves in such an awful shape. (*She goes to the door and looks in*)

What makes you so pale? What are you staring at your-self in the mirror that way for? For goodness sake, wipe that blood off your face! (*With a shudder*) It's horrible. (*In relieved tones*) There, that's better. I never could stand the sight of blood. (*She shrinks back from the door a little*) You better give up trying and go to a barber shop. Your hand shakes dreadfully. Why do you stare at me like that? (*She turns away from the door*) I'll give you fifteen cents — only promise you won't buy a drink with it. Are you still mad at me about that letter? (*Defiantly*) Well, I had a right to read it. I'm your wife. (*She comes to the chair and sits down again. After a pause*)

I knew all the time you were running around with some one. Your lame excuses about spending the time at the library didn't fool me. Who is this Helen, anyway? One of those artists? Or does she write poetry, too? Her letter sounds that way. I'll bet she told you your things were the best ever, and you believed her, like a fool. Is she young and pretty? I was young and pretty, too, when you fooled me with your fine, poetic talk; but life with you would soon wear anyone down. What I've been through!

(*Goes over and takes the coffee off the stove*) Breakfast is ready. (*With a contemptuous glance*) Breakfast! (*Pours out a cup of coffee for herself and puts the pot on the table*) Your coffee'll be cold. What are you doing — still shaving, for heaven's sake? You'd better give it up. One of these mornings you'll give yourself a serious cut. (*She cuts off bread and butters it. During the following speeches she eats and sips her coffee*)

I'll have to run as soon as I've finished eating. One of us has got to work. (*Angrily*) Are you going to look for a job to-day or aren't you? I should think some of your fine friends would help you, if they really think you're so much. But I guess they just like to hear you talk. (*Sits in silence for a moment*)

I'm sorry for this Helen, whoever she is. Haven't you got any feelings for other people? What will her family say? I see she mentions them in her letter. What is she going to do — have the child — or go to one of those doctors? That's a nice thing, I must say. Where can she get the money? Is she rich? (*She waits for some answer to this volley of questions*)

Hmm! You won't tell me anything about her, will you? Much I care. Come to think of it, I'm not so sorry for her, after all. She knew what she was doing. She isn't any schoolgirl, like I was, from the looks of her letter. Does she know you're married? Of course, she must. All your friends know about your unhappy marriage. I know they pity you, but they don't know my side of it. They'd talk different if they did.

(*Too busy eating to go on for a second or so*)

This Helen must be a fine one, if she knew you were married. What does she expect, then? That I'll divorce you and let her marry you? Does she think I'm crazy enough for that — after all you've made me go through? I guess not! And you can't get a divorce from me and you know it. No one can say *I've* ever done anything wrong. (*Drinks the last of her cup of coffee*)

She deserves to suffer, that's all I can say. I'll tell you what I think; I think your Helen is no better than a common street-walker, that's what I think. (*There is a stifled groan of pain from the next room*)

Did you cut yourself again? Serves you right. Why don't you go to a barber shop when I offer you the money? (*Gets up and takes off her apron*) Well, I've got to run along. (*Peevishly*) This is a fine life for me to be leading! I won't stand for your loafing any longer. (*Something catches her ear and she pauses and listens intently*) There! You've overturned the water all over everything. Don't say you haven't. I can hear it dripping on the floor. (*A vague expression of fear comes over her face*) Alfred! Why don't you answer me?

(*She moves slowly toward the room. There is the noise of a chair being overturned and something crashes heavily to the floor. She stands, trembling with fright*)

Alfred! Alfred! Answer me! What is it you knocked over? Are you still drunk? (*Unable to stand the tension a second longer she rushes to the door of the bedroom*) Alfred!

[*She stands in the doorway looking down at the floor of the inner room, transfixed with horror. Then she shrieks wildly and runs to the other door, unlocks it and frenziedly pulls it open, and runs shrieking madly into the outer hallway.*

THE CURTAIN FALLS

MY LADY DREAMS

EUGENE PILLOT

Eugene Pillot was born in Houston, Texas, and was educated at Culver Military Academy, the University of Texas, Cornell and Harvard Universities.

He is a frequent contributor of short plays to magazines.

MY LADY DREAMS

A PLAY IN ONE ACT

By EUGENE PILLOT

Characters

THE LADY
MARIE, HER MAID
LITTLE OLD LADY
THE OTHER WOMAN
THE TWO ADORABLE CHILDREN

MY LADY DREAMS

When the curtain rises we see a lady's boudoir, done in the luxurious manner of Louis Seize, soft pinks, white and gold. There is a fireplace on one side of the room, before it, but somewhat up-stage is a chaise longue piled high with cushions at its rear end. On the same side of the room is a door opening into the adjoining bedroom. On the opposite side of the room is a door leading to an outer hallway. To the rear of this door is a tall wardrobe with doors. At rear center is a dressing table, a long mirror and lights that send a glow down the middle of the room, the rest somewhat in shadow.

Before the mirror sits the Lady, a magnificent, queenly woman in an exquisite negligée. Behind her stands Marie, her maid, a trim little person in black dress and white apron and cap. She is putting the finishing touches to the Lady's hair; and now takes a step back to survey her work and to be sure that all is well.

THE LADY (*appraising the work in the mirror*). I don't think I would do a bit more to it, Marie.

MARIE. No?

LADY. No, I doubt if you have ever dressed my hair quite so becomingly as to-night.

MARIE. Thank you, my Lady.

LADY. And to-night — of all nights, Marie — I must heighten my most telling points. For to-night I start anew on conquest.

MARIE. My Lady means — Lord Varoné — you are not going to — ?

LADY (*determined, almost forcing the words*). Yes, I have decided not to marry Lord Varoné.

MARIE. I'm — sorry.

LADY (*defiantly*). Why should you be *sorry?*

MARIE. Oh, because Lord Varoné seems so — kind.

LADY. Kind?

[*Her voice is very hard at this moment.*

MARIE. Yes. When he stands near you so tall and straight — just like a fine young tree in the forest — and he speaks to you soft and gentle-like — he always makes me think I hear music in a church. And when he looks at you, my Lady! Oh, Madonna! In his eyes are a million stars that say he loves you, *he loves you!* Madonna, how can any woman turn down a man that looks at her like that?

LADY. Lord Varoné is a very selfish man, Marie.

MARIE. Ah, no, not with those eyes.

LADY. Yes, he wants me to do many things — should we marry — that my free spirit would never permit.

MARIE (*persuasively*). But for such a nice man —

LADY. For *no* man will I chain myself to the banalities of a household! What would become of my career, if I did? I have paid with my life blood to build myself up to where I am. I have only to whisper that I have an idea for a story or a novel or a play, and all the editors in the land will risk their lives in the scramble to outbid each other for it, even before I have put the first word on paper. That means power. To-day I am a famous writer, world renowned, almost a great *literateur*. If I marry Lord Varoné and fall in with his old-fashioned ideas, in six months I shall have lost my power in the literary world. I would be domestic.

MARIE. Would Lord Varoné want you to be so?

LADY. If one marries, lives in the country, superintends a country household, and has *children* — and Lord Varoné is *set* upon that point — *well* — !

MARIE. But what does it matter, if you love him, my Lady?

LADY. I will not let my love for him bring domesticity upon me. That is why I am giving him up!

MARIE. With all those stars in his eyes —

LADY. Don't remind me of his *good* points, Marie! I don't *want* to give him up! (*Half-dreamily, as she gazes at his photograph*) If I could only let myself love him as much as I know I love him — ah, Voné, why must you be so wonderful? You must have been a Venetian prince in the olden times. It's torture to think of you — I want you so! But I won't have you, *no I won't!* (*Pushes the photograph aside*) Get out my dress, Marie, hurry up!

MARIE. Something for the dance?

LADY. No, I refused to go to the Ambassadors' Ball with Lord Varoné. It's the opera — I'm going with the Randalls. She will probably wear black. I'd better wear a contrast.

MARIE (*at the wardrobe*). The white metal cloth?

LADY. No, no — too much like a virgin being crucified.

MARIE. The rose or red-violet?

LADY. Bring the new green — that's good for my mood. Green is adaptability, spring, eternal life, or something. Yes, that's it. Let's have it quickly. (*She has slipped out of the negligée and Marie now slips the green gown on her — a superb creation in tones of green, brilliant as the river Nile when the spring sunlight picks out its lighter notes and sends them vibrating everywhere*) I always feel like Cleopatra in green. I wonder if she wore it. It seems to help one to control, to dominate. And Cleopatra was so successful in love. She knew how *not* to love.

MARIE. My Lady looks like a queen.

LADY (*gaily*). The queen who will not let herself love!

[*In the hallway a bell rings.*

MARIE. The front door-bell. All the servants are off to-night. I'd better answer.

LADY. Yes, you'd better, Marie. It might be important.

MARIE. I will be gone only a minute.

LADY. Very well. (*As Marie hurries out, the Lady resumes her seat before the dressing table. Musingly*) Suppose it is Voné? Suppose he wouldn't take "no" for an answer? Suppose he came anyway?

[*As though in answer to her query, both doors of the wardrobe fly open and a strange little old lady steps out. She might almost be one of Barrie's little old ladies come to life, so pinched and quaint and human she is in her gay shawl and poke bonnet with the wiggly rose on it. She walks with a limp and carries a cane to help her.*

LITTLE OLD LADY (*pertly, yet sweetly*). Well, wouldn't you have him, my dearie?

LADY. What? Did somebody speak?

LITTLE OLD LADY (*coming forward so that the Lady sees her*). Well, my voice *is* cracked — most as much as a Sunday cup and saucer I saw once — but still I'd call it speaking, dearie.

LADY (*in her very grandest manner*). Who are you?

LITTLE OLD LADY (*simply*). Oh, nobody much.

LADY. How did you get in here? Was it you who rang the bell? Did Marie let you in?

LITTLE OLD LADY. Ah, no. I never have to be *let* in. I just come; and frequently when I am least expected. I never know when it is going to be, but I'm always there on time.

LADY. How absurd! You must be insane!

LITTLE OLD LADY. Not unless you are, dearie!

LADY. Do you mean to insinuate — ?

LITTLE OLD LADY. Not in *that* way, my pretty.

LADY (*losing her patience*). Well, I want to know — what are you doing here, in my house?

LITTLE OLD LADY. I had to come. You called me.

LADY (*aghast*). *I* called you?

LITTLE OLD LADY. And I always come when I'm called, double-quick.

LADY. Absurd!

LITTLE OLD LADY. No, no, not at all. Just remember back for a moment, if you will, dearie.

LADY. Please don't call me "dearie." It's a little familiar — and cheap.

LITTLE OLD LADY. Oh, no, not cheap. "Dearie" 's not cheap, when there's feeling in the heart behind the word. Anyway, before you heard my wee, pert, cracked cup-and-saucer voice, weren't you sitting there, sort of dreaming-like?

LADY (*not willing to commit herself*). Perhaps I was.

LITTLE OLD LADY. Then that's why I'm here.

LADY. What *do* you mean?

LITTLE OLD LADY. I'm part of your dreaming, dearie.

LADY. W-h-a-t!!

LITTLE OLD LADY. I'm just a memory that comes to you in your dreams.

LADY. Impossible! I never saw you before.

LITTLE OLD LADY. Oh, yes, you have!

LADY. Absurd! People don't dream of what they've never known. I'm modern enough to know that. Absurd!

LITTLE OLD LADY. Not at all, not at all. You've seen the likes of me in the old woman huddled by the lamp-post at the street corner, selling the evening papers. Oh, many times you've seen me there. And once you saw me in the eyes of a scrubwoman that you happened to notice on the floor of an office building, when you went there one morning at an odd hour. Oh, don't be afraid, I'll not tell why you went there. It was the human thing to do, all right. And another time you saw me in the tired little gray lady in the street car. Don't you remember she forgot herself and smiled at you?

LADY (*impulsively, half-musingly*). I have always wondered why she did that?

LITTLE OLD LADY. Only because you were young and pretty, bonny as a wild rose in a desert of scraggly faces.

LADY (*pleased*). O-oh.

LITTLE OLD LADY. You do remember now?

LADY. But how can you be the scrubwoman, the paper lady, *and* the tired little gray lady?

LITTLE OLD LADY. Oh, I'm not really any of them I'm just the ghost of many, many pinched little old ladies that one sees about a great city. All of their thin, wavery shadows are in my soul. But in my eyes they make for you a lady that you *do* know. Look a wee bit, look in my eyes and see if you don't know the lady there, look. [*She leans forward for the Lady to see.*

LADY (*surprised at what she sees*). But you can't be — *her?*

LITTLE OLD LADY (*proudly*). Ah, yes I am! I am Lord Varoné's mother. His very own mother!

LADY. But *she* is a very grand lady, tall, proud, magnificent!

LITTLE OLD LADY. She is all of that to the world, I grant you.

LADY. While you — you're not in the least like her — except the eyes —

LITTLE OLD LADY. Ah!

LADY. Why, you're even so lame you have to carry a cane!

LITTLE OLD LADY. Do you think I mind that? Not for a moment! I'll tell you how it was. When I was still almost young and my boy — Lord Varoné — was just starting his career in the world, I humbled my pride, I broke it in fact, to give him a chance that he *had* to have. It left me lame, that's why I carry a cane.

LADY. But Lord Varoné's mother does not carry a cane. She's tall and straight and walks superbly.

LITTLE OLD LADY. Ah, many a fine-walking lady has a limp in her soul, because of helping somebody that needed her. But do you imagine even one of the grand ladies cares a mite, if she has to carry a prop somewhere inside her? I don't think so. It only makes them walk straighter when they go into the world, and hold their heads high as horses with a checkrein.

LADY. I never thought of that.

LITTLE OLD LADY. How could you, my dearie? Have you ever given up anything that you cherished heart-close?

LADY. Have you come here to insult me?

LITTLE OLD LADY (*very kindly*). Hardly. Varoné's mother's eyes would not do that.

LADY. Then why — ?

LITTLE OLD LADY (*hesitant, for she is not sure of her ground*). I have come to ask you —

LADY. What?

LITTLE OLD LADY. Please marry him.

LADY. I'm sorry — I can't.

LITTLE OLD LADY. He won't make you lose your freedom.

LADY. How did you know it was that?

LITTLE OLD LADY. Ah, mothers know so many things that other people never suspect.

LADY. And at heart — mothers don't usually want their attractive sons to marry. They want to keep them for themselves.

LITTLE OLD LADY. That's only when they fear the girl.

LADY. And you don't fear me?

LITTLE OLD LADY. No one can round out Varoné's life for him as you can.

LADY. Indeed!

LITTLE OLD LADY. You can help him finish the career that I started for him.

LADY (*indignant*). So *that's* the idea! You want me to marry him because I possess qualities that will accomplish things for him! I'm to be a tool to polish the rough edges of his career. You must think I am a fool!

LITTLE OLD LADY. Oh, no.

LADY. And what would become of my own career in the meantime?

LITTLE OLD LADY. You would not lose. Your career would grow richer, along with his.

LADY. I doubt it.

LITTLE OLD LADY. Your whole life would become a sounding board of creation. Think of that, my dearie. You would be a harp of life, singing love to the winds of spring.

LADY. I can't believe it.

LITTLE OLD LADY. Don't say that. I want you to marry my boy. He loves you, you love him. That should be enough.

LADY. Unfortunately, the world makes one take other things into consideration in a marriage these days.

LITTLE OLD LADY (*flaring*). And that's why the whole world is going smash! Nobody will do anything for anybody, unless they get something for it, beforehand if possible. Don't break with Varoné! You will hurt yourself the most.

LADY. Stop saying things like that to me! I won't listen! [*The Lady turns away and sits in chair by the mirror, pouting.*

LITTLE OLD LADY. You know that what I say is true.

LADY (*defiantly*). I don't care.

LITTLE OLD LADY. It isn't often that a mother proposes for a daughter; but you will marry Varoné, won't you?

LADY (*in a rage*). No, no, *no!* I will not marry him, *I will not!*

LITTLE OLD LADY (*edging apologetically toward the hall door*). I shall be hoping so — anyway — dearie —
[*Blows her a ghost of a kiss, and is gone.*
The Lady sits musing by the mirror.
Like a flame from the fire, the Other Woman rises from the fireplace. She is a pulsating, vital creature in a gown as glowing as the flames themselves. As she steps out into the room, the Lady looks up and sees her.

LADY (*again in her grand manner*). And pray, who are you?

OTHER WOMAN. I am the Other Woman in his life.

LADY. The Other Woman? Is there another woman in Varoné's life?

OTHER WOMAN. There is always the Other Woman in every man's life. He may not have met her yet, but she is always there; and usually she is pretty bad.

LADY. Are you?

OTHER WOMAN. I am one of the worst. I have all of the lures, all of the charms that most women know, but few dare to use — unless they are scarlet, as I am.

LADY. You seem to glory in your — color.

OTHER WOMAN. Why shouldn't I? Poppies and flame roses do not hang their heads in shame because nature gave them the color of blood.

LADY. How dare you come here?

OTHER WOMAN. You invited me.

LADY (*aghast*). I?

OTHER WOMAN. You started to wonder about me, after his mother had gone, and to dream about me, then I came.

LADY. The insolence!

OTHER WOMAN. Oh, no! Oh, no! Why shouldn't I come? Aren't we really — sisters?

LADY. Sisters?

OTHER WOMAN. You are pure and gain your ends with guile and in obscure ways. While I — am what people know I am. I take the direct road and gain my ends openly. I am elemental, without fear, vital. No man on earth can resist me!

LADY. I am sure my Varoné would never look at you.

OTHER WOMAN. Ha, you have the false security of a virgin — one of those over-saintly, milk-white ones.

LADY. I would have you understand that my emotions are not milk-white.

OTHER WOMAN. Perhaps not, but your conventions are. You are just the kind that is easiest for me to rob of your men.

LADY. What makes you think that?

OTHER WOMAN. Because I *know*.

LADY. Ha!

OTHER WOMAN. Yes, it's my business to know. How do you suppose it is that women of my — shall we say, *color* — manage to have in their train so many of the most desirable men of a great city? Do you think those men come to us in *preference* to you? Ah, no! It is usually because women like you have placed themselves upon such freezing pedestals that the poor male things can't ever come to a companionable understanding with your kind. You think so well of yourselves that you carelessly discard your men, as one would cards in a game of chance. Then is when we catch them — when their hearts are bruised, crying for sympathy. Then is when we score. We give them everything — and hold them!

LADY. That may apply to the men you know. Not to Varoné.

OTHER WOMAN.   How little you know of life, you who depict it with a pencil and a typewriter!   No wonder magazine stories are so stupidly done to those who know life.   Those stories are written by and for people who know nothing of life.   Well, let me tell you something — for every man like Varoné there is always some scarlet woman waiting around the corner.   And he will be easiest to get just after you turn him down.

LADY (*suspiciously*).   May I ask — do you know Lord Varoné — *now?*

OTHER WOMAN.   No, and I don't even know what he looks like.

LADY.   Then why are you so concerned about him?

OTHER WOMAN (*with great sincerity*).   I want to save him.

LADY.   Save him?   From what?

OTHER WOMAN.   From me — or from women like me   That is why I came here — to beg you not to throw him over. He is pure gold.   Can't you see that?

LADY.   Of course.   I would be blind, if I did not.   But I have a career to think of.   Marriage to any man I loved would send it up in smoke.   I shall marry some one for whom I care nothing.   That's what I shall do.   Then I shall be safe.

OTHER WOMAN.   And Varoné — what will become of him?

LADY.   I shall break with him gently, slowly, so that he will not realize what is happening till it is all over.   By that time it will be too late for you to get him.   He will be reconciled to his fate.

OTHER WOMAN.   You are willing to take a greater risk than I would.   Don't do it.   I want *you* to have Varoné.   You are so worthy of him.   Please take him.

LADY.   No!   I will not be moved by your mawkish sentimentality.

OTHER WOMAN.   Remember — if you don't take him, I will.

LADY.   You cannot move me with such a bluff.

OTHER WOMAN.   Very well.   I gave you the first chance at him. Now I'll take him. And how I shall laugh, and laugh, and laugh at you both — when I crush him — so that he can never rise again! Ha, ha, ha, h-a-a-!

[With a wild laugh, like a dart of flame, she is gone.
The Lady stands nonplussed.

LADY. I wonder if she is right? Could a woman like that get him? I wonder —

[But her musing is broken by a strange, unexpected happening. There is a gay ripple of childish laughter, the pillows on the chaise longue are hurled to the four corners of the room, and the Two Adorable Children leap out, — one from behind the cushions, the other from under the chaise. They are both girls, one blonde, the other brunette, at least eight or nine years old, though they might be almost any age, since they are the rare type that have caught in their hearts the universal spirit of childhood. They have not started to be young ladies in their cradles; in fact, when they have really and truly grown up to the age when one is considered a young lady, they may forget themselves sometimes and bubble forth with some delightfully impulsive remark. Perhaps they are distant cousins of Peter Pan, and will never quite grow up. I don't know. But I hope they won't, for as they now leap from their hiding places, I want them to remain Adorables forever. The Adorable Blonde is in a fluffy dancing frock, simulating a great pink rose, but the Adorable Brunette is in a boy's costume of pink, with her hair well tucked under a boyish cap.

BLONDE *(happily)*. There she is, *there!*

BRUNETTE Ha, ha! *(Clap hands)* You didn't know we were here, did you?

BLONDE *(as they both rush to the Lady)*. Say you didn't know, say you didn't!

BRUNETTE. Say it, say it!

LADY. You dear, adorable children! Of course I didn't know you were here. How could I?

BLONDE *(to Brunette)*. You see, I told you she wouldn't be thinking of us as anywhere at all!

LADY. But I must say — I don't understand. What is it all about?

[*In a rush.*

BRUNETTE. Well, you see —

BLONDE. No, let me tell! It was my idea!

BRUNETTE. But I *did* it! Let me tell her!

BLONDE. No, me, me, *me!*

LADY (*very kindly, for with the advent of the two Adorables she seems to have developed a wonderful gentleness that one would hardly have suspected she had anywhere about her*). You must both tell me, but one at a time. You begin.

[*To Blonde.*

BLONDE. Well, we've just come from dancing school. And — and they had a fancy-dress ball there and — and we fooled everybody there, that is at *first!*

LADY. How did you fool them?

BRUNETTE. Oh, she hasn't guessed yet! Goody, goody, goody!

BLONDE. Ha, ha, ha! We even fooled you, even *you!*

LADY. Yes, but how? How did you fool me? About what?

BLONDE. Look! She isn't a boy at all! (*Jerks cap off Brunette's head and her hair falls in a mass about her shoulders*) Look!

BRUNETTE. I had a dress just like hers, but I wanted to be a boy just for once — to see how it felt — so after we got to the party, I changed clothes with Jimmie Smith. We had a terribly hard time — we had to do it behind Mrs. Smith's back. She's broad enough in the middle, but she doesn't always keep the middle still, you know.

BLONDE. Especially when she laughs.

BRUNETTE. Oh, yes! But Jimmie — you should have seen Jimmie in my dress! He was *too* funny! When he walks, his legs work *in* instead of out. Just like this.

[*Demonstrates Jimmie's walk.*

BLONDE. But everybody thought she really *was* a boy.

BRUNETTE. It was perfect!

BLONDE. Anyhow, she says she felt like a girl all the time just the same.

BRUNETTE. Wasn't that queer?

LADY (*drawing them to her, on the chaise*). You dear, adorable Adorables!

BRUNETTE. Well, aren't you going to undress us for bed?

LADY (*surprised*). I?

BLONDE. We thought you would. We're awfully tired.

BRUNETTE. And sleepy.

LADY. I don't know whether I should. Whose children are you?

BLONDE (*disappointed*). Oh, don't you know?

BRUNETTE. Pshaw, you seemed so kind. We thought it was all decided.

LADY. Decided? What are you talking about?

BLONDE (*with an air of apology*). She's so inexperienced. I guess we'll have to tell her.

BRUNETTE. I guess so.

BLONDE. We're only the kiddies that come to you in your dream.

BRUNETTE. And when your dream wakes up — poof, we are no more.

[*Blows.*

BLONDE. Unless you decide to want us really and truly.

BRUNETTE (*clamoring over her*). Oh, please want us, please, please, *please!*

BLONDE (*slyly*). *He* wants us.

LADY. Who?

BLONDE. Voné!

LADY. Lord Varoné — o-oh.

[*At last she understands.*

BRUNETTE. We know why *you* don't want us. You're afraid you won't be able to write any more, that's why.

LADY. Perhaps it — is.

BLONDE (*gleefully*). Oh, but you don't know how jolly you would write, if you had us! We'd help you!

BRUNETTE. We'd even let you write all about us!

BLONDE. And *for* us!

BRUNETTE. Oh, yes!

LADY. You dears!

[*They are tantalizing fruit, but she still considers them forbidden — to her.*

BLONDE. And they'd be the very best stories anybody ever wrote!

BRUNETTE. Even better than Black Sambo or Peter Rabbit!

BLONDE. And that's saying a good deal, let me tell you.

BRUNETTE. Especially Peter — he's hard to beat.

BLONDE. But *hers* would be better stories. Just think — we'd be in them! And often when she least expected it, there we'd be, saying something terribly clever right in the middle of her story! And people would read them with delight! For they would be just like life.

BRUNETTE. Only heaps better!

BLONDE. And lots more exciting!

LADY (*hugging them to her*). You irresistible ones!

BLONDE (*struggling to free herself*). And — and we'd be lots more fun than that, even in the beginning.

BRUNETTE. Oh, yes! And all the time!

BLONDE. In the beginning — when we are tiny tinies — we'd crow at you from out of pink and blue cradles, and catch at your arm just to see you smile at us. And maybe you'd stop and look at us for a moment, wondering if we understood that you loved us.

BRUNETTE. Of course we would understand. All babies do, if their mothers only knew.

BLONDE. Sure! And later there would be parties! And you would dance with us on the green! Just like this — come, oh do!

BRUNETTE. Oh, do dance with us!

[*They catch the Lady's hands and pull her up. With a child on each side, she does a simple little dance with them, the three ending with an elaborate bow. The moment the dance is over, the children peck a quick kiss on her hands and dart toward the hall door.*

BOTH CHILDREN. Good-by, good-by!

LADY. Where are you going?

BOTH CHILDREN. Away, away!

LADY. Why do you leave me, when I've begun to love you?

BLONDE. You haven't decided to have us!

BRUNETTE. We can't stay unless you decide!

BLONDE. We can't, we can't!

BRUNETTE. Good-by, good-by!

[*The Lady seems stunned, so with gay laughter the two Adorables dash through the door and are — gone!*

LADY. No, oh, no! Don't go! I — (*But the only response is the distant echo of childish glee, which dies away as suddenly as it came*) And I didn't get their names! How can I ever know them again without their names? I must know their names! Wait, wait! Where are you? Gone! Really gone —

[*She sinks down on the chair before the mirror, in the position she had early in the scene. It is at this time that Marie hurries in.*

MARIE. I'm sorry to be so long, my Lady, but —

LADY (*startled*). Marie! Are you in my dream too?

MARIE. Your dream, my Lady?

LADY (*in a burst*). Oh, never mind, don't try to understand — but did you see them? Which way did they go?

MARIE. Which way did who go?

LADY (*almost beside herself*). The children, the children! The Adorable Ones!

MARIE. I went to the front door, but no one was there. It was the telephone that rang.

LADY. But didn't you see the children? Didn't you let them out the front way?

MARIE (*firmly*). I let no one out of the house. And I saw no children.

LADY. But they went that way! Why didn't I follow? Maybe I'm not dreaming now, after all. Marie, come here and pinch me.

MARIE. Pinch you? Where?

LADY. Anywhere. It doesn't matter where. If I feel it, then I know I'm awake. If I don't, then I *am* dreaming. Pinch, Marie, pinch! (*Marie pinches her on the arm. She winces*) Ouch! That settles it! At least I'm not dreaming.

MARIE. On the telephone was Lord Varoné —

LADY. Lord Varoné? Why didn't you tell me before?

MARIE. He is gone now. He did not ask to speak to you, but wanted me to give you a message —

LADY. Yes, yes!

MARIE. He said he would not disturb you, since you had given him a final answer for this evening, but in case you should desire to communicate with him on *another* matter, he is at the Lotus Club.

LADY. Lotus Club? That's only in the next block! Quick, Marie, get into your street coat! I can't telephone such a thing. I'll send a note. Hurry Marie, hurry!

MARIE. Yes, my Lady, yes!

[*Marie flies out the room.*

LADY (*she has already snatched up pen and paper and started to write the important note*). "Dear, dear Voné: (*then as she pauses for a moment*) Oh, if only the dream-ones were here to help me say it, so that it will mean the most — if only —

[*As if in answer to her desire, there appears in the doorway behind her the Little Old Lady, the Other Woman, and the Two Adorable Children. They speak in rapid succession: "We are here to help you!" "We'll always help you!" "We will, we will!"*

LADY. It almost seems as though they *were* here.

CHILDREN. We are!

LADY (*apparently not realizing their presence*). Well, I'll say it the best way I can.

LITTLE OLD LADY. That's it, dearie. He wouldn't want anything better. The best way you can, that's all, dearie.

LADY (*she has been writing rapidly during the above and continues to do so as she speaks*). "And dear Voné, if you don't come and kidnap me the moment this reaches you — well, come, come, *come!* I'm dying to be with you in that darling country house, and the children want you too —" oh, no, I mustn't say *that!* (*She starts to scratch out the words, but her, impulse carries her on*) Oh, never mind — "But most of all, I want you, Voné, *you!*"

[*Hurriedly she seals the letter with a kiss, much to the delight of the little company behind her, who flurry away the moment her task is completed.*

CURTAIN

BLACKBERRYIN'

HOWARD FORMAN SMITH

HOWARD FORMAN SMITH studied the arts of the theatre, under Thomas Wood Steirns, in the College of Fine Arts, Carnegie Institute of Technology, at Pittsburgh. Before graduation he became Technical Director of the school's productions.

In 1922 Mr. Smith was Technical Director of the Virginia Historical Pageant.

BLACKBERRYIN'

A COMEDY IN ONE ACT

By HOWARD FORMAN SMITH

Characters

Mrs. Waste, an old lady of sixty
Phila Granger, a girl of twenty
Mrs. Hathaway, nervous thirty-five
Mrs. Granger, forty, slow-moving and positive
Mrs. Whitmore, owner of the berry house

BLACKBERRYIN'

SCENE. *The berry-house of the Whitmore farm.*

There is a scale in the center, of the common variety, set on wheels with an "L" beam. Boxes, berry crates and baskets lie in confusion at the rear. A door down right leads to the berry fields; a rickety chair stands at the right center; a door upper left leads down the mountain. Down left, against the wall, is a table; underneath it stands a pail of water with a dipper in it. Above, a window pierces the wall.

Mrs. Waste comes slowly in from the berry field. She is an old woman of sixty, bent and gray. She is carrying two baskets. Near the scale, she stumbles and very nearly spills their contents.

MRS. WASTE. Land o' Goshen!

[*She deposits the berries near the scales and hobbles over and scoops herself a drink. Phila Granger comes in from the field with a freight of berries. She is a fresh-looking girl of twenty. She starts to set the baskets down below the door.*

MRS. WASTE. Y're comin' to the berry house regular, Phila?

PHILA. This afternoon is a scorcher, ain't it, Mis' Waste?

MRS. WASTE. It be hot! 'Twon't be Mis' Whitmore's fault if I ain't raw and sunburned by this time.

PHILA. There — that be four, and eight more outside. Purty fair for eight hours' work, ain't it?

MRS. WASTE. Purty fair. Y're young and ye ought to be a fast picker. I got two here and seven more out to the end of the rows. Ye-es, I'm not so spry as I might be. Y're ma's a quick 'un.

PHILA. Ma's been talkin' too much with Mis' Hathaway.

MRS. WASTE. Fast tongue, slow fingers, eh, Phila?

PHILA. Ye hit the nail, Mis' Waste. Any sign of Mis' Whitmore?

[*She goes to the back door and looks out.*

MRS. WASTE (*cautiously*). Be ye anxious to see her?

PHILA. It's about time for her to come up and weigh our berries and pay us off, ain't it?

MRS. WASTE. And ain't it about time fer ye ter tell me somethin'?

PHILA. Eh, what's that?

MRS. WASTE. Mis' Whitmore's a turrible proud woman.

PHILA. She hain't no right to be.

MRS. WASTE (*significantly*). That's a fine house she has down there an' a bunch of money folks say she has — with you an' me doin' her work. D'ye like it?

PHILA. I don't mind so much.

MRS. WASTE. An' there's a reason why — it's that son o' hers.

PHILA. What are ye drivin' at, Mis' Waste?

MRS. WASTE (*in low confidence*). I know all about it, Phila.

PHILA. About what?

MRS. WASTE. About what happened yestiddy.

PHILA. Y're actin' kinda queer to-day, Mis' Waste.

MRS. WASTE. Wal, I was actin' kinda queer yestiddy or I wouldn'ta seen what I did.

PHILA. Well, what were ye doin'?

MRS. WASTE. 'Bout sundown yestiddy, I took the short cut from the Damon's over to Dorcas'. I thought I might get a few blackberries on the way. I was goin' down by the lower end of yer pasture —

PHILA. And yer saw us?

MRS. WASTE. I did. What were Orin Stoddard doin' over this way?

PHILA. Oliver brought him along. Wan't he necessary?

MRS. WASTE. He wur. Y're not wearin' yer ring to-day?

PHILA. I was kind o' feered ter, havin' ter pick fer Mis' Whitmore.

MRS. WASTE. 'Tain't nobody as knows it.

PHILA. Don't they? Orin Stoddard had to go an' talk, of course.

MRS. WASTE. Thet's queer. He was made Justice o' the

Peace 'cause folks thought he was the silentest man in the township.

PHILA. He wan't silent about this. He thought thet it was a funny marriage 'cause I was milkin' and all that. He's gone an' told everybody he saw.

MRS. WASTE. Yer ma know?

PHILA. Pa told her this noon when she went home fer dinner. She ain't said much yet — but — well, I've been keepin' twenty rows away from her.

MRS. WASTE. What about Mis' Whitmore?

PHILA. Somebuddy'll be sure to tell her. Be she comin' now?

[*She runs to door left to look.*

MRS. WASTE. Not as yit. She'll be an angry 'un.

PHILA (*in sudden panic*). Oh, I'm kinda afeered o' her. She'll be angry, 'course she will. What'll I do, Mis' Waste?

MRS. WASTE (*approaching Phila*). Stick her out, o' course. It'll have to be fit sometime.

PHILA. She and Mother'll plump here the same time.

MRS. WASTE. I'll stand by ye, girl. I'll do what I kin, only let 'em take it out on each other.

PHILA. But why should Mis' Whitmore be objectin', always eternally objectin' to me? Ain't I good enough?

MRS. WASTE. It's somethin' your paw or his paw did — I never knew.

[*Mrs. Dorcas Hathaway enters. She is a thin, wiry woman of thirty-five. She talks quickly, drawling the ends of her sentences.*

MRS. HATHAWAY (*plumping down her baskets*). Wal, what's this I'm hearin' about you, Phila?

PHILA (*wearily*). I kin guess.

MRS. HATHAWAY. Guess! Guess! Why I know and should 'a' knowed long 'fore this afternoon. So, that's what ye think o' yer friends. An' married while you was milkin'. That's what ye think o' yer maw, an' ye better be keepin' an eye open fer Mis' Whitmore. She ain't an easy one to do any congratulatin'-n-n-. Married while you was milkin' — that must 'a' been funneee.

PHILA. It wasn't.

DORCAS. I suppose not. I recall my own weddin'. My Evan just did look too meek an' lamblike with his hair all sleeked down an' a red geranium in his buttonhole. He was so comical. I didn't think so at the time, but I nearly dies every time I looks at him now an' recalls him. My, but he was funneeee!

MRS. WASTE. He's funny naow.

DORCAS. Yes, Momer, but he wears good, Evan does. But I suppose weddin's allers appears funny to all folks but them thet's doin' the splicin'. An' they look as sheepish as Scotch collies whether they be married while milkin' or in the hind seat of an automobile.

MRS. WASTE. An' yer might do wus!

[*Mrs. Waste goes out to the berry field.*

DORCAS (*beside Phila, who is sitting on the table*). So ye're married now, Phila? Do ye feel different?

PHILA. I can't say as I do.

DORCAS (*purring*). Sad, ain't it? Sad thet you don't feel different, I mean. I know when I got married, I thought I'd feel so different. But I didn't and I've never gotten over it. Where's your ring?

PHILA. I'm not wearin' it. Oh, I have one.

DORCAS. I don't doubt it. You ain't surprizin' no one. We all kinda expected you an' Oliver to tie up some day, though not so quietlike — or such a funny way. My Evan'll be sayin' as how yer ought to make good in the dairy business. It's somethin' ter be a Mis' Whitmore. I ought ter kiss ye an' congratulate ye all round (*She kisses her*) Now tell us all about it.

MRS. GRANGER (*outside in the berry patch door*). What's thet you be a-sayin'? No, I didn't take no baskets but my own. Look about a bit. You musta lost 'em.

[*During this Phila slips quickly through the back door. Mrs. Granger enters loaded with her berries.*

DORCAS. What's the trouble with Momer?

MRS. GRANGER. Oh, she be a-claimin' thet I took some o' her baskets.

DORCAS. Momer's allers complainin' like thet. When folks is pickin' at a nickel a pound they get light-fingered though. Look at thet scrap I had with Rachel Bates last week. But Momer imagines powerful-l-l.

MRS. GRANGER. Course she do. She don't pick more'n twenty pounds a day. She be a slow 'un.

DORCAS. Gettin' old and gettin' mean, Momer is.

MRS. GRANGER. Where be thet da'ter of mine?

DORCAS. She were here a moment ago. Guess she musta slipped aout.

MRS. GRANGER. Run away, did she? She's been shyin' away from me the hull arternoon. I'd a-gone ter look fer her myself but I didn't want Mis' Whitmore ter think thet my da'ter hitchin' up with her son would slack my berry-pickin' any.

DORCAS. You ain't angered at her fer marryin' Oliver Whitmore, be ye?

MRS. GRANGER. No. Oliver's a good feller. Not good enough for Phila — but better than any of the sheep stock we got in this country.

DORCAS. Think Mis' Whitmore'll be takin' this hard?

MRS. GRANGER. I don't care a rap if she be. If she don't think thet pet son o' hers has done a good thing fer himself, she can't kick up. The thing's done — Where's Phila? (*She goes to the rear window*) Phila-a-a!

DORCAS. She's gone off to meet him, I suppo-ose.

MRS. GRANGER. More'n likely. I want ter hear about it. It's about time fer her ter tell her mother. I should 'a' knowed by the way she shet down on her talk last night. She was mighty quiet-like. I don't wonder, poor girl.

DORCAS. Folks is sayin' Orin Stoddard musta been drunk. He was so amused and talked about it so continual-l-l. [*She is arranging her baskets in corner up-stage right.*

MRS. GRANGER. He married 'em though, an' it's a good joke

on Mis' Whitmore. She mighta knowed they'd do somethin' like thet — she opposin' 'em so unreasonable.

DORCAS (*purring*). But in a pasture —

MRS. GRANGER. I must hear about it! (*She looks out window left*) There she is now! Phila-a-a-a.

(*She goes out door at back.*

Left alone, Dorcas looks about and climbs upon the scale. She starts to weigh herself optimistically, using first the 500-pound weight which makes the scale rattle and her to jump. While she is juggling the balance back and forth on the rod for the next largest weight, Mrs. Granger returns from the mountain path, hot and panting. Dorcas does not see her. She tiptoes downstage behind Dorcas and to the latter's right and plants a broad shoe on the platform. Dorcas beams at the result. Then she spies the foot and bounces off the scale platform)

(*Laughing*) Gettin' fatter, eh, Mis' Hathaway? Real pleased with yerself, wan't ye?

DORCAS. Pshaw! I thought fer a moment my diet o' string beans was workin' — find yer da'ter?

MRS. GRANGER. No, she took off before I sta'ted.

[*Mrs. Waste enters grimly.*

DORCAS. Locate yer baskets, Momer-r-r-?

MRS. WASTE. No, I didn't.

DORCAS. Did y' look?

MRS. WASTE. I looked up and down the berry lot an' into the mowin'.

MRS. GRANGER. Did ye look in the rows?

MRS. WASTE. I went a piece down every row — (*Going to the back where Mrs. Granger has placed her baskets*) Whose be these 'uns here? There be three o' my baskets.

MRS. GRANGER. Them there be my lot. Don't you be touchin' them, Mis' Waste.

MRS. WASTE. But I recalls three of 'em —

MRS. GRANGER (*advancing*). How d'ye know?

MRS. WASTE. Two of 'em had broken handles an one had a green string.

MRS. GRANGER. Them's mine — the hul thirteen!

MRS. WASTE. With three of 'em mine —

MRS. GRANGER Are ye callin' me a thief? I didn't come up here on a hot day to have my berries took from me!

MRS. WASTE. I did have nine. If you takes them, it's only six — I think —

DORCAS. Oh, shut up, Momer, we all know how slow ye pick. Ye're gettin' old.

[*Mrs. Whitmore enters. Silence greets her.*

DORCAS. How be ye, to-day, Mis' Whitmore?

MRS. WHITMORE. Well, thank you.

DORCAS. Been bad goin' to-day-ay-ay-

MRS. GRANGER. Thet bein' the case I've picked thirteen baskets. Want ter weigh 'em?

MRS. WHITMORE. Not yet.

MRS. GRANGER. It's gettin' nigh on to five o'clock. I got a cow to milk.

MRS. WHITMORE. I thought Phila milked your cow.

DORCAS (*after a moment's silence*). Be it five now? My stars, it do stay light evenin's. I don't like it an' Evan don't like it. Lose an hour's work a day, he says (*with increasing momentum*) an' have ye heard about ol' Mr. Haynes down Eastfield way? He's got ter get up at five o'clock ol' time, six o'clock new time, so as to get his store open at six o'clock old time so as the men goin' to work kin buy their things. Then come evenin', when he's fixin' ter close up, folks come in six o'clock old time, seven o'clock new and sets around till seven o'clock old time, eight o'clock new. Then the farmers come in nine o'clock, any time, and sets around till ten'o'clock old time, eleven o'clock new. He's got ter carry two watches an' is plumb done out from sech goin's on. [*She pauses breathless.*

MRS. GRANGER. Should think he would be, poor ol' man.

DORCAS (*continuing*). Y'see, the funny thing about ol' Mr. Haynes —

MRS. WHITMORE (*interrupting her*). Interesting, no doubt. Mrs. Granger, I have recently heard some extraordinary news.

MRS. GRANGER. 'Bout it's bein' extra-ordinary, I dunno. But it didn't shock me none. I was kinda expectin' it, though not in sech a funny way.

MRS. WHITMORE. I was fearing they would attempt some such thing, though not in such an absurd manner. Is the girl here?

MRS. GRANGER (*advancing*). Now, before ye go bullyin' my gal, I want ye ter have yer say with me fust.

MRS. WHITMORE (*crossing to right in front of Mrs. Granger*). Oh, very well, I'm willing.

MRS. GRANGER. Mis' Hathaway, kin ye take a look around fer Phila? I see her down a piece toward the mowin'.

DORCAS (*going*). Don't ye worry. I'll find her. I allers had sharp eyes. Phila-a-a-a-!

[*Dorcas goes out back door. Mrs. Waste approaches Mrs. Whitmore timidly.*

MRS. WASTE. Mis' Whitmore, would ye jest take a peek at these baskets?

MRS. GRANGER (*taking her by the shoulders and shoving her toward door right*). Here, suppose you take a squint along the upper rows o' the blackberry patch.

MRS. WASTE (*feebly obstinate*). But they ain't there.

MRS. GRANGER (*shoving her out the door*). Jest a squint. Ye might find somethin' thet'll surprise ye.

[*Mrs. Granger strides back to stage left.*

MRS. WHITMORE. Mrs. Granger, is this a mistake with the baskets again? I don't want another quarrel like the Bates and Hathaway one. What is the matter with Mrs. Waste?

MRS. GRANGER. Nothin', 'cept age. She's gettin' peevish. Now what's this ye have ter tell me?

MRS. WHITMORE. You seem to know about the whole affair that happened in your pasture last evening?

MRS. GRANGER. Only what I got from Mis' Bates, who got it from Orin Stoddard. Orin married them in aour pasture under a maple tree, near the bars, an' very purty it musta been.

MRS. WHITMORE. Undoubtedly, quite picturesque. It seems that while your daughter was milking, my son drove by. Mr. Stoddard, unfortunately, was along and in a humorous mood. He persuaded my son to let him marry them then and there. Oliver also has a sense of humor, very unfortunately, and the illegal ceremony was performed there by the bars, as you say.

MRS. GRANGER. Illegal?

MRS. WHITMORE. And after it was over, my son drove off and your daughter went back to her milking. There, doesn't the whole thing seem a lark of some sort?

MRS. GRANGER. No, it don't! It seems good and sound, and the fact that your son drove off afterwards seems a want of character. It might 'a' changed him a bit.

MRS. WHITMORE. But your daughter went back to her milking.

MRS. GRANGER. Which is plain hoss sense and I'm proud of her.

MRS. WHITMORE. The entire affair seems too foolish to discuss.

MRS. GRANGER (*advancing to her*). Wal, y'ought to know why they done it so foolish. It was you always eternally objectin' ter my gal who is away too good fer yer family, anyways. When sech a couple takes it in their heads ter get married, why 'course they up an' does. And it comes time fer folks sech as you an' me ter know it. It was yer eternal objectin' thet drove 'em to form holy bonds o' matrimony in a caow pasture.

MRS. WHITMORE. Humph!

MRS. GRANGER. 'Course you an' me is peeved, natural, 'cause we wan't there to witness it. But it bein' done, we got ter swaller it, don't we?

MRS. WHITMORE. I don't propose to swallow it.

MRS. GRANGER (*thunderingly sarcastic*). Allers eternally objectin', ain't ye? It goes back to the time when yer paw an' my paw had some oats together which they fit over. An' to come right down to it, you been thinkin' thet we

Granger folks ain't quite up ter yer ever sence yer man sta'ted rollin' up his bank account an' ye got to go South ter Floridy winters!

MRS. WHITMORE. Perhaps we had better not argue, Mrs. Granger. To save useless talk, I want you to know that I am going to have the marriage annulled.

MRS. GRANGER. Why?

MRS. WHITMORE. It was illegal!

[*Dorcas pushes Phila over the doorstep.*

DORCAS. Here she be — wild as a deer. I don't blame ye, Phila, fer holdin' back

MRS. WHITMORE. Miss Granger?

PHILA. Yes, Mis' Whitmore?

MRS. WHITMORE. Were you married to my son yesterday afternoon?

PHILA. Yes, Mis' Whitmore, I was.

MRS. WHITMORE. Why?

PHILA (*hesitating bashfully*). Because — I love him and I think — he loves me —

MRS. WHITMORE. You think?

MRS. GRANGER. She knows it if thet's what you want!

MRS. WHITMORE. By why in a cow pasture — and especially while you were milking?

DORCAS. It's a good thing fer a girl to mi-i-ilk.

PHILA. Y'see, Mis' Whitmore, we wanted ter get married fer a long time and since — since — my husband . . .

DORCAS. I stuttered first time, too-o-o.

PHILA. Since Oliver was through college, there was really no reason why we shouldn't.

MRS. GRANGER. 'Course there ain't none.

PHILA. But he kept a-sayin' you objected strong. It only made him more anxious, so he got Mr. Stoddard yestiddy. I didn't know nothin' 'bout it. They found me doin' some chores —

DORCAS (*staccato approval*). Y'have a level head, Phila-a-a.

PHILA. He drove off afterwards 'cause I couldn't start on our weddin' trip 'til to-night.

MRS. WHITMORE (*startled*). To-night?

DORCAS (*glancing out of window*). Thet's what you were hidin' over there — a suit case!

MRS. WHITMORE (*pausing*). Did Oliver have a license?

[*Phila nods.*

MRS. GRANGER. I thought as much — all sound and good!

MRS. WHITMORE. Mr. Stoddard was drunk, wasn't he?

MRS. GRANGER. Drunk! This is gettin' ter be a downright shame on ye, Mis' Whitmore!

PHILA. No, Mr. Stoddard was not drunk.

MRS. WHITMORE (*playing her trump card*). People thought so afterward. What witness did you have?

[*Startled silence.*

PHILA (*blankly*). Witness?

MRS. GRANGER. I never heered one was necessary!

MRS. WHITMORE (*turning to Mrs. Granger*). One is necessary. In this case to prove the condition of the person officiating, and also, as the law requires, to witness the ceremony.

MRS. GRANGER. I'm not standin' much more. Y're playin' too hard on my gal's feelin's!

DORCAS (*leaning against the door*). Yes, I recollects. Accordin' to law, it don't pay to be too exclusive in weddin's or funerals-ls.

MRS. WHITMORE. Well, was there any other witnessing person there — besides the cow?

[*Mrs. Waste returns, slow and hot.*

MRS. WASTE. Ain't it a hot day?

DORCAS. It's a very hot day, Momer —

MRS. GRANGER (*in dark rage*). Hain't ye found yer baskets yet?

MRS. WASTE. No, I ain't.

MRS. GRANGER. No use lookin' at mine.

PHILA (*suddenly*). Mis' Waste?

MRS. WASTE. I'm a heerin', Phila.

PHILA (*going to her*). D'ye recall what ye wuz tellin' me 'bout half an hour ago?

MRS. WASTE. 'Course I recollects. As a rule, our family aren't forgetters.

[*She flings a defiant look at Mrs. Granger.*

PHILA. Tell 'em what ye saw on the short cut between the Damon's an' Hathaways, yestiddy afternoon.

MRS. WASTE (*pursing her mouth*). What fer?

MRS. GRANGER. Mis' Whitmore's got the ideer my da'ter ain't married right.

MRS. WASTE. Not married right?

MRS. GRANGER. No!

MRS. WASTE (*speculatively*). Hum-m-m-

MRS. GRANGER. Wal, did ye see anythin'? D'ye know anythin'?

MRS. WASTE (*with sudden vigor*). Don't be too hard on y'self!

DORCAS. Momer, don't be so stubborn!

MRS. WASTE (*sarcastically*). Kinder anxious what I knows, ain't ye?

MRS. GRANGER. Nat'rally — seein' what a fix my da'ter be in!

MRS. WASTE. I'm tellin' if — if

MRS. GRANGER. If?

MRS. WASTE (*sitting back*). Wal, I dunno —

DORCAS (*provoked*). Momer, don't beat about so!

PHILA. Mis' Waste!

MRS. WASTE. Y'see them three baskets, thet's including the two broken handles an' them with the green string? Whose be they?

MRS. GRANGER. Mine.

MRS. WASTE. I allers puts a leaf in the bottom of my baskets.

MRS. GRANGER. Are ye claimin' I'm not straight an' honest? I remember fillin' them baskets.

MRS. WHITMORE. Yes, but mistakes often happen.

PHILA. Ma, let her look.

MRS. GRANGER. Oh, go ahead and look — but she won't find no leaves in the bottom.

[*Mrs. Waste empties a basket and turns confronting Mrs. Granger with a small green leaf.*

MRS. GRANGER (*in genuine astonishment*). Wal, I declare!

MRS. WHITMORE. It seems Mrs. Waste is right.

MRS. GRANGER. It's mighty funny. I wuz ready to take the oath on them bein' mine —

MRS. WHITMORE. It's a shame a thing like this had to happen to you, Mrs. Waste.

MRS. GRANGER. It's a mistake, I tell ye.

MRS. WHITMORE. No doubt.

MRS. GRANGER. Take all three — and three more. I'll make it up to ye, Mis' Waste.

MRS. WASTE. I only want what's mine — that's all.

MRS. WHITMORE. I wish you all would be more careful in the future. Don't leave your filled baskets in the same place. Let us avoid this uncomfortable unpleasantness. Now I must be getting back. Mark your piles and Oliver will be up and weigh them later. You need not wait. [*Starts to go.*

MRS. WASTE (*eyeing her increasing pile*). I'm a-waitin'.

PHILA. Can't — can't ye be a-tellin' us, Mis' Waste?

MRS. WASTE. What was it ye wanted to know?

PHILA. What ye saw yestiddy on the short-cut.

MRS. WASTE (*deliberately*). Oh, that! Orin Stoddard standin' beside the caow straight and solemn —

MRS. WHITMORE. Solemn?

MRS. WASTE. Ain't he allers solemn as a church? This time he were solemner 'n ever an' Oliver an' Phila there joinin' hands. I heered the hull thing — but why do ye ask me? Yer all seem to know —

MRS. WHITMORE (*calmly*). Go on, Mrs. Waste.

MRS. WASTE. Wal, there ain't much ter tell 'cept I happened to see two young folks married sensible like. Oh, yes, an' there was the caow standin' right next to them with the milk pail under her where Phila had left off milkin' —

MRS. WHITMORE (*suddenly*). Which cow?

MRS. WASTE (*bewildered*). I don't grasp ye?

MRS. WHITMORE. I understood from Oliver that one of the two Granger cows is dry. Which cow was the pail under?

MRS. WASTE (*decidedly*). The red an' white 'un. (*Mrs. Whitmore nods dully*) An' after it wuz all over, the young Mrs. Whitmore set down an' finished milkin' the cow she probably started as Miss Granger.

MRS. GRANGER. Ye'll have to give in, Mis' Whitmore. Ye hain't the sta'tin's of a case!

DORCAS. Will ye weigh our berries now-o-ow?

MRS. WHITMORE (*with a sigh*). No, leave them to Oliver. He'll pay you off to-morrow. (*To Phila*) Good-by. You will have a pleasant trip, I know.

[*She kisses Phila awkwardly. All bend forward to watch. She goes out.*

PHILA. Thank ye — mother.

DORCAS. Sayin' thet's mighty awkward first time, ain't it? Let's step down, Mis' Whitmore — war's over.

MRS. GRANGER. You'll be comin' over before ye go, eh, Phila?

PHILA. Yes, mother.

[*Mrs. Granger goes out back door.*

DORCAS. I'll be seein' ye off too. Don't be late, as we get ter bed early these evenin's.

PHILA. No, I won't.

DORCAS. Good-by.

[*She follows Mrs. Granger.*
Mrs. Waste still fumbles with her baskets.

PHILA. Don't be waitin', Mis' Waste. I'll see thet Oliver marks ye right.

MRS. WASTE. Mebbe ye will, gal. Mebbe ye will. I'm not thinkin' harsh o' yer mother.

PHILA. I know. Mother's that way.

MRS. WASTE. She wuz fightin' fer ye.

PHILA. Yes, mother's that way, too.

MRS. WASTE. Wal, good-by, Phila.

PHILA. Good-by, Mis' Waste.

MRS. WASTE (*looking up into her face*). A-startin' on yer honeymoon. I recalls well the time I did. It's the happiest time in life. Phila, let me tell ye. Don't let it slip too fast. Make the most o' yer honeymoon.

PHILA (*happily*). I'm goin' to.

MRS. WASTE. I wish I could warn ye 'bout the little things in life — but warnin's never did me no good — an' probably won't do you.

PHILA. Don't be thinkin' thet.

MRS. WASTE. Pshaw, girl! An old woman's kind er jealous an' don't want ter climb home an' dig pertaters. Good-by. [*She goes out.*

PHILA (*following*). Thank you fer everythin'. Good-by! (*She comes back and picks out a straw suit case from among the clutter of boxes at the back. From without comes a shrill merry whistle. A man's voice calls*) Phila-a-a? [*Phila runs to the door at the back. She waves her hand eagerly — skips out.*

CURTAIN

THE STRONGER WOMAN
MOTHERLY LOVE

AUGUST STRINDBERG

AUGUST STRINDBERG was born January 22, 1849, at Stock-holm, Sweden. Though he wrote in many other forms he is best known as a dramatist. "Motherly Love" (1893) and "The Stronger Woman" (1890) are two of his strongest short plays.

He died May 14, 1912. A striking study is "August Strindberg", by A. J. Uppvall.

THE STRONGER WOMAN

A PLAY IN ONE ACT

By AUGUST STRINDBERG

Characters

MRS. X., actress, married.
MISS Y., actress, unmarried.

THE STRONGER WOMAN

SCENE. *A nook in a ladies' café; two small tables, a red plush sofa and some chairs.*

Mrs. X. enters in winter dress, in a hat and cloak, with a light Japanese basket over her arm. Miss Y. sits in front of an unfinished bottle of beer and reads an illustrated paper, which she subsequently exchanges for another.

MRS. X. How are you, my dear Millie? You look awfully lonely, at this gay time of year, sitting here all by yourself, like a poor bachelor girl.

(Miss Y. looks up from her paper, nods and continues her reading)

It makes me really quite sorry, to look at you. All alone at a café when all the rest of us are having such a good time of it! It reminds me of how I felt when I saw a wedding party once, in a Paris restaurant, and the bride sat and read a comic paper while the bridegroom played billiards with the witnesses. If they begin like this, I said to myself, how will they go on, and how will they end? Fancy! He was playing billiards on the night of his wedding — and she was reading an illustrated paper! Oh, well, but you are not quite in the same box! *(Waitress enters, puts a cup of chocolate in front of Mrs. X., and exits)* I say, Millie, I'm not at all sure you wouldn't have done better to have kept him. If you come to think of it, I was the first to ask you to forgive him at the time. Don't you remember? Why, you could have been married now, and have had a home! Do you remember how delighted you were at Christmas when you stayed with your *fiancé's* people in the country? You were quite enthusiastic over domestic happiness and quite keen on getting away from the theatre. After all, my dear Amelia, there's nothing like home, sweet home — after the profession, of course! — and the kids. Isn't it so? But you couldn't understand that!

(*Miss Y. looks contemptuous. Mrs. X. drinks some spoon-fuls of chocolate out of her cup, then opens the basket and looks at the Christmas presents*)

There, let me show you what I've bought for my little chicks. (*Takes up a doll*) Just look at this! That's for Lisa. Just look, it can roll its eyes and waggle its neck. What? And here's Maja's cork pistol.

(*Loads and shoots at Miss Y. Miss Y. gives a start*)

Are you frightened? Did you think I wanted to shoot you, dear? Upon my word I'd never have thought you'd have thought that. I'd have been much less surprised if you'd wanted to shoot me, for getting in your way. *I know that you can never forget anything*, although I was abso-lutely innocent. You believed, of course, that I worked it to get you out of the Grand Theatre, but I didn't do that. I didn't do it, although you think I did. But it makes no odds my saying all this, for you always think it was me. (*Takes out a pair of embroidered slippers*)

These are for my hubby, with tulips on them which I embroidered myself. I can't stand tulips, you know, but he's awfully keen on them.

(*Miss Y. looks up ironically and curiously from her paper. Mrs. X. holds a slipper up in each hand*)

Just look what small feet Bob has, eh! You should just see, dear, how well he carries himself. But of course you've never seen him in slippers, have you, dear?

(*Miss Y. laughs loudly*)

Look, you must see.

(*She walks the slippers upon the table. Miss Y. laughs loudly*)

Just see here. This is the way he always stamps about whenever he's out of sorts, like this. "Eh, that damned girl will never learn how to make coffee! Ugh! And now the confounded idiot has trimmed the lamp wrong!" The next minute there's a draught and his feet get cold. "Oof, how cold it is, and that blighted fool can never manage to keep the fire going."

(*She rubs the soles of the slippers one against the other. Miss Y. laughs out loud*)

And this is how he goes on when he comes home and looks for his slippers: which Mary puts under the chest of drawers.

Oh, it's a shame for me to sit here and give my husband away. He's a good sort, at any rate, and that's something, I can tell you. Yes, you should have a husband like that, Amelia; yes, you, my dear. What are you laughing at? Eh? Eh?

And I'll tell you how I know he's faithful! I am sure of it, for he told me so of his own accord. What are you giggling at? Why, when I went for a trip in Norway, that ungrateful Frederique ran after him and tried to seduce him — can you think of anything so disgraceful! (*Pause*) I'd have scratched the eyes out of the creature's head, that I would, if she'd come playing around when I was on the scene! (*Pause*) It was lucky that Bob told me of his own accord, so that I didn't get to hear of it first from a lot of sneaking scandalmongers. (*Pause*) But Frederique was not the only one, you may say. I didn't know it, but the women are absolutely crazy over my husband. They think he is awfully influential in getting engagements just because he holds an official position! It may be that you, too, have tried to run after him — I don't trust you more than need be — anyway. I *know* that he doesn't bother about you and that you seem to have a grudge against him, and consequently against me, the whole time! (*Pause; they look at each other with embarrassment*)

Come around and see us to-night, dear, just to show that you don't feel badly about us, at any rate about me! I don't know why, but somehow I feel that it would be particularly ungracious of me to be unfriendly towards you of all people. It may be because I cut you out. (*Speaking more slowly*) Or — or — I can't tell the reason. (*Miss Y. stares at Mrs. X. curiously. Mrs. X. continues reflectively*)

But everything went wrong, when you came to our house, because I saw that my husband couldn't stand you — and I felt quite uncomfortable as though there was a hitch somewhere, and I did all I could to make him show himself friendly towards you, but without success — until you went and got engaged, and then a keen friendship sprang up, so that it seemed for a moment as though you had only first dared to show your true feelings when you were in safety — and then it went on! — I didn't get jealous — strangely enough — and I remember the christening when you stood godmother and I made him kiss you. Yes, I did that, and you got so embarrassed — I mean I didn't notice it at the time — I haven't thought of it since then either, I haven't thought of it from then till now. (*Gets up sharply*)

Why don't you say something? You haven't said a word the whole time, but have just let me sit here and talk; you have sat there with those eyes of yours and picked up all my thoughts — thoughts! — hallucinations, perhaps — and worked them into your chain, link by link. Ah, let me see. Why did you break off your engagement, and why, from that day to this, have you never come any more to our house? Why won't you come in, in the evening?

(*Miss Y. seems as though she were about to speak*)

Stop! You needn't say it! I quite understand now. It was because and because and because. Yes, it all fits in! That's what it is. Ugh, I won't sit at the same table with you. (*Moves her things to another table*) That was why I had to embroider tulips on his slippers, though I couldn't stand them; that was why. (*Throws the slippers on the floor*)

That was why I had to spend the summer at Lake Malarn, because *you* couldn't stand sea air; that was why my boy had to be called Eskil, because it was your father's name; that was why I had to wear your colors, read your authors, eat your favorite dishes, drink your drinks, — chocolate, for instance; that was why.

Oh, my God! it is ghastly to think of, ghastly; everything I got came from you to me, even your passions! Your soul crept into mine like a worm into an apple, ate and ate — burrowed and burrowed, till there was nothing left but the rotten core.

I wanted to avoid you, but I could not; you lay there like a serpent with your black eyes of fascination — I knew that you would succeed at last in dragging me down; I was lying in a swamp with my feet tied, and the more violently I struggled with my hands, the deeper did I work down, down to the bottom, while you lay there like a giant crab and gripped me in your claws; and now here I am at the bottom!

Oh, how I hate you, hate you, hate you! But you, you just sit there and say nothing, quiet, indifferent — indifferent. It is all the same to you if it is the beginning or the end of the month; Christmas or New Year; if the rest of the world is happy or unhappy; you can neither hate nor love; you sit as stolidly as a stork over a rat-trap. But you couldn't capture your prey, mind you; you couldn't pursue it; you could only wait for it.

Here you sit in your lair — this nook, you know, has been called the Rat Trap — and you read your papers to see if somebody's having a bad time of it, if somebody's had a misfortune, if somebody's been sacked from the theater. Here you sit and survey your victims, reckon out your chances like a pilot his shipwrecks; take your toll.

My poor Amelia, do you know, I feel quite sorry for you, because I know that you are wretched, wretched, like a wounded creature, and malicious because you are wounded. I cannot be angry with you, although I should like to be, because you are the weaker — why, as to that little affair with Bob, I am not bothering about that — what did it really matter to me? Supposing it was you or somebody else who taught me to eat chocolate, what does it matter? (*Drinks a spoonful out of her cup*) Besides, chocolate is very wholesome, and if I did learn to dress myself in your model, well *tant mieux* — it only strengthens my hold upon my husband — and you were the loser by it while I was the winner.

Why, I had ample grounds for coming to the conclusion that you had already lost him — but it was you still thought that I should go my way! But now you carry on as though you were sitting and repenting; but, you see, I don't do that. One mustn't be petty, you know.

Why should I just take what nobody else will have? Perhaps you — taking it all round — are stronger than I am at this particular moment — you never got anything out of me but you gave me something of yourself. Oh, it's really a case of thieving, in my case, isn't it? — and when you woke up I had possessed myself of the very thing you missed.

How else does it come about that everything you touched became worthless and sterile? You couldn't keep any man's love, with those tulips and those passions of yours — but I could; you weren't able to learn the art of my life out of your authors, but I learnt it; you haven't got any little Eskil, although your papa was called Eskil.

Else why do you sit there without a word, and brood and brood and brood? I thought it was strength, but perhaps the reason is just that you haven't anything to say, that's because you couldn't think of anything to say. (*Rises and takes up the slippers*)

I'm going home now — and taking these tulip things with me — your tulips, my dear; you couldn't learn anything from others — you couldn't yield, and that's why you crumpled up like a dried-up leaf. I didn't do that. I must really thank you, Amelia, for the excellent training you have given me — thank you for teaching my husband how to love. And now I'm going home to love him. [*Exits.*

CURTAIN

MOTHERLY LOVE

A PLAY IN ONE ACT

By AUGUST STRINDBERG

Characters

THE MOTHER
A DRESSER
THE DAUGHTER
LISE

MOTHERLY LOVE

The Mother and the Dresser are smoking cigars, drinking stout, and playing cards. The Daughter sits by the window and looks out with intentness.

MOTHER. Come along, Helen — it's your deal.

DAUGHTER. Oh, please let me off playing cards on a fine summer day like this.

DRESSER. That's right. Nice and affectionate to her mother, as usual.

MOTHER. Don't sit like that on the veranda and get scorched.

DAUGHTER. The sun isn't a bit hot here.

MOTHER. Well, there's a draught, anyway. (*To the Dresser*) Your deal, dear. Righto!

DAUGHTER. Mayn't I go and bathe this morning with the other girls?

MOTHER. Not without your mamma; you know that once for all.

DAUGHTER. Oh, but the girls can swim, mamma, and you can't swim at all.

MOTHER. That's not the question, whether a body can swim or can't, but you know, my child, that you mustn't go out without your mamma.

DAUGHTER. Do I know it? Since I've been able to understand the simplest thing, that's been dinned into my ears.

DRESSER. That only shows that Helen has had a most affectionate mother, who has always tried her best. Yes — yes, no doubt about it.

MOTHER (*holds out her hand to the Dresser*). Thank you for your kindly words, Augusta — whatever else I may have been — that — but I was always a tender-hearted mother. I can say that with a clear conscience.

DAUGHTER. Then I suppose it's no good my asking you if I can go down and have a game of tennis with the others?

DRESSER. No, no, young lady. A girl shouldn't sauce her mamma. And when she won't oblige those who are nearest and dearest to her, by taking part in their harmless fun, it's in a manner of speaking adding insult to injury for her to come and ask on top of it, if she can't go and amuse herself with other people.

DAUGHTER. Yes — yes — yes. I know all that already. I know — I know!

MOTHER. You're making yourself disagreeable again. Get something proper to do, and don't sit slacking there in that fashion. A grown-up girl like you!

DAUGHTER. Then why do you always treat me like a child if I'm grown up?

MOTHER. Because you behave like one.

DAUGHTER. You have no right to rag me — you yourself wanted me to remain like this.

MOTHER. Look here, Helen; for some time past I think you've been a bit too bloomin' smart. Come, whom have you been talking to down here?

DAUGHTER. With you two, amongst others.

MOTHER. You don't mean to say you're going to start having secrets from your own mother?

DAUGHTER. It's about time.

DRESSER. Shame on you, you young thing, being so cheeky to your own mother.

MOTHER. Come, let's do something sensible instead of jangling like this. Why not come here, and read over your part with me.

DAUGHTER. The manager said I wasn't to go through it with any one, because if I did, I should only learn something wrong.

MOTHER. I see; so that's the thanks one gets for trying to help you. Of course, of course! Everything that I do is always silly, I suppose.

DAUGHTER. Why do you do it, then? And why do you put the blame on me, whenever you do anything wrong?

DRESSER. Of course you want to remind your mother that she ain't educated? Ugh, 'ow common!

DAUGHTER. You say I want to, aunt, but it's not the case. If mother goes and teaches me anything wrong, I've got to learn the whole thing over again, if I don't want to lose my engagement. We don't want to find ourselves stranded.

MOTHER. I see. You're now letting us know that we're living on what you earn. But do you really know what you owe Aunt Augusta here? Do you know that she looked after us when your blackguard of a father left us in the lurch? — that she took care of us and that you therefore owe her a debt which you can never pay off — in all your born days? Do you know that? (*Daughter is silent*) Do you know that? Answer!

DAUGHTER. I refuse to answer.

MOTHER. You do — do you? You won't answer?

DRESSER. Steady on, Amelia. The people next door might hear us, and they'd start gossiping again. So you go steady.

MOTHER (*to Daughter*). Put on your things and come out for a walk.

DAUGHTER. I'm not going out for a walk to-day.

MOTHER. This is now the third day that you've refused to go out for a walk with your mother. (*Reflecting*) Would it be possible — Go out on to the veranda, Helen. I want to say something to Aunt Augusta.
(*Daughter exits on to the veranda*)
Do you think it's possible?

DRESSER. What?

MOTHER. That's she's found out something?

DRESSER. It ain't possible.

MOTHER. It might 'appen, of course. Not that I think anybody could be so heartless as to tell it to her face. I

had a nephew who was thirty-six years old before he
found out that his father was a suicide, but Helen's
manner's changed, and there's something at the bottom
of it. For the last eight days I've noticed that she
couldn't bear my being with her on the promenade.
She would only go along lonely paths; when any one
met us she looked the other way; she was nervous,
couldn't manage to get a single word out. There's
something behind all this.

DRESSER. Do you mean, if I follow you aright, that the
society of her mother is painful to her? — the society
of her own mother?

MOTHER. Yes.

DRESSER. No; that's really a bit too bad.

MOTHER. Well, I'll tell you something which is even worse.
Would you believe it, that when we came here, she didn't
introduce me to some of her friends on the steamer?

DRESSER. Do you know what I think? She's met some one
or other who's come here during the last week. Come, we'll
just toddle down to the post office and find out about
the latest arrivals.

MOTHER. Yes, let's do that. I say, Helen, just mind the
house a minute. We're only going down to the post for
a moment. [*Daughter reënters from veranda*)

DAUGHTER. Yes, mamma.

MOTHER (*to Dresser*). It's just as though I'd dreamt all this
before.

DRESSER. Yes; dreams come true sometimes — I know
that all right — but not the nice ones.

[*Exeunt right.*

*Daughter gives a nod out of the window; Lise enters. She
wears a tennis costume quite white, and a white hat.*

LISE. Have they gone?

DAUGHTER. Yes; but they're soon coming back.

LISE. Well, what did your mother say?

DAUGHTER. I haven't even had the pluck to ask her. She
was in such a temper.

LISE. Poor Helen! So you can't come with us on the excursion? And I was looking forward to it so much. If you only knew how fond I am of you.

[*Kisses her.*

DAUGHTER. If you only knew, dear, what these days have meant to me since I've made your acquaintance and visited your house — have meant to a girl like me, who's never mixed with decent people in her whole life. Just think what it must have been for me. Up to the present I've been living in a den where the air was foul, where shady, mysterious people came in and out, who spied and brawled and wrangled; where I have never heard a kind word, much less ever got a caress, and where my soul was watched like a prisoner. Oh, I'm talking like this about my mother, and it hurts me! And you will only despise me for it.

LISE. One can't be made responsible for one's parents.

DAUGHTER. No, but you've got to pay the penalty for them. At any rate they say that very often one doesn't find out before the end of one's life the kind of people one's own parents, with whom one's lived all one's life, have really been. And I've picked up this as well, even if one does get to hear about it, one doesn't believe a word.

LISE (*uneasily*). Have you heard anything?

DAUGHTER. Yes. When I was in the bathhouse three days ago I heard through the wall what people were saying about my mother. Do you know what it was?

LISE. Don't bother about it.

DAUGHTER. They said my mother had been just a common creature! I wouldn't believe it; I won't yet believe it. But I feel that it is true; it all fits in — to make it probable — and I am ashamed — ashamed of going near her, because I think that people stare at us — that the men throw us looks. It's too awful. But is it true? Tell me if you think that it's true?

LISE. People tell so many lies — and I don't know anything.

DAUGHTER. Yes, you do know — you do know something. You won't tell me, and I thank you for it; but I am equally miserable whether you tell me or whether you don't.

LISE. My darling friend, knock that thought out of your head and come home to us — you'll find you'll get on splendidly with every one. My father arrived early this morning. He asked after you, and wanted to see you — I ought, of course, to tell you they have written to him about you — and Cousin Gerhard as well, because I think —

DAUGHTER. Yes, you — you have a father and I had one too, when I was still quite, quite tiny.

LISE. What became of him, then?

DAUGHTER. Mother always says he left us because he was a bad lot.

LISE. It's hard to find where the truth lies. But — I tell you what; if you come home to us now, you'll meet the director of the Imperial Theatre, and it's possible it might be a question of an engagement.

DAUGHTER. What do you say?

LISE. Yes, yes — that's it. And he takes an interest in you — I mean Gerhard — and I have made him take an interest in you, and you know quite well what trifles often decide one's whole life; a personal interview, a good recommendation at the right moment, — well, now, you can't refuse any longer, without standing in the way of your own career.

DAUGHTER. Oh, darling, I should think I did want to come. You know that quite well; but I don't go out without mamma.

LISE. Why not? Can you give me any reason?

DAUGHTER. I don't know. She taught me to say that when I was a child. And now it's got deeply rooted.

LISE. Has she extracted some promise from you?

DAUGHTER. No, she didn't have any need to do that. She just said "Say that!" and I said it.

LISE. Do you think then that you're doing her a wrong if you leave her for an hour or two?

DAUGHTER. I don't think that she would miss me, because when I am at home she's always got some fault to find with me. But I should find it painful if I went to a house when she wasn't allowed to come too.

LISE. Do you mean to say you've thought of the possibility of her visiting us?

DAUGHTER. No, — God forgive me, I never thought of it for a moment.

LISE. But supposing you were to get married?

DAUGHTER. I shall never get married.

LISE. Has your mother taught you to say that as well?

DAUGHTER. Yes, probably. She has always warned me of men.

LISE. Of married men as well?

DAUGHTER. Presumably.

LISE. Look here, Helen; you should really emancipate yourself.

DAUGHTER. Ugh! I haven't the faintest desire to be a new woman.

LISE. No, I don't mean that. But you must free yourself from a position of dependence which you have grown out of, and which may make you unhappy for life.

DAUGHTER. I scarcely think I shall ever be able to. Just consider how I've been tied down to my mother since I was a child! that I've never dared to think a thought that wasn't hers; have never wished anything but her wishes. I know that it's a handicap; that it stands in my way, but I can't do anything against it.

LISE. And if your mother goes to rest, one fine day, you'll be all alone in the world.

DAUGHTER. That's how I shall find myself.

LISE. But you've got no set, no friends; and no one can live as lonely as all that. You must find some firm support. Have you never been in love?

DAUGHTER. I don't know. I've never dared to think of

anything like that, and mother has never allowed young men even to look at me. Do you yourself think of such things?

LISE. Yes. If any one's fond of me and I should like to have him.

DAUGHTER. You'll probably marry your cousin Gerhard.

LISE. I shall never do that — because he does not love me.

DAUGHTER. Not love you?

LISE. No; because he's fond of you.

DAUGHTER. Me?

LISE. Yes, — and he has commissioned me to inquire if he can call on you.

DAUGHTER. Here? No, that's impossible. And besides, do you think I would stand in your way? Do you think I could supplant you in his regard, you who are so pretty, so delicate. (*Takes Lise's hand in hers*) What a hand! And the wrists! I saw your foot when we were in the bathhouse together. (*Falls on her knees before Lise, who has sat down*) A foot on which there isn't even a crooked nail, on which the toes are as round and as rosy as a baby's hand. (*Kisses Lise's foot*) You belong to the nobility — you're made of different stuff from what I am.

LISE. Leave off, please, and don't talk so sillily. (*Gets up*) If you only knew — but —

DAUGHTER. And I'm sure you're as good as you're beautiful, we always think that down below here when we look at you above there, with your delicate chiselled features, where trouble hasn't made any wrinkles, where envy and jealousy have not drawn their hateful lines —

LISE. Look here, Helen; I really think you're quite mad on me.

DAUGHTER. Yes, I am that, too. I wish I were like you a bit, just as the miserable whitlow-grass is like an anemone, and that's why I see in you my better self, something that I should like to be and never can be. You have tripped into my life during the last summer days as lightly and as delicately as an angel; now the autumn's come; the day after to-morrow we go back to town — then we shan't know each other any more — and we mustn't know each other any more. You can never draw me up, dear, but I can draw you down — and I don't want to do that! I want to have you so high, so high and far away, that I can't see your blemishes, and so good-by, Lise, my first and only friend.

LISE. No, that's enough. Helen, do you know — who I am? Well — I — am your sister.

DAUGHTER. You — What can you mean?

LISE. We have — the same father.

DAUGHTER. And you are my sister, my little sister? But what is my father then? But of course he must be captain of a yacht, because your father is one. How silly I am! But then he married, after. Is he kind to you? He wasn't to my mother.

LISE. You don't know. But aren't you awfully glad to have found a little sister — one, too, who isn't so very loud?

DAUGHTER. Oh, rather; I'm so glad that I really don't know what to say. (*Embrace*) But I really daren't be properly glad because I don't know what's going to happen after all this. What will mother say, and what will it be like if we meet papa?

LISE. Just leave your mother to me. She can't be far away now. And you keep in the background till you are wanted. And now come and give me a kiss, little 'un. [*They kiss.*

DAUGHTER. My sister. How strange the words sound, just like the word father when one has never uttered it.

LISE. Don't let's go on chattering now, but let's stick to the point. Do you think that your mother would still refuse her permission if we were to invite you — to come and see your sister and your father?

DAUGHTER. Without my mother? Oh, she hates your — my father so dreadfully.

LISE. But suppose she has no reason to do so? If you only

knew how full the world is of concoctions and lies and
mistakes and misunderstandings. My father used to tell
a story of a chum he used to have when he first went to
sea as a cadet. A gold watch was stolen from one of the
officers' cabins and — God knows why! — suspicion fell
on the cadet. His mates avoided him, practically sent
him to Coventry, and that embittered him to such an
extent that he became impossible to associate with, got
mixed up in a row and had to leave. Two years afterwards the thief was discovered, in the person of a boat-
swain; but no satisfaction could be given to the innocent
boy, because people had only been suspicious of him.
And the suspicion will stick to him for the rest of his life,
although it was refuted, and the wretch still keeps the
nickname which was given to him at the time. His life
grew up like a house that's built and based on its own bad
fame, and when the false foundation is cut away the
building remains standing all the same; it floated in the
air like the castle in "The Arabian Nights." You see —
that's what happens in the world. But even worse things
can happen, as in the case of that instrument-maker in
Arboga, who got the name of being an incendiary because
his house had been set fire to; or as happened to a certain
Anderson, whom people called Thief Anders, because he
had been the victim of a celebrated burglary.

DAUGHTER. Do you mean to say that my father hasn't been
what I always thought he was?

LISE. Yes, that's just it.

DAUGHTER. This is how I see him sometimes in dreams,
since I lost all recollection of him — isn't he fairly tall,
with a dark beard and big blue sailor eyes?

LISE. Yes — more or less!

DAUGHTER. And then — wait, now I remember. Do you
see this watch? There's a little compass fastened on to
the chain, and on the compass at the north there's an eye.
Who gave me that?

LISE. Your father. I was there when he bought it.

DAUGHTER. Then it's he whom I've seen so often in the theater when I was playing. He always sat in the left stage box, and held his opera glasses trained on me. I never dared tell mother because she was always so very nervous about me. And once he threw me flowers — but mother burned them. Do you think it was he?

LISE. It was he; you can count on it that during all these years his eye has followed you like the eye of the needle on the compass.

DAUGHTER. And you tell me that I shall see him — that he wants to meet me? It's like a fairy tale.

LISE. The fairy tale's over now. I hear your mother. You get back, I'm going first, to face the fire.

DAUGHTER. Something dreadful's going to happen now, I feel it. Why can't people agree with each other and be at peace? Oh, if only it were all over! If mamma would only be nice. I will pray to God outside there to make her soft-hearted — but I'm certain He can't do it — I don't know why.

LISE. He can do it, and He will, if you can only have faith, have a little faith in happiness and your own strength.

DAUGHTER. Strength? What for? To be selfish? I can't do it. And the enjoyment of a happiness that is bought at the cost of some one else's unhappiness cannot be lasting.

LISE. Indeed? Now go out.

DAUGHTER. How can you possibly believe that this will turn out all right?

LISE. Hush! (*Enter Mother*) Madam.

MOTHER. Miss — if you don't mind.

LISE. Your daughter —

MOTHER. Yes, I have a daughter, even though I'm only a "Miss," and indeed that happens to many of us, and I'm not a bit ashamed of it. But what's it all about?

LISE. The fact is, I'm commissioned to ask you if Miss Helen can join in an excursion which some visitors have got up?

MOTHER. Hasn't Helen herself answered you?

LISE. Yes; she has very properly answered that I should address myself to you.

MOTHER. That wasn't a straightforward answer. Helen, my child, do you want to join a party to which your mother isn't invited?

DAUGHTER. Yes, if you allow it.

MOTHER. If I allow it! How can I decide what a big girl like you is to do! You yourself must tell the young lady what you want; if you want to leave your mother alone in disgrace, while you gad about and have a good time; if you want people to ask after mamma, and for you to have to try and wriggle out of the answer, "She has been left out of the invitation, because and because and because," now say what you really want to do.

LISE. My dear lady, don't let's beat about the bush. I know perfectly well the view Helen takes of this business, and I also know your method of getting her to make that particular answer which happens to suit you. If you are as fond of your daughter as you say you are, you ought to wish what is best for her, even though it might be humiliating for you.

MOTHER. Look here, my girl, I know what your name is, and who you are, even though I haven't had the privilege of being introduced to you; but I should really like to know what a girl of your years has got to teach a woman of mine.

LISE. Who knows? For the last six years, since my mother died, I have spent all my time in bringing up my young sisters and brothers, and I've found out that there are people who never learn anything from life, however old they get.

MOTHER. What do you mean?

LISE. I mean this. Your daughter has now got an opportunity of taking her place in the world; of either getting recognition for her talent or of contracting an alliance with a young man in good position.

MOTHER. That sounds all very fine, but what do you pro-pose to do about me?

LISE. You're not the point; your daughter is! Can't you think about her for a single minute without immediately thinking of yourself?

MOTHER. Ah, but, mind you, when I think of myself I think of my daughter at the same time, because she has learnt to love her mother.

LISE. I don't think so. She depends on you because you've shut her off from all the rest of the world, and she must have some one to depend on, since you've stolen her away from her father.

MOTHER. What's that you say?

LISE. That you took the child away from her father when he refused to marry you, because you hadn't been faithful to him. You then prevented him from seeing his child, and avenged yourself on him and upon your child.

MOTHER. Helen, don't you believe a single word of any-thing that she says — that I should live to see such a day! For a stranger to intrude into my house and insult me in the presence of my own child!

DAUGHTER (*comes forward*). You have no business to say anything bad about my mother.

LISE. It's impossible to do otherwise, if I'm to say anything good about my father. Anyway, I observe that the con-versation is nearly over, so allow me to give you one or two pieces of advice. Get rid of the procuress who finds herself so at home here under the name of Aunt Augusta if you don't want your daughter's reputation to be abso-lutely ruined. That's tip number one. Further, put in order all your receipts for the money which you had from my father for Helen's education, because settlement day's precious near. That's tip number two. And now for an extra tip. Leave off persecuting your daughter with your company in the street, and, above all, at the theater, because if you don't she's barred from any engagement; and then you'll go about trying to sell her favors; just as, up to the present, you've been trying to buy back your lost respectability at the expense of her father.

[*Mother sits, crushed.*

DAUGHTER (*to Lise*). Leave this house. You find nothing sacred, not even motherhood.

LISE. A sacred motherhood, I must say!

DAUGHTER. It seems now as though you've only come into this house to destroy us, and not for a single minute to put matters right.

LISE. Yes, I did! I came here — to put right the good name of my father, who was perfectly guiltless — as guiltless as that incendiary whose house had been set on fire. I came also to put you right, you who've been the victim of a woman whose one and only chance of rehabilitation is by retiring to a place where she won't be disturbed by anybody, and where she on her side won't disturb anybody's peace. That's why I came. I have done my duty. Good-by.

MOTHER. Miss Lise — don't go before I've said one thing — you came here, apart from all the other tomfoolery — to invite Helen out to your place.

LISE. Yes. She was to meet the director of the Imperial Theater, who takes quite an interest in her.

MOTHER. What's that? The director? And you've never mentioned a word about it. Yes — Helen may go — alone. Yes, without me!

LISE. Well, after all, it was only human nature that you should have carried on like that. Helen, you must come, don't you see?

DAUGHTER. Yes, but now I don't want to any more.

MOTHER. What are you talking about?

DAUGHTER. No, I'm not fitted for society. I shall never feel comfortable anywhere where my mother is despised.

MOTHER. Stuff and nonsense! You surely ain't going to go and cut your own throat? Now just you go and dress so as to look all right!

DAUGHTER No, I can't, mother. I can't leave you now

that I know everything. I shall never have another happy hour. I can never believe in anything again.

LISE (*to Mother*). Now you shall reap what you have sown — if one day a man comes and makes your daughter his bride, then you'll be alone in your old age, and then you'll have time to be sorry for your foolishness. Good-by. (*Goes and kisses Helen's forehead*) Good-by, sister.

DAUGHTER. Good-by.

LISE. Look me in the face and try and seem as though you had some hope in life.

DAUGHTER. I can't. I can't thank you either for your good will, for you have given me more pain than you know — you woke me with a snake when I lay in the sunshine by a woodland precipice and slept.

LISE. Give me another chance, and I'll wake you with songs and flowers. Good night. Sleep well.

[*Exit.*

MOTHER. An angel of light in white garments I suppose! No! She's a devil, a regular devil! And you! How silly you've been behaving! What madness next, I wonder. Playing the sensitive when other people's hides are so thick.

DAUGHTER. To think of your being able to tell me all those untruths. Deceiving me so that I talked thus about my father during so many years.

MOTHER. Oh, come on! It's no good crying over spilt milk.

DAUGHTER. And then again, Aunt Augusta!

MOTHER. Stop it. Aunt Augusta is a most excellent woman, to whom you are under a great obligation.

DAUGHTER. That's not true either — it was my father, I'm sure, who had me educated.

MOTHER. Well, yes, it was, but I too have to live. You're so petty! And you're vindictive as well. Can't you forget a little taradiddle like that? Hello! Augusta's turned up already. Come along, now let us humble folk amuse ourselves as best we can. [*Enter Dresser.*

DRESSER. Yes, it was he, right enough. You see, I'd guessed quite right.

MOTHER. Oh, well, don't let's bother about the blackguard.

DAUGHTER. Don't speak like that, mother; it's not a bit true!

DRESSER. What's not true?

DAUGHTER. Come along. We'll play cards. I can't pull down the wall which you've taken so many years to build up. Come along then.

[*She sits down at the card table and begins to shuffle the cards.*

MOTHER. Well, you've come to your senses at last, my gal.

CURTAIN

BIBLIOGRAPHIES

BIBLIOGRAPHIES

A LIST OF BOOKS ON THE THEORY AND TECHNIQUE OF THE THEATRE AND THE DRAMA

[The Editor has not attempted to make a complete bibliography of books relating to the drama and the theatre. The titles listed are those which contain matter of importance to amateurs.]

GENERAL

Macgowan, Kenneth. "The Theatre of Tomorrow." Boni & Liveright, New York.

Appia, Adolphe. "Die Musik und die Inscenierung." Bruckmann, Munich.

Archer, Wm. and Barker, Granville. "A National Theatre." Duffield & Co., New York.

Moderwell, H. K. "The Theatre of Today." John Lane & Co., New York.

Pichel, Irving. "On Building a Theatre." Theatre Arts, Inc., New York.

ORGANIZATION

Beegle, M. P. and Crawford, Jack. "Community Drama and Pageantry." Yale University Press, New Haven.

Burleigh, Louise. "The Community Theatre." Little, Brown & Co., Boston.

Dickinson, T. H. "The Insurgent Theatre." B. W. Huebsch, New York.

Cheney, Sheldon. "The Art Theatre." A. A. Knopf, New York.

Hilliard, E., McCormick, T., and Oglebay, K. "Amateur and Educational Dramatics." Macmillan Co., New York.

Mackay, Constance D'Arcy. "The Little Theatre in the United States." Henry Holt & Co., New York.

PRODUCTION

Krows, Arthur Edwin. "Play Production in America." Henry Holt & Co., New York.

Dickinson, T. H. "The Insurgent Theatre." B. W. Huebsch, New York.

Cheney, Sheldon. "The Art Theatre." A. A. Knopf, New York.

DIRECTION

Clark, Barrett H. "How to Produce Amateur Plays." Little, Brown & Co., Boston.

Hudson, Holland. "The Little Theatre Hand-Book." (*In prep.*) Frank Shay, New York.

Stratton, Clarence. "Producing in Little Theatres." Henry Holt & Co., New York.

Taylor, Emerson. "Practical Stage Directing for Amateurs." E. P. Dutton & Co., New York.

Mitchell, Roy. "Shakespeare for Community Players." E. P. Dutton & Co., New York.

COSTUMING

Calthrop, Dion Clayton. "English Costume." A. & C. Black, London.

Mackay, Constance D'Arcy. "Costumes and Scenery for Amateurs." Henry Holt & Co., New York.

"Die Mode: Menschen und Moden im XVII–XVIII–XIX Jahrhundert." 6 vols. Bruckmann, Munich.

'Peasant Art in Italy."

"Peasant Art in Russia."

"Peasant Art in Austria-Hungary."

"Peasant Art in Norway and Sweden." *International Studio:* John Lane & Co., New York.

SCENE PAINTING

Browne, Van Dyke. "Secrets of Scene Painting and Stage Effects." Routledge, London.

Mantzius, Karl. "A History of Theatrical Art in Ancient and Modern Times." 6 vols. J. B. Lippincott Co., Philadelphia.

Mackay, Constance D'Arcy. "Costumes and Scenery for Amateurs." Henry Holt and Co., New York.

Rouche, Jacques. "L'Art Theatral Moderne." Cornelly, Paris.

"Theatrical Scene Painting: a Thorough and Complete Work on How to Sketch, Paint and Install Theatrical Scenery." Appleton Pub. Co., Omaha, Neb.

ACTING

Calvert, Louise. "Problems of the Actor." Henry Holt & Co., New York.

Coquelin, Constant. "Art and the Actor." Columbia University Press, New York.

Filipi, Rosina. "Hints to Speakers and Players." Longmans, Green & Co., New York.

Hornblow, Arthur. "Training for the Stage: Hints for Those About to Choose the Player's Career." J. B. Lippincott & Co., Philadelphia.

Matthews, Brander. "On Acting." Charles Scribner's Sons., New York.

Morse, Elizabeth. "Principles of Expression: a Guide for Developing Readers, Speakers and Dramatic Artists." Nixon-Jones Co.

ANTHOLOGIES — ONE-ACT PLAYS

"Atlantic Book of Modern Plays." Edited by Sterling Andrus Leonard. Atlantic Monthly Press, Boston. Contains fifteen plays.

"Fifty Contemporary One-act Plays." Edited by Frank Shay and Pierre Loving. Stewart Kidd Co., Cincinnati. Contains fifty one-act plays.

"One-act Plays by Modern Authors." Edited by Helen Louise Cohen. Harcourt, Brace & Co., New York. Contains sixteen one-act plays.

"Representative One-act Plays by American Authors." Edited by Margaret G. Mayorga. Little, Brown & Co., Boston. Contains twenty-four plays.

"Representative One-act Plays by British and Irish Authors." Edited by Barrett H. Clark. Little, Brown & Co., Boston. Contains twenty plays.

"Representative One-act Plays by Continental Authors." Edited by Montrose J. Moses. Little, Brown & Co., Boston. (*In prep.*)

"Short Plays by Representative Authors." Edited by Alice M. Smith. Macmillan Co., New York. Contains twelve plays.

"Vagabond Plays: First Series." Norman, Remington Co., Baltimore. Contains six plays.

"Contemporary One-Act Plays 1921–1922." Edited by Frank Shay. Stewart-Kidd Co., Cincinnati. Contains twenty plays.

ANTHOLOGIES — LONG PLAYS

"Chief Contemporary Dramatists: First Series." Edited by T. H. Dickinson. Houghton, Mifflin Co., Boston. Contains twenty plays.

"Chief Contemporary Dramatists: Second Series." Edited by T. H. Dickinson. Houghton, Mifflin Co., Boston. Contains eighteen plays.

"Chief European Dramatists." Edited by Brander Matthews. Houghton, Mifflin Co., Boston.

"Chief Elizabethan Dramatists." Edited by William Allen Neilson. Houghton, Mifflin Co., Boston.

"Representative British Dramas." Edited by Montrose J. Moses. Little, Brown & Co., Boston.

BIBLIOGRAPHIES

"A Second List of Plays and Pageants." Woman's Press, New York.

"Plays and Books of the Little Theatre." Compiled by Frank Shay. Gotham Book Mart, New York.

"One Thousand and One Plays for Little Theatres." Compiled by Frank Shay. Stewart Kidd Co., Cincinnati.

"One Hundred and One Commendable Plays." Compiled by the British Drama League. Poetry Bookshop, London.

PERIODICALS

The Theatre Arts Magazine. Published by Theatre Arts, Inc., 7 East 42d Street, New York City.

The Drama. Published by the Drama League of America, Chicago, Ill.

The Theatre Magazine. New York City.

A LIST OF PLAYS FOR WOMEN

[A selection of some of the more interesting plays, not including those reprinted in this work. The number in parenthesis following the title indicates the number of characters. 2a, 3a are the number of acts.]

Baker, Elizabeth.	"Miss Tassey" (5). Sidgwick & Jackson, London. (Also in "Representative One-act Plays by British and Irish Authors." Little, Brown, & Company, Boston.
Barbee, Lindsay.	"The Call of Wohelo" (10) 3a. T. S. Denison & Co., Chicago.
Barber, M. E.	"Mechanical Jane" (3). Samuel French, New York.
Barnum, M. D.	"The French Maid and the Phonograph," 8w. Samuel French, New York.
Bates, Esther.	"Engaging Janet" (7). Penn. Publishing Co., Philadelphia.
Bretherton, Evangeline.	"The Minister's Messenger" (14). Samuel French, New York.
Bridgham, Gladys R.	"A Modern Cinderella" (16), 2a. W. H. Baker & Co., Boston.
Brown, Alice.	"Joint Owners in Spain" (4). In "Eight One-act Plays." Macmillan, New York. (Separately published by W. H. Baker & Co., Boston.)
Butler, Ellis Parker.	"The Revolt" (8). Samuel French, New York.
Cameron, Margaret.	"The Burglar" (5). Samuel French, New York. "The Piper's Pay" (7). Samuel French, New York.
Campbell, M. D.	"A Chinese Dummy" (6). W. H. Baker & Co., Boston. "An Open Secret" (10), 2a. W. H. Baker & Co., Boston. "Sunbonnets" (11), 2a. W. H. Baker & Co., Boston.
Cannan, Gilbert.	"Everybody's Husband" (6). B. W. Huebsch, New York.

Castell, C. A.   "Snowed Up With a Duchess" (4). Samuel French, New York.

Clifford, Helen C.   "Alice's Blighted Profession" (8). Fitzgerald Publishing Corp., New York.

Crane, Mabel H.   "The Girls" (9). Samuel French, New York.

Dale, Irving.   "Tickets, Please" (4). W. H. Baker & Co., Boston.

Dane, Essex.   "Fleurette & Co." (2). Samuel French, New York.
"Wrong Numbers" (3). Samuel French, New York.

Denton, Clara J.   "To Meet Mr. Thompson" (8). W. H. Baker & Co., Boston.

Doran, Marie.   "The Girls Over Here" (8). Samuel French, New York.

Flexner, Hortense.   "Voices" (2). In "Representative One-act Plays by American Authors." Little, Brown, & Co. Boston.

Forrestre, Emile.   "Mrs. Willis' Will" (5). W. H. Baker & Co., Boston.

Froome, John Redhead. "Listening" (3). *Poet Lore*, Vacation Number, 1917, Boston.

Gale, Elizabeth.   "Aunt Maggie's Will" (10), 3a. Samuel French, New York.

Gale, R. B.   "The New Crusade" (12). W. H. Baker & Co., Boston.

"The Clinging Vine" (16). Norman, Lee Swartout, Summit, N. J.

Gerstenberg, Alice.   "Beyond" (1). In Mayorga's "Representative One-act Plays by American Authors." Little, Brown, & Co., Boston.

⎧ "Overtones" (4).
⎪ "Attuned" (1).
⎨ "Hearts" (4).
⎩ "Beyond" (1).

      In "Ten One-Act Plays." Brentano, New York.

Gibson, Preston.   "Derelicts" (2). Samuel French, New York.

Gould, Felix.   "In the Marshes" (1). In "The Marsh Maiden." Four Seas Co., Boston.

Griffith, Helen S.   "A Man's Voice" (6), 2a. W. H. Baker & Co., Boston.

Halman, Doris F.   "Will o' the Wisp" (4). In "Representative One-act Plays by American Authors." Little, Brown, & Co., Boston.

Hoofman, Phoebe. "Martha's Mourning" (3). In "Representative One-act Plays by American Authors." Little, Brown, & Co., Boston.

Illsey, S. M. "Feast of the Holy Innocents" (5). In "Wisconsin Plays, Second Series." B. W. Huebsch, New York.

Jennings, E. M. "Mrs. Oakley's Telephone" (4). Samuel French, New York.

"Dinner at the Club" (9). Samuel French, New York.

"Prinzessen von Barnhoff" (8). Samuel French, New York.

"Tom's Fiancee" (5). Samuel French, New York.

Jennings, Gertrude. "Between the Soup and the Savoury" (3). Samuel French, New York.

"At the Ribbon Counter" (3). Samuel French, New York.

Kane, Helen. "A Point of Honor" (5). W. H. Baker & Co., Boston.

"A Russian Romance" (16), 3a. W. H. Baker & Co., Boston.

Kemper, S. "Moth Balls" (3). W. H. Baker & Co., Boston.

Kingsley, Ellis. "The Other Woman" (2). W. H. Baker & Co., Boston.

Macmillan, Mary. "The Futurists" (8). In "Short Plays." Stewart, Kidd Co., Cincinnati.

"The Dress Rehearsal of Hamlet" (10). In "More Short Plays." Stewart, Kidd Co., Cincinnati.

"In Mendelesia." 2 parts (5). In "More Short Plays." Stewart, Kidd Co., Cincinnati.

Macnamara, Margaret. "The Witch" (5). Daniel, London.

Middleton, George. "The Man Masterful" (2). Samuel French, New York.

"The Groove" (2). Samuel French, New York.

M. J. W. "A Brown Paper Parcel" (2). Samuel French, New York.

Muskerry, William. "An Imaginary Aunt." (4). Samuel French, New York.

Nevitt, Mary Ross. "The Rostoff Pearls" (7). Samuel French, New York.

O'Neill, Eugene. "Before Breakfast" (1). Frank Shay, New York.

Reynartz, Dorothy. "Carnival" (8). Dramatic.

Rogers, Maude M.   "When the Wheels Run Down" (3). Samuel French, New York.

Simms, Evelyn.   "The Conspirators" (12), 2a. Fitzgerald Publishing Corp., New York.

Smith, R. C.   "The Rescue" (3). In "Plays of the Harvard Dramatic Club, I." Brentano's, New York.

Thomas, Kate.   "An Evening at Helen's" (7). Samuel French, New York.

"A Bit of Nonsense" (8). Samuel French, New York.

Thompson, Alice C.   "Her Scarlet Slippers" (4). Penn. Publishing Co., Philadelphia.

"An Irish Invasion" (8). W. H. Baker & Co., Boston.

"A Knot of White Ribbon" (3). Penn. Publishing Co., Philadelphia.

"The Luckiest Girl" (4). Dramatic.

"Much Too Sudden" (7). W. H. Baker & Co., Boston.

"Oysters" (6). W. H. Baker & Co., Boston.

"The Wrong Baby" (8). Penn. Publishing Co., Philadelphia.

"Fudge and a Burglar" (8). T. S. Denison & Co., Chicago.

Watson, Evelyn.   "The Mission of Letty" (8), 2a. W. H. Baker & Co., Boston.